MW01644769

WHITE BLAZE LEADERSHIP

Find Your Way to Lead in the Everyday

Peter G. Hodge

Published by Lithodelphis, Atlanta, GA.

www.whiteblazeleadership.com
Contact: peter@whiteblazeleadership.com

ISBN Hardback: 979-8-9917202-0-5
ISBN Paperback: 979-8-9917202-1-2
ISBN ebook: 979-8-9917202-2-9

Library of Congress Control Number: 2024921332

Referenced web links are accurate at the time of publishing but may decay over time.
The occasional British spelling of words is intentional as it reflects my voice.
No generative artificial intelligence was used in the writing of this book.

Cover Design by Megan Kinney
Cartography by Sophie Hodge
Editing by ValMathews.com
Interior Design by Andrea Lard, The Creative 5280

“Solvitur ambulando”

“It is solved by walking.”

*Saint Augustine of Hippo (354–430)**

**Sometimes attributed to Diogenes of Sinope (died 323 BC) as a practical proof that Greek philosopher Zeno’s paradox of motion was false.*

Contents

Appalachian Trail Map & Section Guide

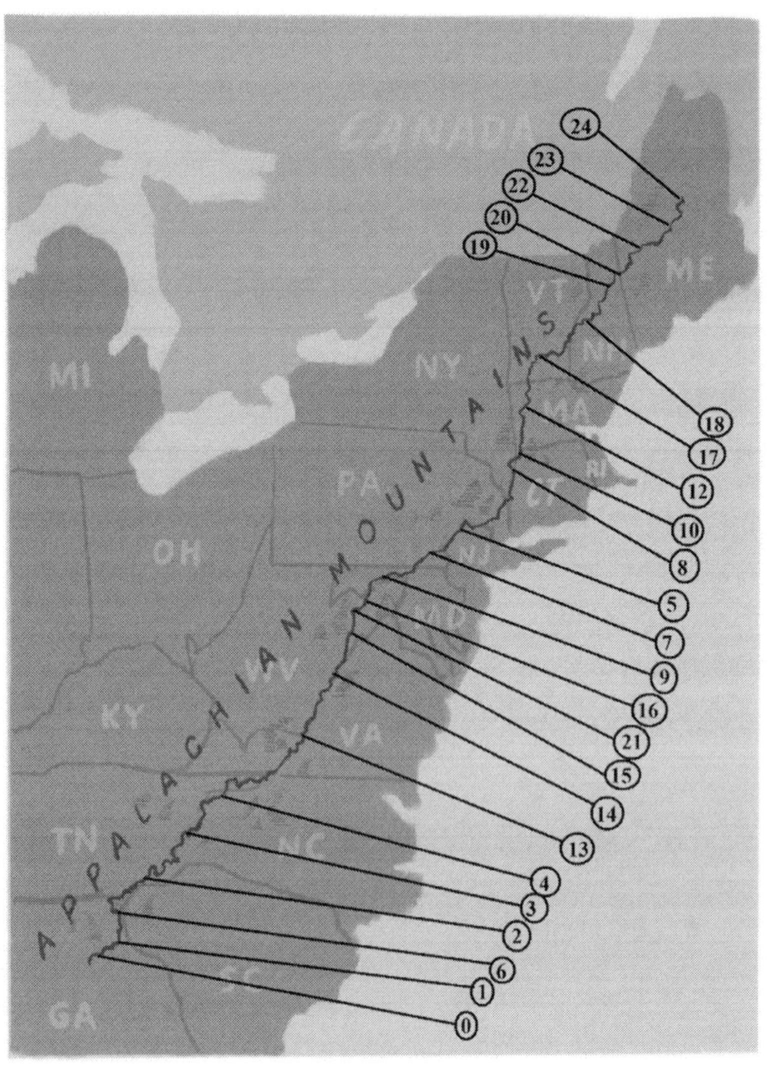

My White Blazes

Question

Inspire

Believe

Value

Act

For Olivia, James, and Sophie.

And All Those Searching for a Cure

Donations to the Cystic Fibrosis Foundation gratefully received at

Introduction

White Blaze Leadership

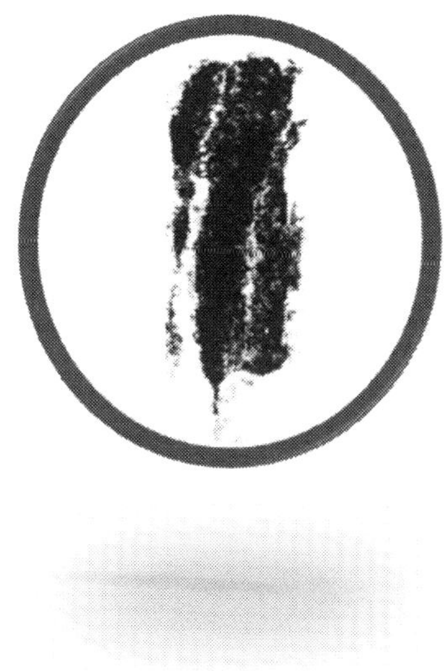

Leadership is not limited to moments of crisis, accelerated change, or intense drama. It doesn't demand excessive courage or hubris. Rather, much of what it means to lead lives in the ordinary and unremarkable moments—in the humdrum of the everyday.

Seizing opportunities to lead in these quiet moments requires us first to recognize the moment when it appears and then to interpret what it's telling us, perhaps in ways we might never have imagined. Finally, to truly seize the opportunity to lead, this moment requires us to take action to show that leadership. White Blaze Leadership is about learning to do this instinctively in three steps: Recognize. Interpret. Lead.

The building blocks of White Blaze Leadership are a set of markers, your White Blazes, that will allow you to perceive those leadership moments as you move through your day-to-day. As you learn to recognize your White Blazes instinctively, they will trigger your ability to consider each moment through the lens of leadership. What is the moment telling you? How do you draw from your experience? How do you translate that into leadership? Learning how to White Blaze will help you grow and shine as a leader.

So why White Blaze Leadership?

White blazes, six inches tall by two inches wide rectangles of white paint, mark the Appalachian Trail as it snakes some two thousand two hundred miles up the eastern side of the United States. These markers are painted on tree trunks, rocks, fence posts, and occasionally sidewalks along the way. Estimates suggest that some one hundred sixty-five thousand white blazes punctuate the length of the Trail.

Each white blaze serves the purpose of informing hikers they are on the Appalachian Trail. The hiker can determine sharp turns, potential obstacles, or important features ahead based on different white blaze variations. The absence of white blazes also serves to inform hikers they might no longer be on the Trail.

Between 2021 and 2024, I section-hiked the entire length of the Appalachian Trail. During those four years, I acquired the skill of instinctively recognizing Appalachian Trail white blazes and modifying my hiking based on the information I absorbed. My quiet time on the Trail allowed me to contemplate the function of white blazes and to consider if I could implement a similar strategy in my personal and professional life. Would it be feasible for me to construct a personal set of white blazes in the real world and use them to enhance my path through it?

White Blaze Leadership comes from this experience. It asks you to consider the White Blazes you have in your life. Which ones are important to you? What set of blazes can you learn to recognize, interpret, and drive meaning from? Are you even on the right path? In discovering your White Blazes, the right path will become clearer.

Through my journey on the Trail, I came to find my personal set of White Blazes: Question, Inspire, Believe, Value, and Act. Yours may well be different or might overlap with these. It's up to you to find your path.

The leadership insights from my White Blazes apply to both how I interact with others and how I look internally at myself. Some White Blaze moments gave me an immediate opportunity to act, while others have deeper meanings and lessons that I carry forward with me.

This book is the story of my hike along the Appalachian Trail. It's a story about the reason I was out on the Trail in the first place: a mission to cure a fatal disease. And it's a story about embracing our potential to lead in the everyday.

My goal in sharing these stories is to showcase the strength of White Blaze Leadership. I'll show you how I learnt to see my White Blazes in everyday experiences and how I learnt to consider and interpret those moments. You will discover how building your set of White Blazes and learning to use them in your day-to-day will help you find your way to lead.

I trust that in coming along on this journey with me, you will find value in White Blaze Leadership, reflect on all those opportunities to lead that arise in the quiet moments of your everyday, and most importantly, find your way to lead.

Section Zero

The First Step

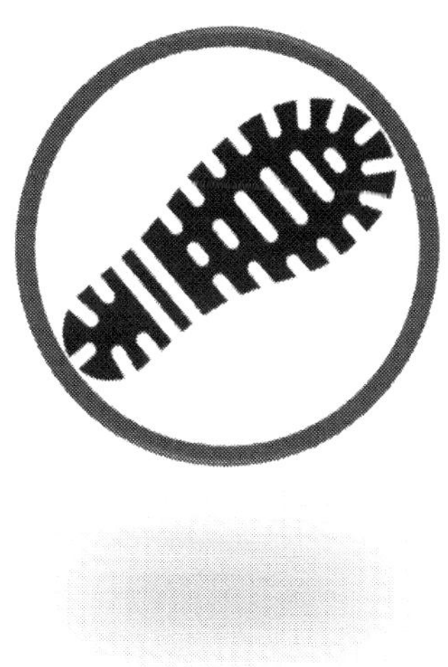

The morning of April 2, 2021, was a chilly 24°F (-4.4°C) at Neels Gap, Georgia. I waved goodbye to my son, who had driven me the hour and a half north from Atlanta, first on highways and then on twisty, narrow country lanes. After leaving the safety of his warm car, I followed a well-worn path up to an access point on the Appalachian Trail.

The frozen ground crunched underneath my hiking boots and my breath steamed outwards in a fleeting display of my inner fears. The stinging cold swirling around me cut into my heady mix of nervousness and excitement. I adjusted the straps on my spotless pack one final time and, looking back, saw the taillights of my son's car disappear, leaving me alone in the gathering morning light.

Then, at 7:34 a.m. I took my first step.

In hindsight, I was underprepared for what lay ahead both physically and mentally—not only for this first day, or this first section, but for the four-year odyssey this would come to be.

I never set out to hike the 2,197.4[1] miles that make up the Appalachian Trail, nor did I intend to write a book on leadership. But the Trail has a way of getting under your feet, getting into your head, and wrapping itself around your heart. It has a way of making you introspective. It gives you the time and the space to reflect and dream. It shifts your perception of the world and, perhaps, how the world perceives you. That first step changes everything.

After my first step, the die was cast, and over the next four years, I would hike the whole of the Appalachian Trail. One section at a time. All fourteen states. All 2,197.4 miles. All five hundred thousand feet of elevation gain. All five million steps.

The First Step

It's the one that matters.

Long before the idea of White Blaze Leadership entered my thoughts, my first White Blaze was clear to me: Act. It was this Act White Blaze that pushed me to take the first step. I found this blaze right at the intersection of intent and action.

You may have the best intent in the world—you will get that promotion, make that career-defining sale, accelerate growth, drive transparency, or redefine your organization's culture. You will change the world. The scale and scope of your intention don't matter because nothing will change unless you take the first step. Unless you act.

Everything you will read in this book happened because I recognized my Act White Blaze. My intent was to change the world, and when I recognized the need to act, to take a first step, I took it. My action was to literally take this first step onto the Appalachian Trail that bitterly cold morning in the spring of 2021.

The Appalachian Trail wasn't new to me. I'd taken part in long one-day hikes on it for years as charity fundraisers for a rare disease non-profit called the Cystic Fibrosis Foundation—a foundation woven into my life story and into the leadership insights played out in this book.

On these single-day hikes, I covered thirty miles over tough terrain in North Carolina. Stepping onto the Trail for these hikes at four o'clock in the morning, I would finish completely spent as the sun went down, knowing we had raised much-needed charitable funds. Our hard-earned dollars funded the science that one day will cure this fatal disease for forty thousand Americans—including my two daughters.

During the dark days of the COVID-19 pandemic, fundraising for many charities proved difficult. Charities that relied on in-person events, such as walks, dinner dances, and golf tournaments, suffered a particularly hard blow. Donations to health-related charities targeting diseases fell 4.2 percent from 2019, according to the Lilly Family School of Philanthropy.[2]

Because of these difficulties in fundraising, I realized it was necessary for me to do something extraordinary to inspire my friends and colleagues to continue to donate to the Cystic Fibrosis Foundation. I needed to draw on my leadership experience and get out there and lead. So, that's how I found myself at Neels Gap.

Hiking the whole of the Trail takes around six months. The Appalachian Trail Conservancy (ATC), which tracks these statistics, estimates over three thousand[3] intrepid hikers attempt this approach per year. These ambitious souls are known as thru-hikers. Most attempt a thru-hike in a south-to-north direction. The ATC estimates only one in four people who start the journey will complete it in any given year. It's a journey not for the faint of heart.

However, I couldn't put my life on pause for six months. Instead, I picked one small part of the Trail and decided to hike it over a long week. Hikers refer to this approach as section hiking. I settled on a section thirty miles from Springer Mountain, the Appalachian Trail's southern terminus. My plan was to hike from Neels Gap, Georgia, for 133 miles northbound to Fontana Dam in North Carolina.

After completing this initial section, the seed was sown, and I gave myself no choice but to hike the full length of the Appalachian Trail. I had no real comprehension of the insights the Trail was preparing to give me or how these experiences would change me. All of those gifts lay in the miles ahead of me.

The Journey

Less is more.

Some of my friends and colleagues reacted with skepticism when I told them my plan, but others were enthusiastically supportive. All wondered, though, what I would get out of too many days spent trudging through remote forests and too many nights spent sleeping in the wilds.

I discovered a piece of the answer to that question when I heard Dr. Preston Campbell, a previous CEO of the Cystic Fibrosis Foundation, speak about his remarkable career as a doctor, executive, and business leader. He focused on a core tenet of his, one of his White Blazes perhaps: Abundance comes from scarcity. Does that White Blaze resonate with you?

In Dr. Campbell's career, the opportunities that came to him from making the unexpected or risky choice made the biggest difference. The path least traveled. These choices put him in situations of scarcity, which led to an abundance of experience and an extraordinary path through life.

Hiking the Appalachian Trail is the epitome of scarcity. One where you're forced to think about food, water, and shelter every step of the way. It's a life experienced at the bottom of Maslow's hierarchy of needs, if you will. And yet, somehow, abundance comes from this.

Prior to taking my first step onto the Trail, I didn't know what my rewards would be, but part of the beauty of taking the first step is that unknowns become known. I would come to find abundance shining brightly on the Trail, revealing leadership insights both personally and professionally.

The White Blazes

It's not the destination; it's what you learn along the way.

As you hike along on this journey with me, we'll cover the miles from Georgia to Maine and together discover my White Blazes and their insights. Along the way, we'll filter a broad stream of topics from history, geology, flora and fauna, literature, leadership, and psychology to more personal subjects such as grit, music, gratitude, and, of course, bear encounters. In each case, the extraordinary wonder that is the Appalachian Trail will serve to remind and inform us of our responsibilities as leaders and of our opportunities to lead.

We'll experience over a hundred vignettes during our time together on the Trail. These short stories will relate memorable moments, experiences, and perspectives, each one retold to illustrate how I recognized one of my White Blazes and the unique aspect of leadership it offered. Through the words, images, and emotions, each vignette will push us to a deeper understanding of what it means to lead. I offer each one to help you pause and consider what leadership means to you.

After completing the Appalachian Trail, I was able to confirm my set of White Blazes that had guided me along this journey:

Each individual insight throughout the book is coded with these icons so that you can relate it back to these White Blazes.

If you're just starting on your leadership journey or are highly experienced and well along the trail, you can consider how my White Blazes led me to think about leadership and how the opportunity to lead can present itself in our everyday lives. And in turn, consider how you, too, can build your set of White Blazes and develop the skill of interpreting what the moment is telling you.

The Book

Have it your way.

Initially, I wrote about my time on the Appalachian Trail on LinkedIn, the business-focused social media platform. The simplicity of the insights, or a primeval need to connect with the land, resulted in the positive response I received to these articles. My writing about the Trail struck a deep chord with my colleagues and network. Perhaps, a little tired from the constant noise of day-to-day, they yearned for the adventure of the outdoors.

This book, *White Blaze Leadership*, is a curated collection of these articles fully reworked to pull them together as a whole. The sections follow a chronological order, written shortly after each hike, rather than ordered in geographical sequence. This results in a journey that broadly follows a south-to-north direction along the Trail, but not always. Terrain, weather, and logistics played into when I would hike certain sections.

"Hike your own hike" is a phrase I hear often on the Appalachian Trail. The idiom signifies no right or wrong way to hike between point A and point B. Similarly, I encourage you to read this book in a way that makes sense to you. You could do a full "thru-hike" of the book, starting with this section and working your way to the end. Or you could jump into individual sections when and if you have the time, as each section stands alone. You might even have a favorite section that you keep revisiting, which I would love to hear about if you do.

If your goal is simply to better understand the concept of White Blaze Leadership, you might want to pick just a few sections to illustrate the concepts and approaches within.

Take your time with each section, much like I took my time hiking them. The individual insights presented in each are worth pausing and pondering how they might apply to you as a leader. When you consider the days or weeks it took me to hike each section, it makes sense that spending time contemplating what you've just read will be a rewarding investment.

Out on the Trail, I find the deepest and most meaningful conversations happen at the end of the day while sitting around a roaring campfire with other hikers who happen to have chosen the same spot as me to camp for the night. The intoxicating smell of smoke, the chamomile tea in my mug, and the sound of laughter fill the air. The companionship of strangers and shared experience of the journey encourages people to open up and offer considered thoughts and feelings about whatever topic is at hand. In this way, both the fire and the conversation illuminate the darkness.

To mimic this experience, I've included a page at the end of each section with questions designed to prompt you to jot down your ideas, actions, and thoughts based on your interpretation of the section. These are *our* campfire conversations. They offer an opportunity for introspection about your approach to leadership. An opportunity to ponder your White Blazes. An opportunity for your unknowns to become known.

The Trail

See the stars, see how they shine for you.

Hiking the Appalachian Trail is like coming full circle for me. I grew up in a small rural village on the coast of North Wales in the U.K. No internet, no cellphones, only four channels on the television and one of those was in Welsh. The mountains, and what seemed like untamed country, were always within reach and the stars shone fiercely in a sky devoid of light pollution.

Life was quiet and measured.

Then, I took a first step and headed off to college. I earned a computer science degree from what is today the University of Greenwich, London. That took me on a path that led to New York, Denver, Miami, and the technology powerhouses of Boston, Seattle, and Silicon Valley. High-tech consulting, selling to Fortune 500 companies, and leading high-performing teams all provided opportunities to travel the world and experience megacities as diverse as Tokyo, Mumbai, and Mexico City. I built my personal and business networks so that we could build the technology and systems that would connect the world.

Later, when my children were born and cystic fibrosis entered my world, it was not the fear and turmoil of this deadly genetic disease that I would remember most. Rather, it was the gift it gave me to be a better father, to view the world from a less selfish perspective, to connect and build a community focused on finding a cure.

And yet, it's out on the Trail, in all its solitary magnificence, embraced by the silence of the forest, that I feel most connected. It's as if I've stepped back to the innocence of my childhood, one where I would lie in bed watching the billions of stars in the Milky Way arc across the night sky and wonder what my future will hold, what *our* futures will hold.

The Trail is where life, once again, is quiet and measured.

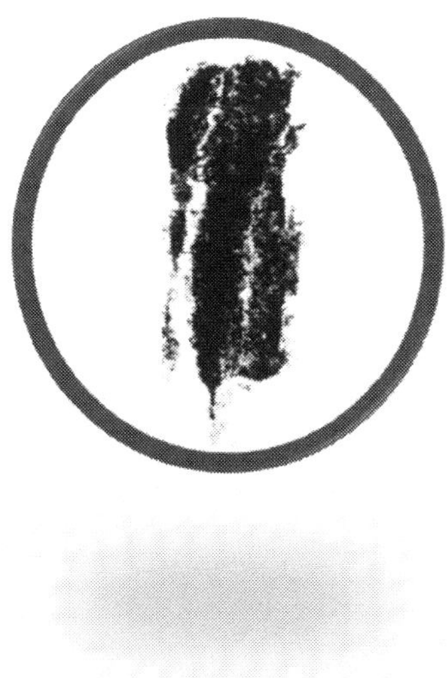

Whatever path you choose to hike this book, I thank you for considering *White Blaze Leadership*, for opening the pages, and for being willing to spend your valuable time with the insights into leadership that are within.

Not all my experiences may resonate. Not all my White Blazes and insights might apply to your situation. You might not even agree with some of them, and if you don't, I would love to get your thoughts and feedback. And, when we make it to the end of the Trail together, if you're inspired to tell me about your set of White Blazes, I would love to hear about them.

I'm confident you will enjoy this journey with me and perhaps, as I did, learn something from the simplicity of the experiences I took from my time on the Appalachian Trail.

As American naturalist Henry David Thoreau so perfectly stated: "I went to the woods because I wished to live deliberately, to front only the essential facts of life, and see if I could not learn what it had to teach, and not, when I came to die, discover that I had not lived."[4]

Section One

A Single Dove Chocolate Got Me Up a Mountain

The Appalachian Trail, at 2,197.4 miles, is a daunting task for anyone considering hiking its totality. I, however, began with a much more modest goal, which was to get to Fontana Dam in North Carolina, 133 miles away from my starting point. It was fortuitous that on my initial section hike, the idea of hiking all the way to Mount Katahdin in northern Maine, the northern terminus of the

Appalachian Trail, was something I had never even entertained. Otherwise, the sheer magnitude of that endeavor might have caused me to never take my first step.

Over nine days I dragged myself and my forty-pound pack up thirty thousand feet of elevation gain and a similar amount of descent. I hiked ten hours a day and slept on the ground in my flimsy tent deep in the woods. I went hungry and thirsty. At times, I felt thoroughly cold and miserable. In the end, I came close to my goal of reaching Fontana Dam but fell fifteen miles short, only making it as far as Stecoah Gap instead. I had been overly optimistic about my abilities to put miles behind me. It was my first realization that the Trail could be harder than it looked on paper and also my first realization that the Trail doesn't negotiate.

Yet somehow, the Trail gave back to me in ways I never imagined it could. My first section gave me a glimpse into the extraordinary insights in personal and business leadership I could draw from my experiences. It gave me the time to contemplate, which, for most of us, is a rare luxury. It gave me the perspective to appreciate the simple things and the time to recognize them. All the while, the Trail was preparing itself to get so far into my brain and my heart that I would have no choice but to keep on hiking.

The first set of leadership insights are, unsurprisingly, some of the simplest and most fundamental insights into what it means to be a leader. These insights that follow while elementary are the ones I would build on and come back to over the next four years as I continued my journey along the Appalachian Trail. These are the ones that allowed me to first glimpse my White Blazes.

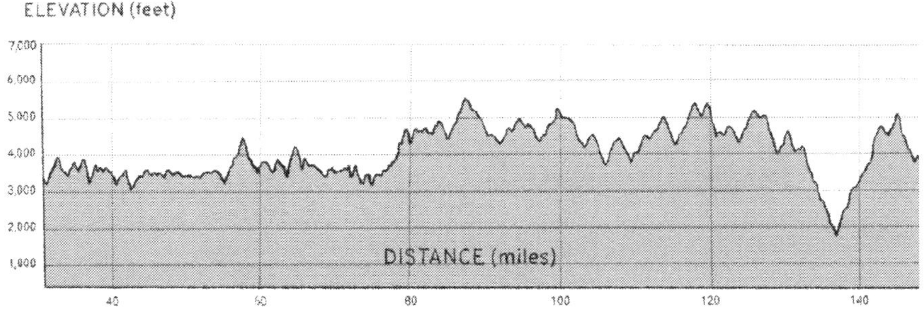

Figure 1 Neels Gap, GA, to Stecoah Gap, NC

Lighten the Load

Understand what you need to succeed and lose the rest.

Pack weight is among the most critical success factors in long-distance hiking. Every ounce you carry requires calories to move it. And calories add more weight that needs to be carried. Thru-hikers quickly figure out what they don't need to carry. I chatted with one such hiker who lugged around a pound of coffee beans and a grinder with him. He rapidly decided that freeze-dried coffee, weighing in at a fraction of his hipster coffee supplies, "would do just fine in the morning."

Conversely, it doesn't take long for thru-hikers to realize what they are also missing. I met several hikers who were already changing out their shoes, surprisingly, at the first chance they got. It turns out hiking day after day differs from a quick stroll around the park while breaking in the trendiest pair of zero-drop trail runners.

In hindsight, my pack was far too heavy for this first outing, but I didn't know what I didn't know. Each time I would hike over the subsequent months and years, my ability to reduce my pack weight continued to improve. My experience and knowledge taught me what was essential and what I could leave behind. As I look back on this first hike from the lens of time and distance traveled, I ask myself, "What was I even thinking with all the stuff I packed?"

Challenge the status quo.

In our business lives, we carry much that doesn't add value to the mission at hand. Those Zoom calls no one knows why they are on. That report no one reads. The tool, system, or machine that is a wrong fit or perhaps creates more effort to operate than it does in the value it produces. Knowing the difference between what's required today and what's not is a critical leadership skill.

For example, I can point to actions in my work experience that have helped to lighten my load—simple things, such as making sure I'm only joining meetings where I have value to add or understand why I'm invited. I remember an occasion when I was providing analysis on leading indicators for the business on a monthly basis. Due to ongoing changes in the market, I was certain these were the wrong data points. After conferring with the stakeholders, we re-engineered the indicators to gain a new perspective on the business. This lightened my workload and improved our understanding of our performance.

The example above also illustrates how identifying activities that add little to no value goes hand in hand with being prepared to make the needed changes. Inertia is a powerful force inside any mature organization. This force can complicate and slow down any type of change to the status quo. Sometimes, driving change might even require harnessing the political capital required to force the change, especially when strong resistance to it exists. In leadership, we need to forcefully communicate the reasons for change and articulate a path forward for that change.

When I think about leaders who push back on the status quo, one of my heroes comes to mind. I had the privilege of meeting Navy Rear Admiral Grace Hopper, the legendary computer scientist, in person when she spoke at the university I attended in London. Although she died in 1992, she still is a towering figure in the field of computing and in the advancement of women in computing. A 1976 *Computerworld* magazine article quotes her: "The most dangerous phrase a DP (data processing) manager can use is 'We've always done it that way.' "[5] The clock on the wall in her office ran counterclockwise to emphasize that point to her engineering staff.

Challenging your peers and teams with a simple question of *why* something is the way it is can be an eye-opening experience for everyone involved and a powerful leadership skill.

Trail Magic

Small personal actions can have a significant impact.

Late into the day, a steep mile stood between me and my campsite for the night. Huffing and puffing up to the summit of Blue Mountain, I caught a glimpse of a clear freezer bag hanging on a tree with a single Dove chocolate left in it. Trail Magic! It gave me the go juice I needed to get that last difficult mile done.

Trail Magic permeates the culture of the Appalachian Trail. It's best defined as unexpected acts of kindness or generosity. During my time on the Trail, I enjoyed multiple acts of selfless kindness from complete strangers known as Trail Angels. Trail Magic could be anything from this single piece of chocolate to a full-scale breakfast buffet in the middle of the woods. Or from an ice cream bar to random beer, water, and soda cans left at trailheads. Any kind of Trail Magic was much appreciated. You never expect Trail Magic, but when it happens, its impact is massive on your day.

It's not just about food and drink; rather, it's anything that gives energy, encouragement, or a pick-me-up when you need to keep going. Other examples include a piece of valuable knowledge from another hiker, a ride to or from a trailhead, or the unseen work of trail maintenance workers who have cleared a fallen tree out of your way. Sometimes, you don't even know you need that piece of Trail Magic until the gift is given to you.

Unleash the power of small, thoughtful, personal interactions.

We sometimes forget how much of an impact a simple personal action can make in the workplace. It can be as simple as taking the time to pause and listen to someone, compliment someone on their work, or ask what someone is working on and then focus on hearing their response. Though seemingly trivial, these actions could be exactly what someone on the other side of the interaction needs. Each of us has the opportunity to practice and refine this skill many times a day, and as leaders, we should be conscious of it.

For example, I was sitting in the waiting room at a dentist's office recently, waiting for a friend who I was giving a ride. The receptionist was making call after call to remind people of their appointments and was doing a wonderful job—polite, engaging, and professional. I took a moment to tell her how much I appreciated someone being terrific at their job. Months later, my friend told me the receptionist still talked about that interaction and how much it meant to her.

Leaders recognize the power of Trail Magic and actively go out of their way to apply it effectively. Stop for a moment and recall a time someone helped your day, or your entire career, with a small piece of thoughtful interaction applied at the exact right moment. Imagine what it will feel like to offer up some Trail Magic of your own.

Hike Your Own Hike

Everyone's journey is unique.

There's no single right way to undertake a hike from Georgia to Maine. Some folks are up-early-and-at-it types, while others, like me, enjoy a leisurely breakfast as part of their routine. Some carry ultralight packs, while others carry a slew of luxury items. Some, like the extraordinary Tara Dower (who at the time of this book's publication holds the fastest known supported time to complete a thru-hike of the Appalachian Trail), push the limits of human endurance. For comparison, Dower averaged over fifty miles a day and finished her north-to-south record in forty days and eighteen hours. I consider seventeen miles a day to be good going.

The point is that every person hikes what is right for them at the moment. Their speed, number of miles covered, frequency of rest days, and a myriad of other factors are unique to each individual. At the end of the journey, two people taking different approaches can still reach Maine and complete the Trail.

In the early days of my Appalachian Trail hiking, a key part of hiking-my-own-hike was morning coffee and a brief respite before heading out to face the hardships of the day. Later in my four-year journey, though, I would learn to leverage this coffee time to significant advantage, transforming the ritual into something far more powerful. That transformative lesson, however, lay many tough miles ahead of me.

Chamomile tea at the end of the day always served its purpose of slowing me down and preparing me for a well-earned sleep. I thoroughly enjoyed taking the extra ten minutes to indulge myself every morning and evening.

Guide career paths by understanding individual journeys.

Leaders understand everyone is going through different journeys too. It's important to understand where someone is in their life and career, what they want, what they need, and what external factors play into those decisions. Everyone just needs someone to believe in them.

Now might not be the right time to push someone to take extra responsibility. Perhaps now is the right time to push someone to overcome their confidence gap. Perhaps you need to encourage someone to transfer to a different group if you don't have the opportunities to keep up with their pace.

This understanding all comes down to listening and recognizing that just as one size does not fit all on the Trail, one size doesn't fit all in life or the work environment either.

Take Time to Enjoy the View

Stop and remind yourself of what you have accomplished.

While on the Trail in North Carolina, I climbed a steep mountain deep inside the Nantahala National Forest. This magnificent forest is one of 154 extraordinary forest areas the United States Forest Service manages on our behalf and for generations yet to come. The name Nantahala comes from the Cherokee, meaning the Land of the Mid-day Sun, so-called because some valleys in the area are so steep the sun only reaches the forest floor when it's directly overhead.

Step, breathe, step. I was two hours into what would be a three-hour climb of close to three thousand feet. The dense trees were closing in around me, but I kept my focus on the muddy path rising in front of me. The leg-sized tree roots crisscrossing the Trail seemed to be intent on tripping me up or, at a minimum, breaking my stride with their awkward placement. I was determined to push my way to the top without taking a break. Glancing to my left, a gap in the trees opened to a stunning vista.

I paused and then took fifteen minutes to sit and enjoy the view, looking out over the Nantahala National Forest with peaks and valleys going on forever. The vista was every bit the classic Appalachian postcard, with peaks rolling into the distance and the greens of the trees and blues of the sky blending into the horizon. After my brief stop, I felt refreshed and, surprisingly, reached the summit around the same time as if I hadn't taken a break. And that's the key point right there.

Reflect on and communicate your team's accomplishments.

Pausing for a moment doesn't necessarily mean a major impact. In this case, I still arrived at my destination at the same time. Nothing lost, but much gained. Taking the time to stop and reflect on everything you have accomplished is a skill not enough leaders focus on. Teams work hard performing the day-to-day activities of our jobs. Pausing and asking everyone to lift their heads and see the difference they make is so empowering.

For example, the difference might have been in fulfilling some aspect of the business's mission or in the communities touched by what they do. It might be in volunteer work, the social impact of the organization, or perhaps in the daily lives of colleagues and their families. Empower yourself and your teams by pausing to appreciate the view. What might a pause look like for you right now? What difference do you make that's worth bringing into focus?

It Takes All of Us

Leaders strive to be inclusive.

On the Trail, we are family, or *tramily* as thru-hikers call it. We are one family, a trail family. No judging. If you're open to sharing your story, great. If not, that's fine too. I met an eighteen-year-old who was a gas station attendant and a seventy-five-year-old whose whole life had been as a lobsterman in Maine. I've met successful middle-aged couples escaping the everyday and veterans trying to re-engage with the America they went overseas for. Tramily. Every hiker helps and encourages fellow hikers to reach Maine unconditionally.

In addition, thru-hikers also take on a trail name, which represents who they are on the Trail. A trail name is distinct and separate from the real world. Often, hikers start without a trail name and earn it from a habit, a physical attribute, or some amusing incident that occurred along the way. On the Trail, I'm known as *Coach*. It's a trail name I've earned from encouraging friends, colleagues, and anyone who will listen to me to come hike with me as I raise the funds required to cure cystic fibrosis. I try to live up to the name while I'm hiking.

For many thru-hikers, their tramily becomes the close-knit community that gets them through this adventure. A tramily provides mutual support, safety in numbers, companionship, and the unique power of a shared experience. Strangers, to start with, become lifelong friends by the time they get to their journey's end.

This camaraderie has also been true in my journey with the cystic fibrosis community. In 1955, a small group of parents created the Cystic Fibrosis Foundation to research this terrible disease. A genetic defect causes the buildup of sticky mucus in the lungs, one of many impacts the disease has on the body. Repeated infections and inflammation damage the lungs so severely that median life expectancy was only four to five years of age in the 1950s.

In the decades since then, thousands of parents, friends, strangers, scientists, caregivers, and those with cystic fibrosis have all come together and hiked a metaphorical long trail to find a cure. We have forged considerable progress along this trail over the intervening years and are closer to the finish line than ever before. A child born between 2017 and 2021 now has a median predicted age of survival of 53 years.[6] Incredible progress but not yet a cure.

It's the extraordinary people I have met along the way and the totality of the cystic fibrosis community that fueled me to take the first step and each one after that, no matter how hard they were.

Embody the principles you advocate.

A heightened sense of social responsibility over the last few years has enabled organizations to focus on their internal communities. Businesses are saying we must give everyone the support, opportunity, and encouragement to contribute to their fullest. Even as conversations around diversity, equity, and inclusion have become politicized we still cannot avoid thinking about the full value our colleagues bring with their unique experiences and perspectives.

Many organizations and individuals have found the courage to say, "We're not doing good enough," and aspire to do better.

When everyone has the opportunity to give their best, it's the most effective way to compete and win in any market. A strong leader understands this and will commit to it.

In a fascinating *Harvard Business Review* article from March 2023 titled "How Investing in DEI Helps Companies Become More Adaptable,"[7] the authors found that small increases in diversity, equity, and inclusion ratings lead to a significant increase in the ability of an organization to change. In turn, this ability has a strong correlation to improvement in revenue growth, shareholder return, and Earnings Before Interest and Taxes (EBIT) margins.

Leadership, both in business and personal affairs, necessitates recognizing sometimes the world we want doesn't happen on its own. Rather, we need to actively encourage the behavior we want to see in order to achieve these goals through action, example, and direction. That change starts with you and those you inspire. The famous anthropologist Margaret Mead captured that sentiment: "Never doubt that a small group of thoughtful, committed citizens can change the world; indeed, it's the only thing that ever has."[8]

I'm optimistic if we do our part—if *you* do your part—these efforts will change our outlook so that one day, equality in our daily lives will be as normal a concept as tramily is on the Appalachian Trail.

No, It's Not Lonely at the Top

Remember the people there with you.

Hiking solo for hours upon hours might seem like a lonely endeavor. In fact, it's far from that. Hiking gives me the time to clear my mind from the clutter of the everyday and allows me to focus on what matters the most. In this case, my mission to cure cystic fibrosis.

A mission I need to complete so my daughters don't have to face that disease. So they don't have to endure endless hospital stays and countless doctor visits. So they never have to worry about what their current lung function is or what bacteria is growing in their sputum. Instead, they can plan their life adventures to the fullest.

It also gave me time to think about the people whose support allowed me to be on the Trail: From my son James, who drove me to the trailhead that first day, to my friend Patrick, who met me along the way with egg sandwiches and fresh coffee, and all my unseen friends and colleagues who followed along, donating and wishing me well on this adventure.

Prioritize collective success.

Leaders understand that even though they are the ones on stage, presenting to a client or sitting in that board meeting, behind them are many friends and colleagues who have supported them and still support them in their role. Effective leaders lean into those relationships, pulling people along with them. They make sure everyone knows whatever part they play is valued and reflected in that moment.

In return, that support can act to empower a leader with the energy, confidence, and drive to perform at their best because it's not just about them; it's about everyone involved. Leaders embody the proverb: "If you want to go fast, go alone. If you want to go far, go together."

Leaders Have to Lead

Sometimes, as a leader, you need to be out front.

OK, so this one might win me a Captain Obvious award, but bear with me. My reason for this hike was simple. I needed to inspire. I needed to inspire my family, friends, and colleagues to donate to the Cystic Fibrosis Foundation, a charity that one day will cure my daughters' disease. More urgently, I needed to inspire other fundraisers who would normally join me for our annual Xtreme Hike event.

I'm a Volunteer Leader for this organization, having led multiple initiatives, such as the National Annual Fund. I've sat on regional chapter boards and spoken at dozens of walks, golf events, and black-tie galas. When asked for help, my response is always an emphatic "Yes!"

A whole year into the COVID-19 ordeal, I was tired of the uncertainty and frustrated at the impact the pandemic was having on our fight toward a cure for cystic fibrosis. I decided going big was the type of leadership that was needed to inspire and motivate others to push COVID-19 behind them and get back to fundraising.

Lead from the front with big, bold, visionary action.

Leaders must lead from the front sometimes. Take big, bold, visionary actions that will inspire their teams and those around them to stand up, get motivated, and give their best. As a leader you can't—nor should you— be out front all the time, but trust that you will know when the time arrives for you to step forward and go big.

It could be during times of intense market change or crisis. It could be when changes in people or products have everyone on edge, or it could be because an extraordinary idea of great magnitude needs to see the light of day.

During my career, I have witnessed leaders step up and take these types of actions in response to internal or external forces. The type of bold leadership we saw when COVID-19 turned our world upside down. The type of leadership that guided firms through the dot-com crash of the early 2000s and the stalwart leadership we saw in the days and weeks following 9-11.

Bold leadership also happens in response to competitive market conditions on a far more frequent basis. You only have to look at visionary leaders who brought us into the modern world with breakout products like smartphones, self-driving cars, and mRNA therapies. As the Roman poet Virgil wrote, "*Audentes Fortuna iuvat*" (Fortune favors the bold).[9]

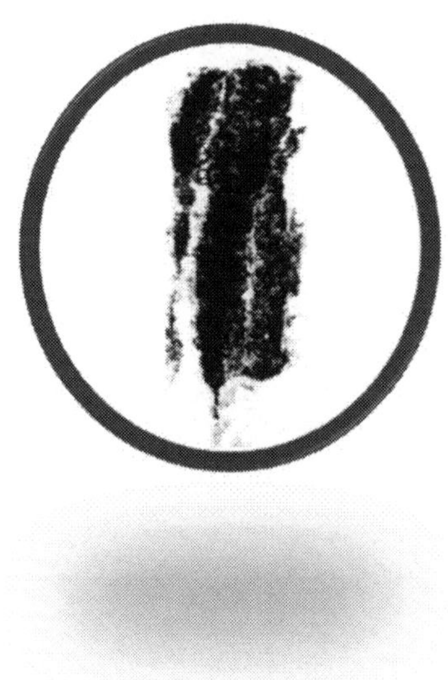

This section of the Trail gave me basic insights into hiking and leadership. My first step led to these reminders that the simplest of tasks can be the ones that are the most valuable. For me, these insights represent a solid foundation, one I kept coming back to as I hiked along the Appalachian Trail.

They also serve as a reminder that taking the first step isn't complicated, even if it's daunting. I know that only by taking the first step can I move closer to completing my mission and my dream of finding a cure for cystic fibrosis.

Examining how these insights emerged from the simple act of hiking into the woods was also the start of my White Blaze Leadership journey. For the first time, I considered how I could translate these experiences into meaningful thoughts and ideas. This goes beyond merely a good story or shared experience. It gets to the heart of what White Blaze Leadership is: Recognize. Interpret. Lead.

Section One Campfire Conversations

- How would you describe the key qualities that shape your approach to leadership?
- In what ways do you find or create time in your schedule for reflection?
- Can you share an experience when you gave or received trail magic? Perhaps share something unexpectedly kind or helpful.
- What strategies or actions do you think could help you lighten your load?
- Are there any bold ideas you've been exploring or at least considering?
- What first steps are you thinking about taking toward your goals, and how will you act on them?

Section Two

How a Sasquatch Taught Me Gratitude

It was early November 2021, and I found myself squinting right at a Sasquatch, who must have been at least eight feet tall. I didn't fully believe what I was seeing, and for his part, he was staring intently right back at me. It was cold, and it had been raining on and off for the last thirty-six hours. Thick ice covered the fir trees at this altitude. Maybe I was hallucinating because of the horrible weather and my fatigue, but I was fairly certain he was physically standing right in front of me.

Kuwohi in the Great Smoky Mountains National Park is the highest point on the Appalachian Trail at 6,643 feet. The mountain was renamed from Clingmans Dome in September 2024 to its original name of Kuwohi, which means *mulberry place* in Cherokee. Kuwohi is also the mid-way point on my section hike of 125 miles, straight across this majestic landscape. It had been a relentless thirty-five-mile climb from Fontana Dam to this peak. Even in the miserable weather, the views across the Smokies and the changing patterns of the old-growth forest drew me onwards and upward. Somewhat incongruously, as I reached the mountain's summit, the Trail dropped me right into a parking lot.

There, busloads of visitors were disgorged to take in the views from the observation tower. The tower, officially known as the Clingmans Dome Observation Tower, was built in 1959 and is listed in the National Register of Historic Places.[10] Its modern architectural style of a long concrete spiral ramp and circular viewing platform seems utterly out of place. I felt like it was a brutal intrusion into the wilderness I'd been immersed in for the last few days. From that perspective, the tower is perhaps more valuable as a reminder of our history with the Cherokee than a viewing platform for day-trippers from Gatlinburg.

It's right here, near the tower's base, where I encountered the Sasquatch. My brain finally forced me to accept it's an actor in an excellent Sasquatch costume. For the briefest of moments, though, my mind questioned if this was real. The swarms of tourists posing for pictures with him, however, were a dead giveaway. This wasn't the making of an Unexplained Mysteries television special.

Still, part of me continued to imagine it was an actual Sasquatch trying to make a living in a gig-economy world. I snapped my selfie, said thank you, and moved on to answering tourist questions about whether I was a real hiker or not. I think I am! The thought of the Sasquatch going home to his Sasquatch family after an exhausting day of smiling for cameras made me happy for most of the afternoon's hike.

Later, I reflected on that casual "Thank you" I gave the Sasquatch. It led me to think more deeply about what gratitude is, how I could improve my ability to extend gratitude, and how I could harness the power of this simple act.

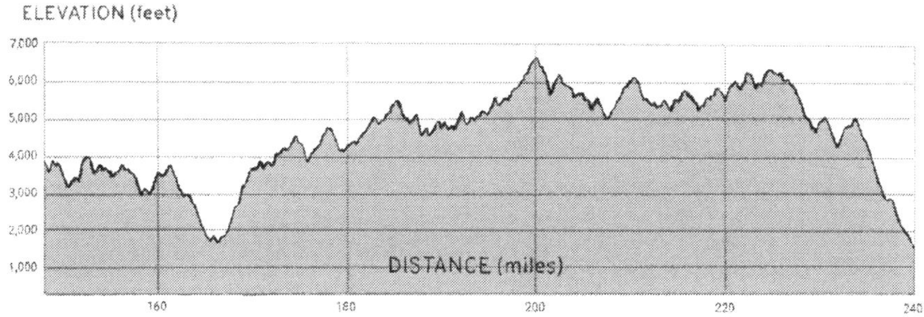

Figure 2 Stecoah Gap, GA, to Standing Bear, TN

Gratitude Needs Context

Adding depth to "Thanks" significantly enhances its meaning.

Yeti, Almas, Yowie, Bigfoot, and Sasquatch. Stories of large ape-like creatures roaming dense forests exist all over the world. The Angus Reid Institute published a public opinion poll[11] showing twenty-six percent of Canadians believe cryptids, animals we don't have proof exist, such as the Sasquatch, are "definitely" or "probably" real.

Every year, thousands of aspiring cryptid wranglers try their hand at Bigfoot Calling competitions held nationwide at Bigfoot festivals. So far, no one has been successful, but you can watch plenty of calling attempts on YouTube. It's a solid way to waste an hour of your life that you can't get back.

As I hiked, I seldom listened to anything other than the silence of the forest: no music blasting, no e-book in my ears, no desire to learn how to speak Italian. I felt safer this way. More connected. I could hear the crack of fallen branches as unseen wildlife moved in the shadows or the footsteps of another hiker moving along the Trail. Walking in silence helped me to concentrate on the surrounding environment, where I did the mental math to calculate distances and timing, weighed options for water stops, and got comfortable inside my head. It also provided a much better chance to hear a bear or Sasquatch sneaking up on me.

If I'd seen this Sasquatch in the woods rather than the parking lot, I would have been terrified. Instead, we were hamming it up for Instagram-worthy photos like a couple of teenage girls at a Taylor Swift concert. I snapped the perfect photo, offered my thanks, and moved out of the way to let someone else create a memory.

The Sasquatch thought I was thanking him for letting me take a photo with him, but I was thanking him for being the waypost that informed me I'd reached the pinnacle of my climb to Kuwohi. My "Thank you" was one of hundreds I'm sure he received that day. What if I'd added a few words of context? I could've said, "Thank you for representing the pinnacle of four days of hard hiking and for making me smile. I appreciate you." That would have been memorable.

Strengthen your gratitude muscle with consistent practice.

We should encourage our colleagues and teams to be more specific about gratitude by adding context to it. "I appreciate you because we wouldn't have won this deal without your input." "Thank you for covering that meeting for me. It allowed me to be present for a critical client call," or "You're the best when you lead these team calls because you're so prepared." This extended "Thank you because" carries so much more impact than a plain "Thank you." Although a simple thank you is one thousand percent better than no thank you at all.

As the occasion arises, I will also send old-fashioned handwritten thank-you notes. Nothing too fancy, but a simple, plain card with a straightforward note of thanks, sent for the right moment, can have a memorable impact.

Type-2 Fun

We should be grateful even when things aren't perfect.

Later into my hike that week, I was climbing back down and down and down from the top of Kuwohi. My right knee was killing me, my fingers were numb from the cold, the rain had poured continuously for the last forty-eight hours, and I'd accidentally stepped in some bear poop. *Argh!* Type-2 fun!

Type-2 fun is the type of fun that, in the moment, makes you want to quit, hang up your soaking wet backpack and your disgusting hiking boots, and head home. However, later, around a campfire or sipping on a beer, it's the stuff of legend that gets bigger with each retelling. I really didn't know it at the time, but I had a lot of type-2 fun ahead of me in the coming months and years I would be out on the Trail.

I hiked into Standing Bear Hostel that evening feeling quite miserable. But after a warm shower and some hot food, I was ready to take my spot by the welcoming campfire and share my type-2 fun stories.

Find the power gained from the toughest situations.

Imagine the power we could impart if we encouraged our teams and colleagues to be grateful for type-2 fun right in the moment when it's happening. It might be a project gone off the rails, a client meeting that went horribly wrong, or a can't-lose proposal that went to the competitor.

I unearthed this inspiring quote from the poet Maya Angelou: "Courage allows the successful woman to fail—and learn powerful lessons from the failure—so that in the end, she didn't fail at all."[12] In this simple statement, Angelou captures not only the essence of the value in adverse circumstances but also the fact that even to experience type-2 fun, you must have shown the courage to take the first step.

Sensing the value of type-2 fun in the moment and the reward of experience from it is valuable. We should be grateful for that experience and the knowledge it will arm us with for the next time. After all, in our professional careers, we'll all step into proverbial bear poop.

The More You Know

Understanding and gratitude go hand in hand.

Ox, a trail maintenance worker, gave me a ride in his truck to the Fontana Dam trailhead at the start of my day. He is one of the thousands of volunteers who maintain the Trail year-round. We talked about the dam and how it was built during World War II to provide electricity for much-needed aluminum production. We talked about the ghost towns submerged under the water—Forney, Judson, Fontana, and Bushnell sacrificed to the greater need of the war effort. But mostly, we talked about the Trail because that's what hikers do.

Ox enjoys educating hikers on what it takes to maintain the Trail. "Once they understand," he said, "they care more for it and are more thankful for what they have."

Cultivate gratitude by understanding what you're grateful for.

That's such a powerful insight. As leaders, if we can help our teams understand to a greater degree what they are being grateful for, then that gratitude will be deeper and more meaningful, both in the giving and the receiving. For example, an extra couple of hours working late on a project might have meant a missed kids' soccer game or a late train home. Perhaps the reworked presentation meant someone missed a friend's birthday party, or that proposal, which needed to be in on Monday, meant someone delayed their vacation by a day.

I was thankful for the ride to the trailhead from Ox. He understood it meant a mile less of a walk for me that day with my heavy pack. My expression of gratitude for him was richer for listening to his stories of working on the Trail. As I hiked that week, I took more notice of trail maintenance and improvement work, and I was also more grateful for it.

In simply taking the time to consider this interaction with Ox, I started to understand the power of White Blaze Leadership. That's the recognition of the process—the ability to say, "That was a meaningful moment," and then decide what to do with it.

The Glue That Binds Teams

Gratitude requires emotion, and emotion drives us all.

Out on the Trail, I've received Trail Magic and am grateful for each occurrence. For instance, a stronger hiker who passes me on the Trail and takes a moment to check if all is good. Or a fellow hiker around the campfire who offers a piece of chocolate or shares information about how far to the next flowing stream on a sweltering day. These simple acts of kindness instill gratitude in me for being there and being part of the community on the Appalachian Trail.

In return, I've also given back to the Trail community as circumstances allow—from kind words and encouragement to shared supplies and, in one case, the gift of my spare water filter to a distraught hiker on the verge of tears. Although they were trivial interactions within the grand scheme of hiking the Appalachian Trail, the impact of each was acknowledged with strong gratitude and an easy smile.

In all cases, the deep simplicity of time on the Trail allows us to see gratitude more clearly for what it is. It's an acknowledgment that we are better when we are *in this together*, regardless of if we are giving or receiving.

Recently, I read a thought-provoking paper called "Pay It Forward: Gratitude in Social Networks."[13] It was published in a wonderfully named scientific journal: *The Journal of Happiness Studies*. (We should all subscribe.) The paper looked at how simple acts of gratitude can multiply across a social network through a mechanism called Upstream Reciprocity. Here, people who receive gratitude feel compelled to *pay it forward* by replicating that act to other people they encounter. Upstream Reciprocity ultimately strengthens the structure of the entire organization.

Embrace the power of genuine gratitude.

Gratitude is a powerful force. The best leaders and the most capable organizations understand this instinctively. It's vital we help our colleagues understand this as well and translate gratitude into meaningful words and actions supported by authentic emotion. Sincere gratitude can't be faked and therefore demands understanding.

In February 2015, Oliver Sacks, the famed neurologist and writer, authored an op-ed essay in the *New York Times* titled "My Own Life,"[14] where he wrote about his recent cancer diagnosis. Knowing he only had a few months left to live, he offered us this: "I cannot pretend I am without fear. But my predominant feeling is one of gratitude. I have loved and been loved; I have been given much and I have given something in return; I have read and traveled and thought and written."

In the end, I believe Dr. Sacks knew exactly what he was talking about.

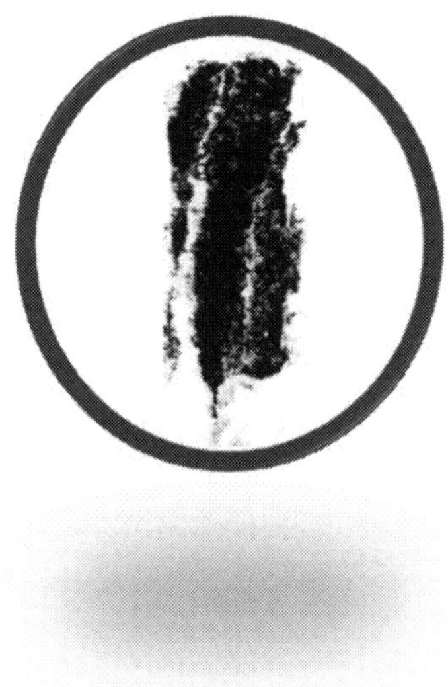

This section of the Trail allowed me to consider gratitude in a new light—see it in ways I had never even considered. It makes sense that the Trail would take me down this path this early into the journey, as I'm sure that gratitude is a requirement for completing my mission. I already know I will need to lean on friends, strangers, and colleagues to get me all the way to Mount Katahdin. So, it makes sense that I need to embrace gratitude.

I do have much to be grateful for in my life: Wonderful family and friends who support me in this endeavor. Colleagues and an organization that encourages me to bring my authentic self to work every day. The gift of a purpose and of a mission to fulfill it. For these things, I'm deeply grateful.

As the journey progressed, I came to understand that gratitude, on its own, is not one of my White Blazes. Rather, gratitude is wrapped into and around my other White Blazes. Perhaps it strengthens them and makes them more readily visible to me. This was an interesting self-discovery as gratitude is often held out in its own right as a leadership trait, and it's certainly one that I aspire to use.

This is one aspect of White Blaze Leadership that I would come to learn over the coming years: It will help you to better understand yourself and what drives you forward.

One thing I was decidedly grateful for on this section of the Trail was that it was just the bear poop I encountered and not the actual bear.

Section Two Campfire Conversations

- What are some ways you could increase your practice of gratitude?
- How do you work to foster a culture of gratitude within your organization?
- What are you feeling grateful for right now, and how might you express that gratitude?
- Can you think of a challenging moment—perhaps a type-2 fun experience—that, in hindsight, you might have handled differently?

Section Three

Of Mice and Men and Owls

Cold-weather hiking seemed to be a frozen bridge too far for me. However, over a cold long weekend, I decided to brave the elements, don every piece of hiking clothing I owned, and just do it. It was colder than I expected and colder weather than I ever wanted to be outside in. The nighttime temperatures dropped to 5°F (-15°C). For me, that's cold. Like, really, really cold. It's even colder when the task at hand is getting out of your sleeping bag in the middle of the night to go pee. A mental and logistical test of endurance!

In 1914, Sir Ernest Shackleton and his crew of twenty-seven sailed the three-masted barquentine *Endurance* down to Antarctica. I'm sure he felt the same way about the temperatures as he famously posted a wanted ad for sailors to join him: "Men wanted for hazardous journey. Small wages, bitter cold, long months of complete darkness, constant danger, safe return doubtful. Honor and recognition in case of success." The spoilers over at the Smithsonian seem to think he never actually placed this ad in the *London Times*,[15] but what do they know?

Alfred Lansing's epic book, *Endurance: Shackleton's Incredible Voyage*,[16] recalls the heroic story of Shackleton's adventures in this frozen wasteland. Shackleton's mission, The Imperial Trans-Antarctic Expedition, set out to make the first land crossing of the continent. However, when *Endurance* sank soon after arriving, the mission turned to one of determination and survival. I recommend this as your next book on leadership.

I know my weekend expedition was a pale shadow of Shackleton's adventure, but even so, I felt as if I had answered his advert and signed up for his mission as I headed out into the darkness and bitter cold.

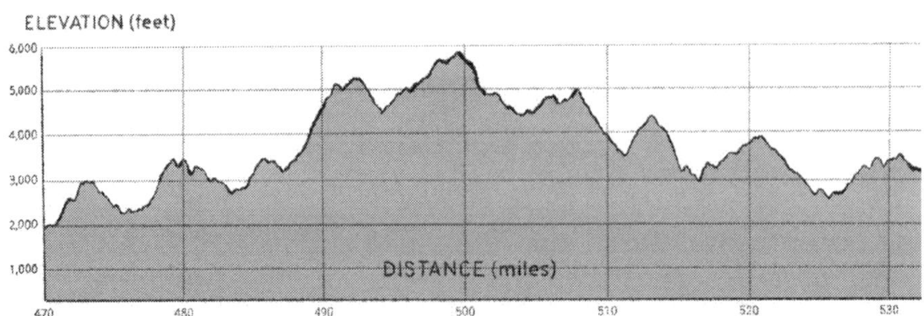

Figure 3 Damascus, VA, to Partnership Shelter, VA

There Is No Cold

The higher the stakes, the more the need to prepare.

There's an often-told hiker saying designed to impart wisdom: "There is no cold, just a failure to prepare for cold." As a resident of South Florida for thirty years, trust me, cold is real. Local news stations in South Florida issue severe weather temperature warnings when it plummets close to 50°F (10°C). "Bring in your plants and small pets," they advise. My Floridian wardrobe consisted of shorts, T-shirts, and a few coats I'd owned for decades. Knowing I would face much colder temperatures on this section of the Trail, I did what any self-respecting hiker would do and drove to REI to buy stuff. If you're unfamiliar with REI, it's a co-operative selling everything you might need—and a whole bunch of equipment and accessories you don't technically need but want—to do some serious outdoor recreation.

Founded in Seattle in 1938 by Mary and Lloyd Anderson, REI has grown from importing a single type of Austrian ice axe to being among the largest outdoor product retailers in the United States. I didn't buy an ice axe on this visit to REI but sort of wished I had. Next time you visit an REI, you might pause to notice that in a classy nod to their history, the door handles on the entrance to their stores are ice axes.

My trip to REI netted me a sleeping bag liner, which added an extra fifteen degrees of protection, and a pair of gloves a NASA astronaut would be proud of. Both items were essential to a favorable outcome on this section.

The bigger the stakes the more preparation matters.

In life and business, as in hiking, preparation increases in importance as the stakes rise. Preparation is not my strongest asset, but being unprepared at 5°F (-15°C) could have deadly consequences. As leaders, we can help our teams to better understand why the investment in time required for preparation is necessary.

Be it business meetings, planning, or presentations, taking the time to prepare correctly increases with the stakes at hand.

I see this firsthand at my organization every day. Colleagues spend considerable effort preparing for orals, which is the main stage in presenting proposals to clients. The more focused the preparation, the better the outcome. Presenting your slides in advance to a group of colleagues and directly receiving their critical feedback can feel a little awkward at first. The outcome, however, is a presentation that's fine-tuned for your message and a more effective use of the time your client is investing in the meeting with you.

I read a thought-provoking article in the Journal of Experimental Social Psychology titled "Feeling Prepared Increases Confidence in Any Accessible Thoughts Affecting Evaluation Unrelated to the Original Domain of Preparation."[17] The article studies how being prepared in one domain can lead to feeling confident in your thoughts completely unrelated to what you have prepared for. What I took from this paper was that spending the time to prepare for success in one field can amplify the value you get from that investment by giving you confidence across everything you do. It's the mindset of, "If I can do that, I can do anything."

When I was preparing to write this section, I researched the famous quote from Abraham Lincoln on preparation: "Give me six hours to chop down a tree, and I will spend the first four sharpening the axe." It turns out this is something he most likely didn't say. The initial attribution to Lincoln didn't occur until 1960, according to Quote Investigator,[18] and was in an advertisement for drilling equipment. At least we know Washington chopped down that cherry tree, right?

From Ice Comes Water

To change the status quo, you must apply energy.

One night I was sleeping in a Trail shelter, an open wooden structure with a floor, roof, and three walls. There are about 280 of these shelters or lean-tos dotted along the Appalachian Trail. The shelters range from spacious and well-maintained to some that could best be described as functional. I was cocooned in my sleeping bag and sleeping bag liner, with just enough of a gap left for me to breathe. The Trail shelter was silent except for the occasional scurrying of mice and the creaking of my air mattress as I tossed and turned in my sleep.

By the time morning finally broke through the dense forest surrounding the shelter, everything was frozen solid. My water bottles and my hiking boots were bricks. However, I anticipated this and filled my coffee mug with water the night before.

Thankfully, I had done research on operating my stove at these temperatures. The standard fuel for a canister is propane mixed with isobutane or n-butane. These gases become liquid when kept under high pressure in the canister. Opening the valve causes the liquid in the canister to boil and return to a gas state, which can then be ignited. However, this requires the liquid fuel to be warmer than its boiling point, which for isobutane is 10.94°F (-11.7°C). Since the ambient temperature was colder than this, you can see my problem.

Fortunately for me, propane has a much colder boiling point than isobutane, at around -43.6°F (-42°C). But this would potentially leave me with weak gas flow or, worse yet, if the propane burned off before I was done, no gas at all. Thankfully, the solution was straightforward. My gas canister, along with my water filter and electronics, slept inside my sleeping bag with me.

Once the stove was set up and lit, the block of ice inside the mug transformed into water, which then became much anticipated morning coffee. Unfortunately, the only way to unfreeze my hiking boots was to put them on and start moving.

Change requires the application of energy.

There's a strong leadership insight here: If you aspire to change the state of something, anything, you must apply energy. Even though the previous sentence is painfully obvious, it's still worth re-reading.

The bias to inertia is a potent force in both personal and business settings. "Why change if it works?" "What if I make a poor decision?" "I can't possibly get a consensus on this!" In researching the topic of organizational inertia, all the scientific papers I could find acknowledged the same message. Apply energy and you get something valuable in return.

Our responsibility as leaders is to overcome this inertia bias through the application of energy. Energy can take many forms, from inspirational words and ideas to action and leadership from the front. The clarity of what might happen if you don't change can also be a powerful energy to shift momentum.

A quote commonly attributed to business icon Jack Welch but actually found in the foreword to GE's 2000 Annual report states, "We've long believed that when the rate of change inside an institution becomes slower than the rate of change outside, the end is in sight. The only question is when."[19]

To overcome inertia, understand the various types of energy at your disposal and identify the other assets and resources available to you. Apply them in a focused and relevant way and in the quantities needed to stay ahead of external change. Then, you and your team can turn your ice into coffee, too.

The Road Less Traveled

Stepping out of your comfort zone will bring long-term rewards.

Hiking in these conditions, I saw far fewer people than on sunny summer days. One day, I hiked for a full eight hours and encountered only two other hikers. It was literally the road less traveled. In return, though, I received the gift of solitude and extraordinary winter landscapes I would never have seen otherwise. Patches of recent snowfall still lay in areas that were untouched by sunlight, and the lack of moisture in the air sharpened everything around almost as if I was wearing a new pair of glasses.

I learnt unanticipated skills for hiking and camping in these types of temperatures, such as re-using my favorite old COVID mask to keep my face and nose warm. I also learnt how to slow my pace on icy downhills following my second spill of the day.

My favorite skill was learning how to build a campfire that would last through the night. Using the upside-down method, I created a fire with the largest logs at the bottom and worked my way up with smaller and smaller logs. When I lit this fire at the top, it slowly burned its way down the structure, taking hours to finish and providing me with hot embers and an easy fire to get going in the morning. Usually my fires are short-lived, designed to provide me with less than an hour of company before I go to sleep, so it was a challenge to build this new type of structure.

Getting a fire started at the end of a long day is an activity I look forward to and try to make the time for. It's a skill I pride myself in. At the point when I just know the fire is going to catch and burn well, I always find myself smiling. The crackling of the burning wood, the golden colors of the flickering flames, and the long shadows the fire cast bring me a sense of control over my surroundings. Along with that control comes comfort. I might be deep in the woods and really out of my element, but "Look!" I can create fire.

Embrace the road less traveled.

A strong leadership quality is helping people to recognize the road less traveled has its rewards. It could mean requesting a team member to work on an unconventional project or motivating them to pursue a career move that may not seem logical to them. It might also include encouraging colleagues to put their hands up for nascent opportunities or to take on community roles outside their comfort zones.

Early in my career, I took a road less traveled and offered to work on a project no one else was interested in. I became heavily involved in developing a telecommunications networking protocol solution called Signaling System 7,[20] (SS7) for a major technology vendor.

Prior to SS7, the information about a phone call, the call setup information, was embedded in the same signal used for the call itself, i.e., *in band*. SS7 allowed network operators to put this information into a separate network, i.e., *out-of-band*, which was separate from the call itself. This provided for a more secure network and allowed for the development of an innovative set of services, such as toll-free calling and call waiting, and for the foundation of the World Wide Web, which was to follow. For me this *out-of-band* career experience was also the foundation of my professional career in the cyber security industry.

Over the course of a lengthy career, it's those out-of-band experiences that will differentiate you from others and open up diverse opportunities that will support and strengthen you as a leader. It's your ability to hike into the woods of life and ignite a bright leadership fire that will make a difference.

Of Mice and Men and Owls

Meeting diversity where you find it is critical.

A notable aspect of winter hiking I hadn't fully appreciated is that my hiking day is a lot shorter. I hike until an hour before sundown for safety reasons, but when the sun sets at five o'clock, that can make for a much shorter hiking day. After a solid day of hiking, I decided to sleep in another Trail shelter for the evening, which saved me the effort of pitching my tent. This is something I will do sometimes if the weather is bad or if I arrive close to dark.

As the night progressed, my company turned out to be the ever-present shelter mice scurrying along the walls of the shelter. I knew they could smell my food, and they knew, that I knew, that they could smell my food. Two years later, I would meet a thru-hiker who was traveling with his cat, Fenn. Seems a little overkill for the mice problem, but hey, hike your own hike.

Shortly afterward, an enormous owl turned up in a tree nearby and spent hours hooting into the night. Based on its call, it was a Great Horned Owl, one of the most common nocturnal owls in North America. Its booming hoot can be heard for long distances in the forest, and it's ranked pretty high on the badass scale of *Owls to be Concerned About* if you're a smaller mammal. Of the twenty species of owls in North America, only the Snowy Owl and Great Grey Owl are larger, but their territories do not extend this far south.

The owl was shouting at the mice—or me. I'm not sure which. Either way, it was just me, the mice, and the owl passing the long hours in freezing temperatures in the middle of a dark winter forest.

The owl helped me to think about listening more intently to the surrounding forest. I could hear its hoot echoing and counted out the frequency of its call. Once I had learnt its voice, I could calculate and anticipate when it would next hoot and how many times. The owl also helped me to focus on the silence, rushing in to fill the void once the echoes of the hooting faded away.

The mice helped me to think about the forest on a different scale. About the sheer amount of biodiversity that can be found within a forest like the one I was in. I wondered what the mice eat when there are no hikers to supply them. How many different food chains exist to even create an ecosystem where these mice thrive? It was a scale of thinking I hadn't explored before.

Both the owl and the mice helped me think about the forest in ways I had never really considered before. I thought we made a fantastic team getting through the freezing night together as if we were in the newest cartoon buddy movie.

Power in diversity.

The leadership point I want to make here is about the power of a diverse team, both from the perspective of diversity in thought and diversity in people. These two aspects are tightly coupled, as different cultures, demographics, and life experiences all bring different viewpoints and ways of thinking about how to solve problems. When you push yourself outside your comfort zone, you will meet people who you would never typically meet. Harnessing these different perspectives presents an opportunity for competitive advantage. This requires meeting diversity as you find it—and as it finds you.

An essential quality of a strong leader is recognizing this idea of diversity as a strength and leaning into it. Do you create teams that have different perspectives? Perhaps, teams who raise an issue, risk, or opportunity that your background might not highlight? Are the different experiences of your customers represented so that you can understand their perspectives?

As a long-time member of the Tennessee Squire Association, a sort of fan club for Jack Daniels Whiskey, I have been deeply impressed with the distiller's approach to embracing diversity. In 2020 they set up an organization alongside a direct competitor, Uncle Nearest. These two distilleries have a common heritage dating all the way back to the 1850s when Nathan "Nearest" Green, a freed enslaved man, taught Jasper "Jack" Daniels how to make great whiskey. Today, the Nearest & Jack Advancement Initiative "aims to advance diversity within the American whiskey industry and includes the creation of the Nearest Green School of Distilling, the Leadership Acceleration Program, and the Business Incubation Program."[21] I'll drink to that!

When it comes to engaging in the diversity experience and the value it will deliver, I encourage everyone to lead from the front.

Here's My Number

Share whatever useful information you can.

At the end of this section, I arrived at the ramshackle hiker hostel that lay a few hundred yards off the Appalachian Trail. Ramshackle is a generous description. I had scheduled a trail shuttle to pick me up the next morning and deliver me back to civilization.

Up and down the Appalachian Trail, a small cadre of drivers caters to thru-hikers. They will pick hikers up at the most remote of trailheads, allowing them to get to some level of civilization where they can shower, pick up supplies, or do laundry. Like gifts brought home from a vacation, thru-hikers eagerly share phone numbers of shuttle drivers along the Trail. That small piece of information can make a huge difference in how a hiker's day, or week, goes. Even if we don't end up needing to use the number, just having it provides a little extra comfort.

Hiking the Appalachian Trail would be much harder without this informal network of shuttles and the transparency that hikers show in sharing that information. I offer my thanks to all the hard-working drivers—even if your car does have a faint whiff of smelly hiker.

My first stop after getting my bunk bed sorted out for the evening was a shower. Peeking into the enclosure, the light from my cell phone illuminated various half-full bottles, which I assumed were hair products. The shower was a dark wooden box with no lights, and its floor looked ready to collapse under me. But the water was gloriously hot! It was one of the most refreshing showers I've ever enjoyed. Refreshed and clean, I slept the sleep of champions.

Be transparent with your information within the boundaries set.

Leaders are transparent about information within the constraints of the normal practice of business, such as regulatory or competitive limitations. When you're transparent about information, your teams and peers will trust you more and respond to the information more appropriately. It could be financial information on how your business is performing or information on a new product or new market that your business is entering. The more you can share, the more everyone will feel that they, too, are part of the process.

I have seen this firsthand in how the Cystic Fibrosis Foundation works with patients and donors to the charity. This organization has always been transparent about where the money we raise is being spent, about what the long-term goals are, and about the successes and failures that we have experienced along the way. This transparency isn't just about showing how the donations are spent, but it's also about giving hope to the tens of thousands fighting cystic fibrosis that we can and will cure this disease.

I have also met many extraordinary doctors along this journey who have been completely transparent as well. These doctors carry the burden and responsibility of being completely transparent, and they're doing a remarkable job at it, especially when the news is difficult.

Encourage your teams and colleagues to be as transparent as they can be within the boundaries that you set. This will build stronger teams and make you a stronger leader.

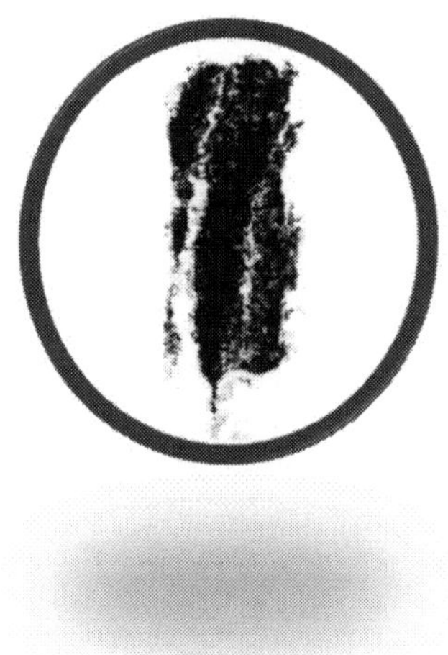

This section of the Trail brought home more insights I will need to hold close if I am to get to Mount Katahdin. It taught me that I must have the courage to push outside my comfort zone, the courage to prepare for that discomfort, the courage to bring the energy needed to do what I set out to do, and the courage to share what I know. This could all be summed up as having the courage to lead.

As I was now starting to better understand how to navigate the Trail, the idea of White Blaze Leadership began coming into focus. I was thinking more about my experiences and what they were telling me. It still wasn't coming instinctively to me, but just like any approach or method, these things take time to become part of who you are.

As I thought about the idea of courage, my Believe White Blaze started to form. Belief in my own abilities, combined with the belief that *the Trail will provide*, gave me the courage to head out and take on the mission.

If you're unsure how to get into a mindset of courage, might I suggest starting with a refreshing hot shower?

Section Three Campfire Conversations

- In what ways might your organization be experiencing inertia, and how could this impact your goals?
- What kinds of energy or resources are available to you to support and drive change?
- How are you approaching and embracing diversity within your organization?
- How would you assess your level of preparation for current and future challenges?
- What steps are you taking to ensure transparency of information across your teams?
- How do you bring courage into your leadership, and what does that look like in practice?

Section Four

Decision Making Under Stress

From above, this part of southern Virginia must resemble a crinkled cut chip. The Appalachian Trail runs diagonally across these hills, rising to a ridgeline, following it along for miles, then dropping back into the next valley.

From atop a ridge, the view was unobstructed across to the next ridge, and in the early morning, a layer of fog hung in the valley below as if covering it in fluffy white cotton to protect whatever lies beneath. It's deep into this wilderness that

I have gotten myself into a bit of a pickle.

Like most things that go wrong, it's not one mistake or miscalculation; it's the sum of several that has led me to this point, like a messed-up parlay bet where each small win adds up to something monumental.

As I considered my options to get safely out of this self-created mess, I thought to myself, "This will make for riveting leadership insights, assuming I survive." Rest assured, I did indeed survive to tell the tale.

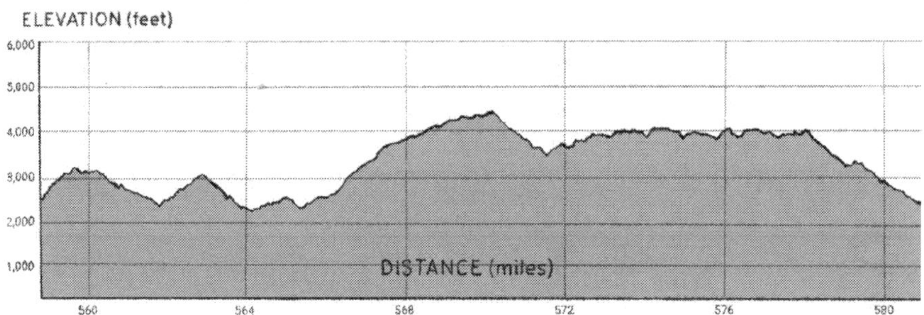

Figure 4 Jenkins Shelter, VA, to Bear Gardens, VA

A Battle Plan Never Survives Contact with the Enemy

Recognize early when your plan is impacted.

I was out of camp by five o'clock that morning. Much earlier than usual, as my plan was to hike a long twenty-two miles to complete the day rather than my usual seventeen miles. That distance would get me to Bear Gardens Hostel, my destination for the night.

My headlamp sliced out a cone of safety into the freezing darkness of the early morning as I hiked through the Beartown Wilderness and up to the Chestnut Knob Shelter some ten miles away. The four-thousand-foot incline up to the shelter was a daunting start to the day. My clothes, still damp from the day before, steamed as my body heated up from the effort. In this way I moved along the dark Trail like some ethereal forest ghost.

My pace is slow uphill, and I own that fact, which is why I calculated in the extra time with the early start. That rugged climb was harder going than I anticipated, and I could best describe my pace as glacial. In hindsight, I should have been more aware my pace was putting me behind my plan for the day. I knew this piece of information soon after starting out that morning, yet I failed to act. This was my first mistake of the day.

Recognize small things that could lead to big things.

As leaders we can help our teams recognize the small things that can impact our bigger plans, when and as they happen. Not every event brings problems, but acknowledging and being aware of potential issues is important.

For example, imagine a team member goes out sick and you say, "Oh, they can just make up the time when they get back next week." But what if they are out for longer? What if they have a vital piece of information you need to move something else forward? How would you handle this situation? It's critical to capture the issue and anticipate consequences, even if it requires no immediate action.

A prime example of this is the Challenger Shuttle disaster. On a chilly Florida morning, January 28, 1986, Challenger launched on its tenth mission, STS-51-L. The launch, commanded by Dick Scobee with a total crew of seven, including schoolteacher Christa McAuliffe, was widely televised throughout the United States and in schools across the country. Minutes later the shuttle was nothing more than wreckage at the bottom of the Atlantic Ocean and its crew were all lost souls.

The Rogers Commission report concluded that while the actual cause of the accident was a faulty O-Ring valve, this was an accident *rooted in history.*[22] Despite sufficient information to address the problem, no one recognized the importance of acting on the minor errors that ultimately caused this catastrophe. The Rogers Commission report makes for fascinating reading if you have time.

Two Plus Two Equals Five

Make sure your data points are accurate.

By the time I reached the Chestnut Knob Shelter, I was way behind schedule, but I was confident I could make up the time because what goes up must come down. The next section of the Trail was five miles of down, descending some two thousand five hundred feet. My goal was to get back on track by picking up the pace. A couple of miles into the descent, my knee was killing me. A frequent problem for hikers on big descents, it's not serious, but it's painful and slows you down.

There are several reasons for this type of knee pain, but the primary reason is that hiking downhill puts undue stress on your knees, and everything associated with them. In a detailed scientific paper called "Downhill Walking: A Stressful Task for the Anterior Cruciate Ligament?"[23] we learn that the tibiofemoral compressive force is seven times body weight for males and eight and a half times for females. I don't understand the biomechanical implications, but anything in a multiple of your body weight sounds excessive. As for the title of the paper, I can only assume the author lacks real downhill walking experience; otherwise, why put a question mark on the paper title?

By the time another hour of slow hiking had passed, I was sure I'd be unable to make the hostel anytime close before dark. I checked the maps and calculated my remaining time, distance, and elevation. I couldn't figure out why so much elevation remained, but I knew the hostel was out of my reach given the distance and still another ten thousand feet of elevation change. This was my second mistake. I misread the data, and the remaining elevation change was only half of what I thought it was.

My inability to calculate accurately was caused by a combination of pain, fatigue, and self-doubt in my abilities. I instinctively sensed the data was off, but instead of questioning it, I accepted the result as it was. I allowed doubt to guide my decisions, and in doing so, I chose data that affirmed my nagging belief that I wasn't capable enough.

If the data doesn't seem right, question it.

It's a vital leadership skill to recognize when we need to help ourselves and our teams to question and recheck critical data points when the data *smells off*. We know two plus two doesn't equal five, so why accept that result at face value?

It could be a sizable overrun in the effort needed to deliver a project, the cost of an event, or something as simple as the time required to get to a meeting. I remember sending a large software quote back to be rechecked by the team, as the dollar value seemed too high. The subcontractor accidentally included the same line item twice, once as a stand-alone item and once bundled into a package. As such, neither of us spotted it initially.

If the numbers don't seem right, double-check them. Making sure they are accurate is time well spent.

I'm a Celebrity, Get Me Out of Here!

Critical communication needs to be crystal clear.

I avoid hiking after the sun goes down. Typically, my plan is to be at camp an hour before sunset. This gives me time to set up camp in daylight and supports a margin of error if something unforeseen slows me down. If I hiked into the nighttime hours and something goes wrong, it could be ten hours or more before another hiker comes along. My hour-before-sunset rule seems like solid risk management to me.

Realizing I couldn't reach the hostel before dark, I texted them to arrange a shuttle pickup at the forest service road a few miles ahead. The problem was cell service was non-existent in the area. While I was sure the text had been sent, I had no way of getting a response. The basic text I sent said, "Can you pick me up at 4:00 p.m." at the location I was headed for. This was mistake number three.

My communication was terrible. In hindsight, I should have sent a text saying, "I will be at this location at 4:00 p.m. I will wait until 5:00 p.m., and if you can't make it, I will shelter on the Trail for the evening." Definitive, clear, and useful. I gave myself an F-minus for the text I actually sent.

Make your communication unequivocal and purposeful.

When events get stressful for whatever reason, it's critical, as leaders, that we communicate unambiguously. The ability to compose your messages so they meet the criteria of clear, useful, and concise is a foundational leadership skill.

The United States Air Force Academy describes its class on clear communications[24] as: "Clear communication is a complex, nuanced, and teachable practice essential for successful officers and leaders of character. Effective use of oral, visual, written, and aural modes of communication signifies the professional competence and knowledge expected in a leader while engendering the trust of those being led." Does reading that make you want to sit up a little straighter, too?

I grew up in the U.K. speaking and writing British English, which now causes me to experience a clear communication problem daily. That problem is how to correctly format dates. In the United States, the normal date format is month/day/year, but in the U.K., the format is day/month/year. This means that dates, such as 6/1/24, can be ambiguous to me. To solve this problem, I almost always write out the month, i.e., June 1, 2024. This way, no confusion can happen about my meaning. The dates are clear, and no mistakes are made.

Back in rural Virginia, the hostel received the text but couldn't get to the pickup location anyway. I only discovered this upon reaching the hostel much, much later.

Options, What Options?

Manage your risk and your response objectively.

I arrived at the forest road crossing at four o'clock as forecast. No rescue squad was waiting to drive me to a luxurious shower. In fact, nothing waited for me except a clearly seldom-traveled dirt road. At this point I was tired, having eleven hours of hard hiking under my belt, sore from the descent, and aware I had gotten myself into a bit of a pickle.

Here is where I made an admirable decision. I took a fifteen-minute nap. This might sound counter-intuitive given that time and daylight were my enemies, but I knew I needed to reset myself, and power naps were a specialty. So, I set my watch for fifteen minutes, rested up against a tree, and closed my eyes.

The canopy of leaves rustled in the slight breeze, and the wrinkled bark of the tree pushed into the back of my head. As I drifted off, I heard the song of a distant bird who seemed happy about something. My breathing slowed, and I paused right on the line between awake and asleep to try and understand what the bird was telling me.

Fifteen minutes later I was wide awake and working through the options in my head.

First, I considered the fixed components of the equation. I couldn't change when the sun went down, and I couldn't change the fact a bridge was out of service a mile ahead over a stream I would now need to wade through. It's not something to be done in the dark. I rechecked my data for the remaining seven miles and realized the elevation change wasn't as brutal as I thought it would be. I came up with a plan to leave at five o'clock, giving time for the hoped-for shuttle to show up. This would allow me to ford the stream in the light and get to a shelter a few miles further on where I could spend the night.

Optimize decision-making with facts and time to weigh options.

Some circumstances require us to act immediately, right in the moment. In these situations, leaders draw instinctively on experience and gut feelings. If it's not one of those hair-on-fire moments, taking the time to thoroughly examine the options is a rewarding leadership skill. Building an action plan around the immovable objects will help everyone understand the plan better, buy into your decision-making, and gain consensus around preferred actions.

One last note on napping. Although I could not find the source material, numerous articles on the web discuss NASA research showing pilots who nap showed alertness improvements of fifty-four percent and job performance improvements of thirty-four percent. "Napping leads to improvements in mood, alertness, and performance [such as] reaction time, attention, and memory,"[25] according to Kimberly Cote, Ph. D, professor of psychology and neuroscience at Brock University. She recommends between ten and twenty minutes as optimal. I agree with you, Dr. Cote.

Believe in Yourself

Action speaks louder than words.

Five o'clock came and I acted on my plan. I forded the freezing cold stream with plenty of sunlight still left. This involved tying my pack to a rope suspended across the water. Then I waded across, in the thigh-deep waters, holding onto the rope with one hand and pulling along my pack with the other. The insistent current pulled at my legs, forcing me to focus on each step, on my balance, and on the remaining distance to the opposite bank.

Invigorated by the cold waters and my hour of rest, I felt stronger than I had all day. I hiked on for about two more hours, and as night descended, I finally reached the Trail shelter. There, another decision awaited me: Stay or push on for another hour and a half to the hostel. I made sure my spare headlamp was charged and double-checked the terrain. Ahead of me, the Trail was mostly a gentle downhill and looked straightforward.

I took all the risks into consideration and decided to push on. The one other hiker already at the shelter called me a badass, and I somewhat felt like one as I moved out into the cold, dark forest. Thankfully, he also hollered after me when I started back out of the shelter but going in the wrong direction. Not so much of a badass, after all.

I crawled into Standing Bear Hostel at around 8:30 p.m. that evening with fifteen and a half hours of hard hiking behind me. Raiding the hostel's fridge, I pulled out my favorite post-hike beverage. It was the tastiest can of Dr. Pepper I ever gulped down.

Believe in yourself.

As a leader, you must believe in the actions you choose. Execute them confidently and adapt if events change your path.

A significant insight I gained from this trip was to focus on believing in myself more. I knew I could do the distance, but I allowed doubt to creep in and throw me off. The key here is recognizing when you have allowed doubt to have a voice. What are the circumstances that are your triggers? Can you use those events in a positive way? Something that informs you but doesn't distract you?

I'm still working on recognizing when I have handed over the steering wheel to doubt. I know I can do better at managing this distraction. I know I can do better at believing in who I am and what I am capable of. It's a mental muscle that I can work on like any other muscle.

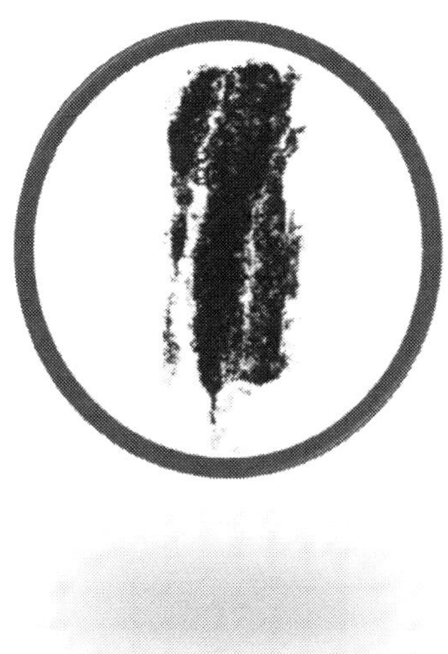

This section of the Trail put me in a situation where extremely valuable insights into survival were given without any serious damage being done. It brought home to me the need to be an effective communicator and to be honest with myself about progress and risks. It also allowed me to focus on believing in myself.

It wouldn't be the last time the Trail threw a lesson in self-belief at me, and it wouldn't be the last time that my Believe White Blaze shone brightly.

Ultimately, you must believe in yourself and your abilities, and if you're struggling with belief, perhaps a fifteen-minute power nap might be exactly what you need.

Section Four Campfire Conversations

- In what ways does your self-belief influence your leadership approach, and how might it shape your effectiveness?
- What aspects of your communication style are you working to develop or refine?
- How are you fostering a culture that emphasizes data-driven decision-making within your team or organization?
- What strategies or approaches do you find most helpful when managing stressful situations? Why?

Section Five

How You Doin?

"I have died. I've gone to Hell. It's New Jersey. Oh, the mosquitoes." This was an entry in the logbook at the Pochuck Mountain Shelter dated August 8, 2021. I had a lot of sympathy for the unknown author but for different reasons.

Over the last twenty-four hours, I'd experienced torrential rain, hail, snow, and sleet. My feet felt like two blocks of frozen meat. Even the mosquitoes weren't crazy enough to come out, and they chose violence every single day. I was beginning to think hiking New Jersey would not be an enjoyable hike at all.

However, by the end of my time on the Appalachian Trail in New Jersey I would develop a surprisingly different perspective and was grateful for the leadership insights she gave me.

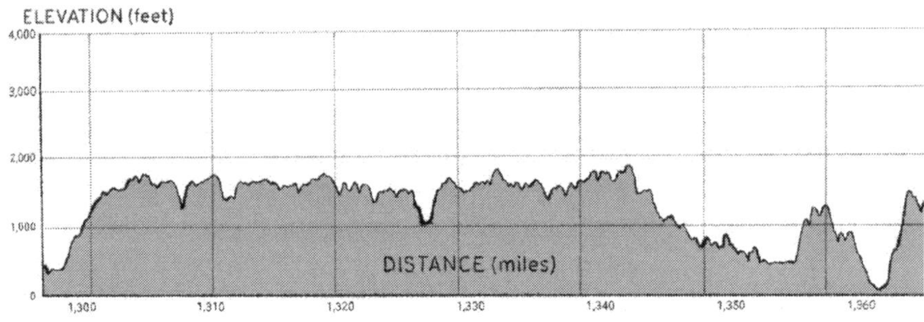

Figure 5 New Jersey

Jungleland

Don't let your preconceptions get in the way.

When I say New Jersey, you likely automatically think Newark Airport, Springsteen, The Sopranos, and that posh bit at the bottom of the state where they say they're from Philadelphia, but we all know they are actually from New Jersey.

New Jersey is a beautiful state. There, I said it. It's full of extraordinary scenery and ecosystems. Over five days of hiking, I experienced some of this beauty up close and personal. From majestic Bald Eagles patrolling a reed-lined marshland to extraordinary views offered from atop the ridges the Trail runs along. Perched high on one of these ridges, I could see for miles across both New Jersey and Pennsylvania. It was easy to pick out the Red-shouldered Hawks effortlessly riding the uplifts. Below the ridges, the water towers of hundreds of small communities in the distance reached up into the sky like giant golf tees.

New Jersey is the *Garden State*. The term originated in the 1800s to advertise its farmland, and New Jersey is still an agricultural powerhouse today. There are over nine thousand farms in the state, and in what can be considered a splendid fact to know, New Jersey ranks third in the production of spinach. The state provides a handy guide to spinach,[26] including pictures and tips such as, "You can prepare spinach as a salad, a hot vegetable, a creamy soup, a soufflé, add it to vegetarian lasagna or combine it with cheese as a stuffing for ravioli, among other things."

Excellent job, State of New Jersey! You had me at souffle.

Own the difference between fact, perception, and assumption.

In life and business, we can't help but bring our preconceptions to the table. But we can help how we deal with them and encourage our colleagues and teams to do the same. The first step here is acknowledging that leadership isn't an absence of bias; it's recognizing our biases and acting accordingly.

I remember a valuable lesson I learnt earlier in my career when I let a bias drive my decision-making. I pushed through selecting a subcontractor based on a prior relationship rather than fairly evaluating the set of proposals we had in hand. The decision proved to be poor as they did not have the experience needed to do the work to the required level of quality. This ended up with us having to spend time and hard-earned dollars on damage control, something that could have been avoided if I hadn't let my bias cloud my judgment.

So next time you're sitting in a meeting and think *Sopranos*, why not take a minute and find out what's really going on.

Can I Eat That Mushroom?

Leveraging what's around you.

The answer to the question "Can I eat that mushroom?" is, of course, "Sure you can." The answer to the question "Should I eat that mushroom?" is decidedly "No, you shouldn't." While crossing New Jersey, I met an inspiring young woman who was a professional forager. Yes, it's a proper occupation. She was close to finishing a three-month tour of the East Coast investigating alternative ways of living off the land.

We talked about different resources in the forest that were readily available for hikers to liven up an endless stream of ready-to-eat meals and protein bars. Ramp, violets, dandelion, chickweed, garlic mustard, and purple dead nettles are common in the New Jersey forests, and she assured me they are edible and even tasty. She was much more wary when we talked about mushrooms. She said, "There is a fine line between those you can eat and those that will kill you." Duly noted. I'll play it safe and leave the mushrooms where they bloom.

Use the resources available to you to their maximum impact.

Later that day, as I swiftly moved along the quiet Trail, I considered the idea of corporate foraging. Were there tools, data, and processes that litter the corporate landscape, waiting to be effectively used? How many useful applications has your organization developed that you don't know about, don't have access to, or used to use but now they won't run on that fancy latest-gen smartphone?

In this analogy, customer data might be the mushrooms of the corporate forest floor. It looks as if it's something that could be tasty, allowing you to know more, respond better, and beat the competition. However, customer data comes with significant responsibility and regulatory requirements around privacy and consent, especially globally. It's easy to step over the line and find yourself in a world of hurt if you're unsure of exactly what you're doing.

Consider taking the time to explore this idea of corporate foraging with your colleagues and teams. At a minimum, it's a fun exercise, and who knows, you might uncover a truffle or two out there.

Follow the Yellow Rope

Apply critical thinking.

Deep into the day, I slowly picked my way down an especially hazardous rock-strewn descent. Imagine someone tossed a million shoebox-sized Lego bricks across a hillside. That's an illustrative visual of the terrain.

To my right was a yellow rope tied to a tree. "Hmmm," I thought. "A yellow rope in the middle of the woods," and then I continued on my way.

About ten minutes later, I came to the other end of the rope and, looking up, saw it marked an easier path down the scree than the one I had just endured. If only I had paused to consider more deeply why a yellow rope was tied to a tree in the middle of the woods. It was blindingly obvious once I discovered the other end.

“Why?” is the most critical question you can ask.

Sometimes we are so absorbed in the task at hand, that we fail to see what is right in front of our faces. As leaders, we can set a notable example by applying critical thinking when we see a yellow rope. “Why?” is a powerful question, but we don’t use it enough. This simple yellow rope in the middle of the woods ended up illuminating my Question White Blaze when I spent the time considering everything it was telling me.

I read a fascinating scientific paper that studied the impact of nurses’ ability to apply critical thinking to their accuracy in handing over a patient during shift change.[27] The research reveals that when an incident did occur, up to sixty-five percent of those incidents could have been prevented if the nurses made better decisions.

Education is the common denominator that correlates critical thinking and good decision-making. This research is a firm reminder that being prepared, inquisitive, and knowledgeable leads to favorable outcomes.

I recently took a class in critical thinking but clearly failed to apply the lessons I learnt about pushing on something until you get to the truth. I suspect part of the reason was I was tired as this was late in the day, and I hiked “heads down.” It was a valuable insight into myself that I need to hold my head up sometimes rather than try to power on through.

We might not always get to the answer, but encouraging our teams to keep asking, “Why?” is a powerful leadership skill.

Fire Tower Bob

Know who's in your ecosystem.

When I met him, Bob was perched up on the observation deck of the Catfish Fire Tower. From sixty feet above, he hollered for me to come on up.

Fire towers are dotted along the length of the Trail and serve the purpose of allowing rangers to detect smoke or fire across remote regions of the forest. Some are old and abandoned, their steel lattice framework rusting away, crumbling under my fingertips as I can't help but touch the decaying metal. Some are closed to inquisitive hikers for safety reasons, and some are welcoming to those who wish to climb to the top for a view above the canopy. The Catfish Tower was originally erected in 1922, and if you're in the Delaware Water Gap National Recreation Area, I would strongly recommend visiting it.

Bob shared with me how he's manned that tower for almost forty years and can spot fires across one hundred square miles. He's one of thousands of state employees and volunteers who keep us safe out on the Appalachian Trail. With climate change, urban sprawl, and a host of other issues to deal with, the Forest Service does an admirable job with limited resources.

He also proudly told me about his ex-military fire truck sitting at the base of the tower. In service for thirty-five years, the truck oozed as cool-looking retro Bronco vibe as you could get. I stayed and chatted with him for about thirty minutes before I pushed onwards, but I could've stayed and listened to his stories all day if the Trail wasn't calling my name.

Safeguard your success and maintain your integrity.

As I hiked toward my end point for the day, I thought about the Fire Tower Bobs I converse with in a business environment—those people whose unseen job it is to keep us safe.

A strong leadership skill is understanding who lives in these roles in your ecosystem. As someone whose career has been at the pointy end of deal making, I've grown to have a significant respect for our legal teams, quality review experts, and human resource professionals. Along the way, they have thankfully prevented me from starting any major forest fires, although I'm guilty of waving around a flamethrower on more than one occasion.

Take some time and think about who your Fire Tower Bobs are, share that knowledge with your teams, and educate them on the importance of their roles. Then maybe go give your Fire Tower Bobs a hug.

The Boss

Mosquitoes can get really big.

I thoroughly enjoyed my time on the Trail in New Jersey. Crossing it southbound, as I did, leads inexorably to the extraordinarily beautiful Delaware Water Gap.

In the mid-1800s, the Hudson River School art movement flourished in the New York region. It was a group of painters who took the European Romanticism style and applied the same form to the idyllic landscapes that were now in reach of more Americans. The Delaware Water Gap was one of their favorite places to paint, and landscape artists such as George Inness, Asher Brown Durand, and Thomas Doughty all created iconic works depicting the beauty of the gap.

These paintings show us a bucolic scene of the river and the gap in the mountains. In some of the paintings you will see the first signs of the encroachment of civilization as barges and steam trains start to seep into the artwork.

However, New Jersey can't quite help herself, and today the Trail dropped me onto I-80, where I walked alongside the interstate for the last mile, separated only by a short barrier. No oil painters, no steam trains, no majestic silent barges in sight. Only the roar of freight trucks speeding by me as they headed into Pennsylvania, hauling cargo to points west.

I have Springsteen's "Wrecking Ball" stuck in my head. It might be the best song ever written about New Jersey and certainly the best song with mosquito references, as Springsteen claims they are as big as planes. Although, to be fair, Nirvana's "Smells Like Teen Spirit" has to be a close second for the mosquito references.

The largest mosquito you will actually find in New Jersey is the Asian Tiger Mosquito, which only grows to about 0.2 inches. For the record, the largest mosquito in the United States is the excellently named shaggy-legged gallinipper (Psorophora ciliate), which is thankfully rare and thrives only after heavy, heavy rain. A University of Florida article[28] references several papers that describe its "relatively intimidating heft and persistent biting behavior" and "its legendary aggressiveness." Sigh.

When in doubt, listen to the Boss.

This isn't a leadership lesson you will find in many MBA programs, but making sure your teams know the Boss's music would greatly contribute to ensuring everyone's success.

The thing is, knowing what motivates everyone is something you should aspire to. For some it might well be Springsteen or their favorite music. For others it could be title, travel, or compensation. For some, like me, it could be a deeper purpose.

The more you can understand what drives someone, the better you can relate to them. This makes you a more effective leader and serves to build more effective teams.

In a paper titled "The Behavioral Neuroscience of Motivation: An Overview of Concepts, Measures, and Translation Applications,"[29] the authors describe motivation as "the energizing of behavior in pursuit of a goal." I don't know about you, but that might just be the best description of motivation I've ever heard. They go on to discuss how goal activation needs to be considered within the context of history and our current states: "Motivational drive must be modulated as a function of both internal states as well as external environmental conditions."

This all might seem obvious when written out, but motivation happens when you clearly define a goal and then activate someone to achieve that goal. The activation must be aligned with their internal and external states. Internal state might be their experience of similar events, i.e., "Was I paid on time?" "Did I get the recognition I deserve?" "Did I get asked to join the meeting?" External states might be the correct support or tools being in place to make reaching the goal seem achievable. The more you understand these internal and external states then the more powerful your activation will be, and the vigor of the motivation will increase.

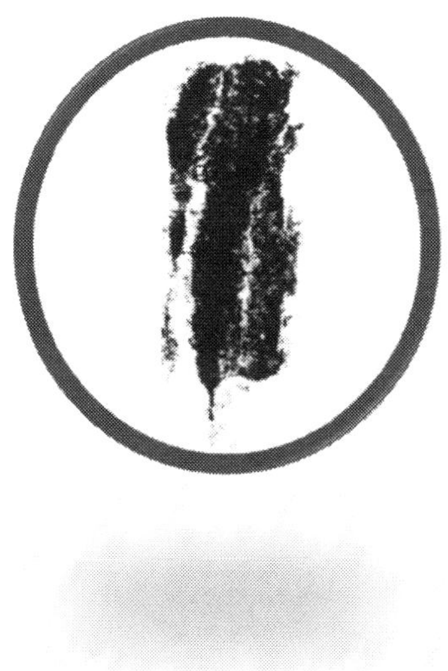

This section of the Trail really helped me to focus on how I think about the world around me and inside of me. By applying critical thinking skills to myself, I get a better understanding of my internal and external states; thereby, creating stronger self-motivation to meet my goals. It also let me focus on how to understand what motivates the people in my orbit, or those I want to inspire or change. All of this led me to think about my Question White Blaze and how that is critical to navigating through my day-to-day life.

New Jersey was good to me. I hope she thinks I'm a good fellow too. If I ever bump into Bruce, I'll be sure to check in on what motivates him. "Hey Boss, I'm doin' good. How you doin'?"

Section Five Campfire Conversations

- How often do you find yourself asking "Why?" and what impact does it have on your understanding or decisions?
- In what ways do you work to distinguish facts from opinions and assumptions in your decision-making?
- What available resources or tools might be used more effectively by you and your team?
- What drives or motivates you in your work and personal life?
- When was the last time you listened to the *Born to Run* album? Listen now and see what resonates?

Section Six

When Bear S**t Hits the Fan

"She has fallen off the trail. She has fallen quite a ways. Her head is bleeding." This was not the text message I wanted to see at that moment. Not ever, really. I was already one beer into my post-hike celebration, having safely brought my team of hikers off the mountain and to the finish line at the Nantahala Outdoor Center (N.O.C.) in North Carolina.

We were at the end of a long day of hiking and fundraising to cure cystic fibrosis. I had integrated this single-day fundraiser into my overall section-hike schedule. At this point, I had completed about twenty of these thirty-miles-in-one-day Xtreme Hike fundraising events since they began in 2011. They were mostly sections of the Appalachian Trail in North Carolina but also Vail in Colorado, the Grand Canyon (rim-2-rim twice), and the Adirondacks in upstate New York.

On that day of that Xtreme Hike event, we contributed hard-earned dollars to the $121 million the Cystic Fibrosis Foundation raised in 2022, the vast majority spent directly on research to accelerate finding a cure. Science is an expensive business. The innovative science we fund—the kind that says, "Just watch me, we will cure this disease"—is astonishingly expensive.

Bijal Trivedis' riveting book *Breath from Salt*[30] tells the history of this search for a cure through the lens of one of the most gracious leaders I've ever met: Joe O'Donnell, a true son of Boston. He and his family raised over $500 million in the fight to cure this disease. Joe lost his son, Joey, to cystic fibrosis in 1986, and he always had the time to give advice, counsel, inspiration, and a smile to anyone struggling with its burden.

The arc of *Breath from Salt* starts with the history of the early doctors and scientists who identified the disease and ends with the FDA's 2019 approval of a miracle drug, Trikafta. This drug, from Boston-based Vertex Pharmaceuticals, has made a life-changing difference for my daughters and tens of thousands of other cystic fibrosis patients. These small molecule drugs directly affect the underlying genetic issue that causes cystic fibrosis rather than treating the symptoms. Not a cure yet, and not a drug everyone with cystic fibrosis can take, but this progress buys time and moves us significantly further down the trail toward a cure.

By the time I received the alarming text message about another team's fallen hiker, my team of hikers were nursing blisters and recanting trail stories of the day as if we had been hiking for weeks. We were celebrating adding to the science and our collective resolve to cure cystic fibrosis. However, our attention was fully realigned now as one of us—one of our own—was in trouble back somewhere on the mountain.

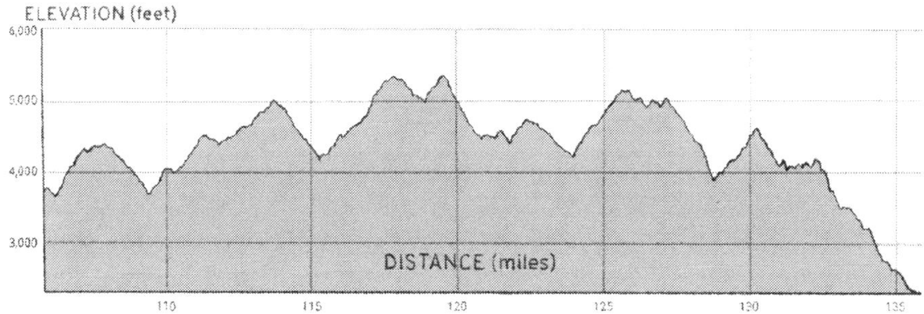

Figure 6 Rock Gap, NC, to N.O.C., NC

Strengths and Weaknesses

Know your limitations.

A severe injury was not on anyone's mind when we had prepared for the long day ahead. Sunburn, blisters, scratches, and insect bites are the hard-won battle scars of a full day of hiking, but nothing more than that. Except that in planning for this long day hike event, we did expect more than that. In fact, we planned and prepared for as many scenarios as possible to ensure all our hikers would have a safe day. All this planning and preparation was led by the extraordinary people at our local Cystic Fibrosis Foundation Chapter.

My Royal Air Force veteran brother told me he always planned missions with the mantra, "Don't expect rescue." I'm not saying "Don't expect rescue" was our actual design point, but it's not a bad starting place either.

Our planning started six months earlier with a team of coaches hiking the full Trail to map it out firsthand. This was then followed up with careful scenario planning so we knew where and how hikers could be extracted along the way if they couldn't go on. On top of that, we notified local authorities of our plans well before the actual hike date.

The evening before the hike, I gave a full safety briefing to all the hikers. Fifty hikers listened patiently with a mix of excitement and anxiety that permeates the air the night before every Xtreme Hike. The briefing included crucial advice on wilderness bathroom etiquette (i.e., pooping in the woods), bear encounters, and responding to injuries. Crucially, we also operate a "No one hikes alone" rule, and deploy coaches, like me, who lead from the front and sweep from behind to make sure help is always close by.

Know your strengths and weaknesses.

The Trail continues to give me unexpected insights and reinforces ones I've previously explored. Here, I have a full-on lesson about knowing my own strengths and weaknesses: specifically, that preparing isn't my strong suit. However, I do understand that preparation matters. It could be a client presentation, a team meeting, or a longer-term project. The more we prepare, the more ready we are to act in the moment, and the better the outcome.

Deloitte uses an approach called Business Chemistry[31] to help teams understand the personalities in a room and how to relate to them. From this Business Chemistry perspective, I'm, unsurprisingly, a Pioneer. This means you're much more likely to hear me say, "Yeah, let's do it!" and then go do it, rather than someone who has a Guardian or Integrator-type persona who would say, "First we should pull the right people together and then figure out if it makes sense to do this."

In business, much like the Trail, there's little room for error. A strong leadership skill is the ability to recognize your strengths and weaknesses, and the strengths and weaknesses in others. Then, adjust your behavior and build your teams to account for both.

I'm fortunate to have colleagues who I can rely on to help with the preparation piece of my job. This means that when the time is right, I can proceed with confidence, knowing the groundwork has been laid. It's valuable that I recognize that deficiency in myself and remain open to receiving the help and be thankful for it too.

Stop the Bleeding First

Prioritize and focus.

The coach hiking with our injured hiker must have been terrified. Watching her friend tumble thirty feet down into a ravine only took an instant but must have felt as if it lasted a lifetime. However, it's in moments such as these that heroes rise to the occasion, which is exactly what she did. Following her first text message alerting the rest of the coaching team, she followed up with the location of the incident, and within two minutes, help was on the way. While she waited for help to arrive, she climbed down to the injured hiker and assessed the situation.

A year prior, I hiked this same section of the Appalachian Trail with a twenty-year combat medic who was recently out of the Army. He told me about how you assess someone for injuries when you first find them. I wish I had listened to him more intently. However, our coach on the scene rose to the situation and did a first-class job of assessing what was going on. She updated the team with a text message indicating a head wound and an arm wound. She then set about bandaging up those visible injuries to stop the bleeding.

Prioritize based on the data you have.

Sometimes the sheer volume of requests and demands coming at you can be overwhelming. Not sure where to start, you might go with the time-honored traditions of procrastinating, making a to-do list of actions you've already done, or picking something easy to do. While satisfying, none of these approaches help to solve the underlying problem.

Insightful leaders will delineate what's critical from what's important, and what can wait. The word *triage* comes from the French meaning to *sort out* or to organize into tiers. It's a useful word. *Tres bien*, France. Triaging a complex workload into well-tiered workstreams is a strong sign of a thoughtful leader who can help create clarity, which can break the inertia that *too much to do* can sometimes instill.

It's also useful to explain the why behind your sorting. This can help you or your teams understand more about the process and the reasoning and help educate for similar situations in the future.

Me: "Help!" Trail: "I Got You."

Do not be afraid to ask for help.

Our downed hiker was approximately two and a half miles from where I was at the finish line. Our team medic and another coach immediately ran up from the finish line back onto the Trail. Thankfully, one of our most experienced coaches, the type of guy I want next to me if something goes wrong, was about three miles further back from the incident. He sped toward the location.

On his way, he passed a campground where thru-hikers were setting up their tents for the night. He paused and called out asking for help with the Trail proven cry of "injured hiker!" Although they didn't need to get involved, five willing hikers rallied to his cry and followed the Trail down toward where our friend lay. While our coach had no way of knowing this, these five good Samaritans were critical in the rescue soon to follow. We needed both their physical help and their skill sets.

Unbelievably, one was a nurse, one was a member of his hometown mountain rescue squad, and one was a total badass. The badass, an Australian, was a combat veteran and the first person to walk unassisted across Australia, the longways. Just him, three camels, and a swag full of determination. He had been there, seen it, and bought several T-shirts. A time-worn Appalachian Trail saying states, The Trail will provide." In this case, it surely did.

Ask for help and listen to the response.

I've learnt from my years of raising donations to help cure cystic fibrosis how to ask for help, even when I didn't want to. Asking for help is not an admission of weakness, rather, it's acknowledging that the goal at hand requires external support.

Along with this goes the salient insight that you can never ever assume you know who will step up to the plate. The simple act of asking yields many surprises, with friends, strangers, and colleagues stepping in when you were sure they were on the not-going-to-help list.

As a leader, being open to asking for help and then listening when people respond is critical. You might not even know you needed the skill, advice, or input someone else is offering or perhaps didn't know that an extra pair of hands could be so useful.

As I hiked and thought deeper about this idea of asking for help, my Believe White Blaze started to crystallize. I better understood that being open to believing that people will help is a self-prophesying act and encourages people to help. In addition, having the belief in yourself that you can accept and be grateful for help strengthens your willingness to reach out for help. Belief in others and myself would become a dominant White Blaze for me through the many miles and trials still ahead.

Lead, Follow, and Sometimes Just Get Out of the Way

Trust in your team.

Everything in me wanted to follow our medic and coach up from the finish line. I know from experience I have a run-into-the-fray response. However, I also knew I could not be additive to the situation at hand. I understood help was on the way to the scene, and at that point I was exhausted from a day that began at 2:30 a.m. The most I could have done was to hobble on up the Trail and most likely caused another problem to be dealt with.

Reluctantly, I stayed at the finish line, monitoring text message chatter for any chance to help remotely. As the minutes went by, I knew our injured hiker was in safe hands and the flow of information confirmed that.

Trusting your colleagues is a virtuous circle.

Being a leader doesn't mean you must always lead from the front. Sometimes that won't be possible. Trusting your colleagues and teams to get a job done—and done right—is a clear vindication of you as a leader.

In a *Harvard Business Review* article,[32] author Abbey Lewis discusses good leadership and trust, and she references work showing some incredible metrics that come from a *Harvard Business Review* study. These metrics include: "People at high-trust companies report 74% less stress, 106% more energy at work, 50% higher productivity, 13% fewer sick days, 76% more engagement, 29% more satisfaction with their lives, and 40% less burnout than people at low-trust companies." We can all agree those figures are a powerful endorsement for valuing and trusting your people.

Building strong, capable teams that can deliver on whatever is thrown at them is your job. The more you trust in them, the more they will trust in you.

Trust Me, I'm a Professional

Know when you need the experts.

Mountain rescues can be complex. Access points to a downed hiker can be limited, and more often than not, remote.

Thankfully, most areas have experienced and qualified rescue teams that put themselves on the line to ensure the safety of those who have experienced unfortunate accidents. It was the phenomenal Swain County Search and Rescue team that came to our aid.

They inserted an ATV about three-quarters of a mile away from the incident. Moving the hiker to the ATV was a painstaking four-hour process and included both low and high-angle extractions involving a pulley system that needed to be moved three times. This is where the thru-hikers support became essential because the pulley system required significant effort to get our friend up and out.

It's OK to ask for help.

I'll draw a distinction here between management and leadership. A significant difference is leaders know instinctively it's OK to ask for help. Rather than a sign of weakness, it's seen as a virtue, as an acknowledgment that a leader is someone who inspires and drives everyone, not necessarily someone who knows everything. In contrast, a manager is supposed to be someone who's in that role because they have the domain experience; hence, they might not be as comfortable asking for help.

Working for a consulting company, I see this day in and day out where our clients know it makes perfect sense to ask for help from us—not because they don't trust their teams, rather they know sometimes you must get the expertise you need externally.

This is especially true when *close enough* isn't good enough. I'm fairly certain if you were stuck down a ravine, all things considered, you'd rather have a professional rescue squad to show up with the equipment and expertise needed to get you out.

All's Well, That Ends Well

Apply what you learnt.

You will be pleased to know all ended well. The local emergency room patched up our injured hiker and released her later that night after some stitches and a cast on her broken leg. The next morning, she rallied for our celebration breakfast along with our new Appalachian Trail thru-hiker friends, our amazing coaches who took part in the rescue, and the rest of our motley crew of hikers.

Our preparation and planning were put into action when needed, and I could not be more impressed with the response of my fellow coaches.

Leadership is a team sport.

Leadership is a team sport and, as a hiking team, we focused on applying what we learnt from the experience—what worked well, what we could improve on, and what we hadn't even considered. In business, as in life, it's beneficial to take the experiences of these unexpected events and use them as powerful learning tools.

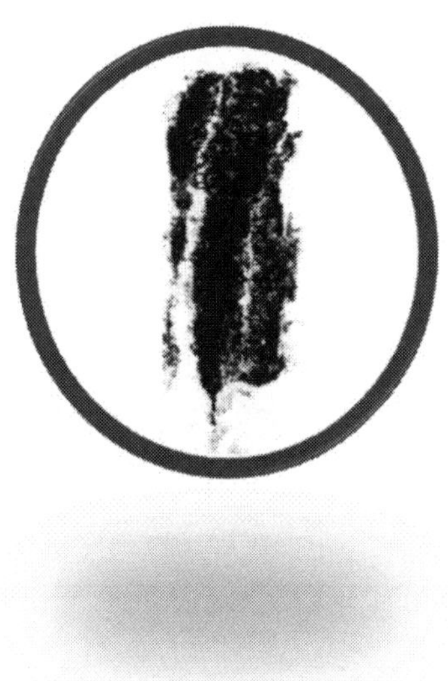

This section of the Trail started to pull together different threads of my nascent White Blazes. It combined my Believe White Blaze insight of recognizing my own strengths and weaknesses, and my Value White Blaze in being willing to ask for help when needed. This helped to get us out of a dangerous situation.

How to plan for risk more consistently and how to build on hard-won experience are also insights that I will bring into my day-to-day leadership so that any situation has a better chance of ending well.

All of this was wrapped up in my Inspire and Act White Blazes as I continue to see the capacity that we all contain—the ability to change the world for the better when we dream and take action. One of my favorite quotes is attributed to the French author Victor Hugo: "Each man should frame life so that at some future hour, fact and his dreaming meet."[33] This encapsulates the idea of these two blazes as inspiration requires action to realize it.

All ended well for this particular adventure on the Trail. *All's Well That's Ends Well* is one of Shakespeare's better-known comedies in which things go awry, but by the end everyone is content with the outcome. In another of Shakespeare's rom-coms, *The Winter's Tale*, he has the most famous line of direction ever given in a play: "Exit, pursued by a bear."

I surely hope that's not how my time on the Trail finishes.

Section Six Campfire Conversations

- How comfortable are you with asking for help, and what impact does it have on your work or relationships?
- What tasks or responsibilities could you delegate to your team today to empower them?
- How would you describe the culture of leadership within your organization, and to what extent is teamwork valued?
- What lessons have you taken away from a recent experience or incident, and how are they influencing your approach to leadership?
- In what ways are your dreams backed by actionable steps, and what does that look like in practice?

Section Seven

Elephant Snot and Pennsylvania Rocks

Somewhere around seventy-five thousand years ago, during the last ice age, the Laurentide Ice Sheet gouged out the Great Lakes in Canada and prepared the ground in Pennsylvania to torment me. I know it's a long time to hold a grudge but bear with me on this.

As the ice sheet retreated, it left scoured rock open to the elements. In a process called mechanical weathering, water seeped into the rocks, and eons of heating and freezing caused the extensive rock seams to fracture into large boulders. These boulders fractured into smaller rocks—exactly like the shoebox-sized rock I just kicked. It was the type of kick that would certainly lead to another painfully lost toenail.

Lost toenails are badges of honor to hikers. Sublingual hematoma, more commonly known as a black toenail, is a tough hike, well executed. It's your pain visibly displayed. The struggle of progress manifested in a very human way. If you have ever had one, you know.

This seemingly never-ending landscape of rocks in northern Pennsylvania was the famous worst part of the Appalachian Trail. It was living up to its name as a destroyer of toenails, hiking shoes, and mental willpower.

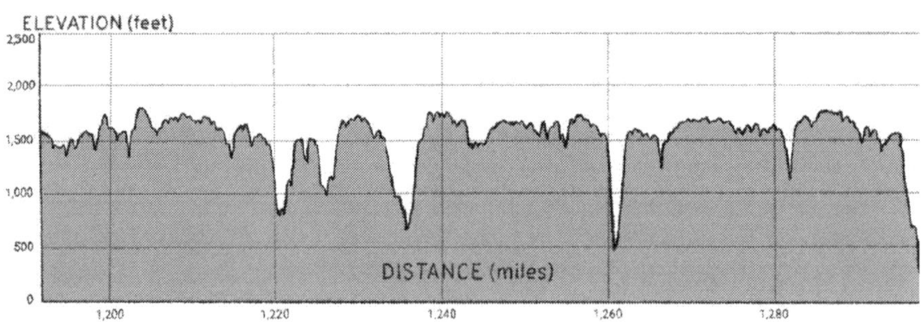

Figure 7 Port Clinton, PA, to Delaware Water Gap, PA

PA Rocks!

If you are going through hell, keep going.

The worst section of the Appalachian Trail, by a long way, is the northernmost one hundred forty miles of Pennsylvania. That's not only my opinion, but it's also the judgment of most anyone who has hiked it. As evidence I point to its ranking at the number one spot on the list of least favorite sections, according to a survey by The Trek.[34]

It's variously referred to as Rocksylvania, or the place where hiking boots go to die. Often I hear pejorative names that would get me a go-directly-to-HR card if I included them here. Like legions of hikers before me I thought, "How bad can it be?" Take my word, hiking across northern Pennsylvania is every bit that bad. While lying awake one night my bones physically hurt. Not my muscles, not my ligaments, but my actual bones, from days of walking on rocks, rocks, and more rocks.

Crossing this terrain, I must be one hundred percent focused, concentrating on every step. Otherwise, a twisted ankle is a certainty. On top of that, the cracks between the rocks will suck down hiking poles in an instant, pulling me off balance. The gaps in the rocks also appear to be the perfect hiding spot for snakes, but I'll leave a discussion on snakes for another time. I ended up developing the Peter-technique for *dancing* over the rocks, which looks, and feels, equal parts absurd and desperate.

Cultivate grit and empathy.

We have all experienced days and weeks like this at work. Where every meeting, every phone call, every task seems as if it will never end, and it's not just work, but hard work. As Churchill famously said, "If you are going through hell, keep going." This quote is likely not attributable to Churchill according to the informative Quote Investigator website,[35] but it makes for a memorable line.

From a leadership perspective we are destined to push our teams and colleagues into situations that are going to require us to dig deep. We must hold to the truth that we have the grit required to push on and that, eventually, the situation will get better. We must hold that truth for ourselves and communicate it in a clear and positive way to everyone else.

We also need to understand that while we have a clear perspective of when we are *walking on rocks*, we might not be aware when someone else is. I like to ask, "How are you?" when meeting someone again. Not as a throw-away line, or as a substitute for a greeting, but as an actual question. "No, really, tell me how you're doing."

Nurturing a leadership style that is open and allows colleagues and team members to be open with you about when they are going through tough periods, when they are feeling the pain of all those rocks, is a vital leadership skill.

Water, Water, Nowhere

The basics can be the most indispensable thing.

If the rock situation isn't bad enough, this section of the Appalachian Trail in northern Pennsylvania is also among the driest sections of the Trail. I typically carry one liter of fresh water and another 750 ml of electrolyte water. Depending on the temperature, I'll stop at a stream to refill three or four times a day. Refilling involves using a filter to squeeze the water out of my dirty water bag and into my safe, clean water bottles.

But the physical act of collecting water is so much more than this. We have all become so used to fresh, clean water at our command that to experience the most basic human task of taking water from a stream somehow becomes significant.

First, it required that I stop and prepare for the moment as if engaging in a time-worn ritual. I took off my pack, set my water bottles down, found the best flow for collection, and then knelt down as if I were at nature's altar. The coolness of the water transformed my hands, melting me into the stream, forcing me to become the same.

Time slowed to the rhythm of the water's flow. Something I had no control over, so I must be present, feel my balance as my feet pressed into the ground. I was grounded in an elemental way.

My instincts understood this was a vulnerable position, nothing more than another forest animal at the watering hole. As such, everything came more into focus. My senses burned with intensity—the pebbles glinting under the water, the smell of the dead leaves on the bank, and the shafts of sunlight piercing the canopy. The crack of a twig or an acorn falling from a tree caused me to swivel my head like a frightened deer and stare intently into the shadows.

And then I was done, replenished with our most basic need. The spell broken, reality collapsed back around me, I stepped away from the stream and moved on.

The water sources along this stretch are few and far between. During the summer months, Trail Angels leave copious amounts of water at trailheads along this section; otherwise, thru-hikers would struggle to complete it. Even though I hiked early in the season, there were still problems with the distance between water sources. Whenever I would meet another hiker on the Trail coming in the opposite direction, the conversation always turned to water. Where is it? Is the water flowing?

Drive team cohesion through meaningful interactions.

As I hiked onwards to the next water source, I pondered about water-cooler conversations in the office and how the COVID-years have removed this vital part of our communication. It was standing around the water cooler or coffee pot that you would build organic networks. You would strengthen the relationships with your colleagues over random, unstructured interactions. Learn about the soccer tournament a colleague's daughter won over the weekend or about how Jones in accounting is quitting to go travel the world. You would learn firsthand about some of the harder personal issues colleagues were going through.

As we move into this era of hybrid working, or work from anywhere, it's incumbent on business leaders to figure out how to fill that gap. How to get the benefits of the water-cooler experience we took for granted, but now doesn't exist in this post-COVID world. I don't have any answers for this observation, but as leaders, we need to acknowledge the issue and work with solid intent to address it. Perhaps you have some thoughts about how to get us to linger a little at the water cooler?

Palmerton

Sustainability is everyone's business.

I head southbound, where the rock climb down into Palmerton is considered among the most challenging descents on the Appalachian Trail. The mountain side is all rocks. More than I've ever seen in one place, and it's a long way down into the Lehigh Valley below. The small town nestled there, Palmerton, is a quaint little place with welcoming folks who are proud of their community, as they should be.

Before I come to this descent, a couple of miles north of Palmerton, I look straight across the narrow valley to Blue Mountain. There, a former zinc smelting operation created a cinder bank comprising of thirty-three million tons of slag running for over two miles and up to one hundred feet tall by a thousand feet wide at points. Over seventy years of operation, the former zinc smelting operation emitted so much heavy metal that it defoliated two thousand acres of Blue Mountain. As a result, the mountain became the site of a Superfund cleanup program.[36]

Only now, forty years since the Zinc smelting factory closed, is a comprehensive program to revegetate the area showing success.

The small water source on the Trail about five miles out from Palmerton comes with a warning only to use in an emergency, as it contains traces of heavy metals. It would have been good to know before I arrived at the location completely parched.

Harness sustainability to differentiate your business.

Sustainability has become a major focus for many businesses. It's seen as enhancing companies' brands and frankly as the right thing to do. For example, in 2021, Mastercard announced they were tying executive compensation to sustainability goals, including carbon neutrality. Well done, Mastercard, priceless.

Leadership in this area can be as bold as what Mastercard has done, or it could be as simple as bringing in a reusable water bottle to work like I do. I've had my trusty water flask for a few years now, and I hope that the dings, dents, and well-used look convey my small contribution to sustainability.

Small, purposeful actions add up over time. Whatever you choose to do, this is one area where leadership by example can help to influence your colleagues, which will help all of us in the future.

Easter Eggs

Giving back to the community matters.

I was fortunate to stay one night at the longest-running hostel on the Appalachian Trail. The Church of the Mountain in Delaware Water Gap has provided shelter to hikers for almost fifty years. The night I stayed, it was only me and an Austrian thru-hiker. He was a hiking machine and at the tip of the spear of 2022 thru-hikers, setting the pace toward Mount Katahdin, some nine hundred miles north of this point.

The pastor of the church invited us to join them that night as they were having their annual Easter potluck dinner. The first in three years because of COVID-19. I gratefully accepted her offer to attend, but it was too much of an American cultural experience for my new Austrian friend.

That evening a wonderful cross-section of the community from Delaware Water Gap welcomed me. I enjoyed a couple of hours with good company—Easter egg coloring alongside some of the local children being a highlight for me—plus plenty of food, and potatoes done more ways than you can imagine. As both a hiker and an outsider, I was treated like a special guest, and they were all so humble in their generosity.

Later that night, as I tried to ignore the snoring of the Austrian guy in the next room, I reflected on how valuable it is to give back to those in your community who might be struggling. After being on the receiving end of hospitality for a few hours, I earned a much deeper appreciation for the volunteer work we do at my organization. Like many organizations, Deloitte actively encourages teams to participate and give back to communities and causes. One day a year, called Impact Day, Deloitte colleagues actively take part in volunteer work across the communities we live and work in. This ranges from cleaning beaches to sitting and playing dominoes with Alzheimer's patients.

The experience also reminded me of why I was out on the Appalachian Trail. Which is to raise the money to buy the science that will one day cure cystic fibrosis. It's my way to give back in a rewarding and tangible manner to a community that has done so much to ensure the health of my daughters and support my journey. I recall the early days of dealing with this disease when I had no real concept of what I was doing or where I was going. New friends who had lost loved ones to cystic fibrosis would have the graciousness to take me under their wings and point me in the right direction.

My trail name of Coach is in part a nod to that selflessness I experienced and now, wiser and older, hope to pay forward with my own coaching.

Inspire a culture of giving back.

Leadership involves being aware of that greater responsibility to give back. And then putting the structure and mechanisms in place that encourage your colleagues and teams to follow through on that responsibility. This is both part of my Inspire White Blaze and part of my Value White Blaze where I have learnt to value everyone's contribution no matter how large or small.

Through my years of volunteering for the Cystic Fibrosis Foundation, I'm especially proud of the young professionals who get involved in philanthropy. Watching them start to understand how powerful getting involved can be is a real gift, as if planting a seed and knowing that it may well bear much fruit in the future.

This involvement helps them to grow both personally and professionally, as it differentiates them in a powerful way. So, if you're reading this and aren't involved in a local community organization, might I suggest you take a bold leadership move? Take a first step, and go get yourself involved. If you don't know how to do that, send me an email and I'd be happy to point you in the right direction.

Elephant Snot

Education and awareness can change behavior.

I received a warning about the problem at Bake Oven Knob. Vandalism. An easy few minutes' walk from a trailhead parking lot, the beautiful rocky overlook had become a favorite spot for graffiti.

Now, I'm going to go on an old man rant for a moment. Graffiti, really? Why would a kid wake up one morning and say I'll pick up a few cans of spray paint, hike into the woods, and spray some rocks at the most beautiful spot around here? *Argh!* Most of the graffiti wasn't even art, just spray painting for the sake of it. I found the question, "Go to the prom with me?" graffitied across six separate rocks, exceptionally annoying. I can only wish and hope she said "NO!" and then told her friends to say "No!" as well.

So, why do kids do stupid acts like this? It must come down to a lack of awareness and education. OK, also hormones, but that's out of scope here.

Ignite progress and transformation through a focus on education.

As leaders, it's not enough to go on *old-man rants* when we see something we don't like. We must step up and figure out how to become a persuasive change agent. How can we use education and drive awareness around the behavior we want to change?

We see this playing out in my industry, cybersecurity. To keep pace with the sheer volume of attacks, we've had to raise awareness of the issue and change everyone's understanding of how breaches occur. Phishing tests, educational classes, and cyber awareness months can help to ensure colleagues think twice about hitting that enticing link for a free iPad or resetting their password via an email request. These are minor examples of driving behavioral change rather than loudly ranting about something.

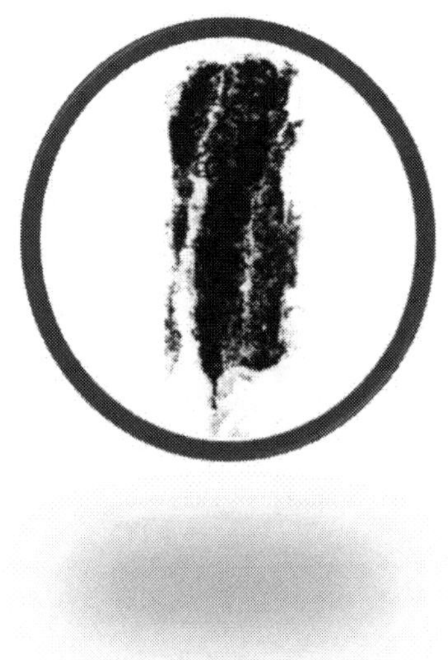

This section of the Trail helped me to focus on the people networks I build in my communities and at work and how to maintain and feed those relationships. To understand how important organic and inorganic networks are to any leader and how to ensure they are preserved long-term. It reminded me that education is at the root of any change we wish to see, regardless of whether it's with yourself, your business, or the broader communities within which you live.

My Value White Blaze allowed me to really take those Trail experiences and learn how to view them from the perspective of valuing them for exactly what they are today and what they mean for my journey ahead.

You'll be pleased to know that in 2022, volunteers and the local fire department organized a day of rock cleaning at Bake Oven Knob. They used the fantastically named Elephant Snot compound to remove years of bad graffiti. That Elephant Snot stuff must be some kind of magic.

Thanks to their hard work, the current graffiti at Bake Oven Knob is not nearly as bad as it used to be, and I sure hope some of the positive press coverage around cleaning up the rocks will help to educate the kids on the folly of their ways.

When I began hiking the Appalachian Trail, I never thought I'd write the words, "That Elephant Snot stuff must be some kind of magic." I'm ever so hopeful that this is the last time I write those words too.

Section Seven Campfire Conversations

- What approaches or practices do you use to keep expanding your knowledge and skills?
- How do you prioritize ongoing education and learning within your team?
- In what ways do you encourage a sense of responsibility for giving back to the communities where your organization operates?
- How might a focus on sustainability enhance your organization and its impact?

Section Eight

Angry Lobsters, Wild Bears, and Naked Hikers

June 21st is National Naked Hiking Day. I know. Really, I understand. I'm as confused as you are about this. *Men's Journal*[37] described it as a "lesser-known holiday observed by a select, but enthusiastic few." You will be delighted to know it's not a holiday I plan to observe. Enthusiastically or otherwise. However, while hiking across New York State, I did come, err, face to face, with a naked hiker on the Trail.

Now, you may wonder how on earth can Hodge extract some leadership insight from this nonsense. Read on, and you can find the answer to that puzzle and learn about the craziness of hiking across the Empire State.

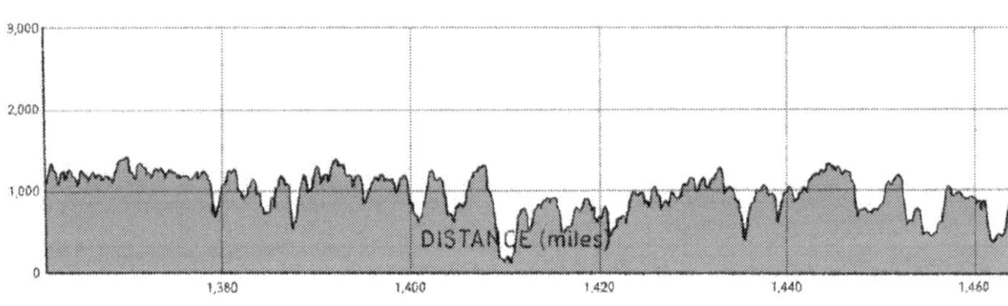

Figure 8 New York

Self-Care

Put your oxygen mask on first.

Hiking the Appalachian Trail northbound from the New Jersey border to the Connecticut border was demanding work. At ninety miles, and with forty thousand feet of total elevation change, the beautiful landscape varies from easier sections to parts that are more rock scrambling than hiking. Over the week I spent out there, the weather included torrential rain, blistering heat, and days so humid it felt like hiking through a steam room. My time also included a vicious summer tropical storm that rolled in faster than expected. Add to this all kinds of bugs that want to suck you dry, and it makes for a tough time out on this New York section of the Trail.

Because of these conditions, self-care is essential. Hikers must be physically able to put in the miles each day, and that requires reacting to injuries as soon as they notice them. For example, moleskin Band-Aids applied to the feet will prevent hotspots from becoming blisters, or a restorative stretch can help alleviate painful IT band issues on the big downhills.

Most importantly, the Trail teaches its hungry travelers how critical it is to combine the right diet with a solid night's sleep. Arriving at camp, I often felt completely exhausted. As if I could never take another step again. But eat some good protein and get a solid eight- or nine-hours' sleep, and I'm up and right at it again the next day. The ability of the human body to repair itself is extraordinary.

I also find the sheer act of hiking, of putting one foot in front of the other for hours on end, incredibly meditative. After a hike, I feel calmed, relaxed, and ready to face the world again—even if my first stop is the local drugstore for another tube of anti-itch cream.

Self-care matters.

Self-care has become a major topic of conversation especially after the impact of COVID-19 on everyone. Organizations are providing tools and options to help employees work on both mental and physical fitness. When carrying the responsibility of leadership, it also means you have an extra responsibility to make sure you're taking self-care for yourself seriously as well.

As they say during an airplane safety briefing, "In case of an emergency, put your mask on first." That will help you operate at a desired higher level. As a result, when you push on your colleagues and teams to prioritize self-care, they can look to you as a phenomenal example.

I've been fortunate to take a couple of self-care classes on the power of sleep, and intellectually I understand that sleep directly affects our health and performance. Abstract classes are great, but the Trail has brought it home to me—nothing is better for self-care than a full night's sleep. So, if you're not sure where to start on self-care, it's as easy as going to bed earlier than usual.

Thinking about the idea of self-care also led me down a path of considering how my White Blazes point outward—being able to act as needed—as well as point inward—believing in myself, inspiring others, valuing who I am and what I have to offer, and being able to honestly question what is going on in my head.

Traditionally, the concept of leadership is mostly directed outward. We lead people, we take on leadership roles, we provide leadership. But my White Blazes were starting to show me that the same attributes of leadership can, and should, be directed inward as well. How do we lead what is going on in our own heads? How do we take control of competing voices and direct them to achieve success?

As this journey continued, I would come to lean into my internally focused White Blazes more than I could ever imagine at this stage of the mission.

Angry Lobsters

Not everything is as it seems.

Sitting smack dab in the middle of the Appalachian Trail was a large and rather angry lobster. Its claws were raised, snapping away at me exactly like we might expect a slightly rude New Yorker lobster to behave. I could almost hear the creature saying, "Hey, I'm walkin' here!"

It was toward the end of a long, muggy day of hiking, with less than a mile to get into camp, when I had this un-nerving encounter. Stopped in my tracks, I considered the situation. What was a lobster doing deep in the woods? Why so angry? Did he fall out of the backpack of some erstwhile hiker who couldn't give up the good life on the Trail? None of this made any sense to me, so I stepped around the beast, without causing a fuss, and went on my way.

Later, after setting up my tent, I chatted with some of the other weary hikers and told them about my bizarre experience. One of the hikers laughed and promptly told me it was a crayfish, which were indigenous to the lakes around there. It must have crawled out of the lake, into the woods, and become lost. He lamented that, had I picked it up, it would have made an excellent supper.

Enhance your understanding of the limitations of assumptions.

As a leader, it's paramount to understand the limitations of making assumptions. Here, I assumed it was a lobster, no matter how improbable that seemed. Crayfish aren't that far removed from a lobster, so it wasn't an awful assumption, maybe a bit misguided, as most anyone knows lobsters live in the ocean and not deep into the Hudson Valley. It wasn't until I asked my companions for more information, and then researched it, that I discovered the truth about the creature.

One big assumption we make is to assume that we mean the same thing when we use the same words. Being British in America, I learnt early in my career to be aware of this problem as many British words have different meanings stateside. Biweekly for example means twice a week in England but every other week in the U.S.

We must be careful about this equivalency, particularly with technical jargon or industry-focused terms. I remember having an argument with a client who insisted I knew nothing about change management while I adamantly insisted that I did. He was referring to the organizational change management that would occur because of the system we were building, while I was referring to managing source-code for the system we were building. The same words, but with different meanings.

Assumptions allow us to decide in a vacuum of information, but we must be aware of the risks that come with that ambiguity. A valuable leadership skill is helping our teams understand when assumptions are okay, how to validate them, and when cold hard facts are critical.

The Bear Necessities

Know before you go.

Large wild bears roam the woods less than forty miles from Manhattan. I know this for a fact, as I came face to face with a large black bear while hiking on the Trail almost within sight of the city.

Fortunately, I accounted for this risk in my preparation, having watched several online videos on what to do in such a situation. I'd also watched a bunch of videos with titles like "When Polar Bears Attack!" Frankly, they weren't that useful but were entertaining on a dark rainy night at home where the Trail seemed far off. I recommend Gordon Buchanan's BBC documentary, *The Polar Bear Family and Me.*[38] For avoidance of doubt, no actual polar bears can be found on the Appalachian Trail.

The trees, heavy with summer leaves, crowded around me, creating an uninterrupted tunnel. I strode up over a small rise only to be met by a large bear sitting right in the middle of the Trail. I vocalized my surprise first without really being able to process what I was seeing. "A bear," I said quietly. And then more forcefully, "It's a bear!" I'm still not sure if it was to inform my hiking buddy, Sting, or to force me to come to terms with what I was seeing. I'm no expert but it was clear this was a large old bear, one used to having his way.

I felt calm—perhaps the calm before the storm or the line right between fight or flight. I want to describe what the bear looked and smelled like, but I have none of those memories. What I do recall is my heart beating faster, my breath deeper, and my full attention on looking for movement from the creature.

While the bear stood there and assessed us, we tapped our hiking poles together and politely asked him to move on. I'm not sure if it was the noise, the commanding British accent saying, "Please, Mr. Bear, would you mind moving along," or perhaps that he just wasn't hungry, but after what seemed a long time, he turned his back and ambled off into the trees.

That was the first, but not the last, bear ass I would see on this trip. With a double shot of adrenalin coursing through my veins, I climbed the next hill in record time.

Yes, luck is at the intersection of preparation and perspiration.

Preparation matters. In cases like my bear encounter, it could be the difference between life and death. In business settings, it's the difference between success and failure, winning or losing a proposal, responding to a critical issue correctly or letting it overwhelm you.

We see this in my field right now, where cyber ransomware attacks continue to cause havoc for clients. However, those who have prepared in advance for how to handle such a situation are in a much better place to weather the digital storm than those who are forced to react to the unfolding situation.

Strong leadership is about educating our colleagues and teams on the need to prepare and also leading by example in this space. Actions as simple as organizing a meeting with a published agenda, doing your homework on a topic, or practicing a skill until you reach a level of proficiency are examples of preparation that set you apart as a leader.

This brings home another important point. All the strategy and preparation in the world is nothing, unless you act on it at the appropriate time. In high school we read Shakespeare's *The Tragedy of Julius Caesar,* and this line always stuck with me: "There is a tide in the affairs of men, which, taken at the flood, leads on to fortune. Omitted, all the voyage of their life is bound in shallows and in miseries."[39] Older and wiser, I feel I now understand I need to have my boat correctly prepared and ready to go at the right time.

Some people say this intersection of action, strategy, and preparation results in a significant business advantage. People with no action, no strategy, and no preparation call the same thing luck.

Deli-Blazing

Cultural Fit Matters.

Appalachian Trail thru-hikers refer to the journey of following the Trail blazes as White-Blazing. In New York, a companion to White-Blazing exists, known to hikers as Deli-Blazing.

Here, hikers can follow the Appalachian Trail and then get on and off to resupply or get food at some the many delis New York is so famous for. It's a part of the cultural make up that is the Empire State. The delis are excellent for breakfast and calorie-loading. Some will even let trail-weary hikers camp right behind the deli, but it can be difficult to sleep with the smell of delicious pizza wafting over your tent. At the start or end of a long day of hiking, counting calories is not a consideration. Take my word for it: You're not likely to go hungry while Deli-Blazing New York.

Trail blaze being an ally for your colleagues.

Strong leadership values are demonstrated when you get the most out of whatever cultural potential you have in your team. It could be the culture of where you're geographically based or the cultural makeup of your team. How do you organize, motivate, and engage to extract the best of what they have to offer? If you do this with intent, it can enhance the overall work experience for everyone on your team. It will also motivate the entire team when you go out of your way to understand, respect, and appreciate their cultural differences.

As a leader, being willing to ask how someone's cultural barriers or norms might enhance or affect a team's operation can help you make informed and appropriate decisions. You can enhance your reputation as a thoughtful leader, and strengthen your team, by stitching together the fabric of these diverse cultures.

Naked Hiker

Not everything that glitters is gold.

On the same day I came face to face with a large black bear, I also came face to face with a naked hiker. Technically, he wasn't fully naked, as he wore boots, a backpack, and a hat. I can only hope he also wore bug repellent, as I know the mosquitoes were doing a job on me that day.

As we approached each other, hiking in opposite directions along the Trail, he offered a friendly "Hi," to which I responded with something like "Hmmm." Next, he said, "Hiking naked is legal in New York State parks." I again responded with "Hmmm," as frankly, I couldn't think of anything better to say. He wished me "Happy trails," as is custom, and then we went on our separate ways. I did at least shout out a "Happy trails!" in return. Looking back over my shoulder, I saw my second bare ass of the day disappear into the woods.

Accept that sometimes there's no value in a situation.

So, I'm sure you're excited to see what insightful leadership insight I drew out of this encounter. Here it is: Sometimes all you can say is, "Hmmm," accept the fact there's nothing of value here, and then move on down the trail. That is a valuable leadership lesson right there.

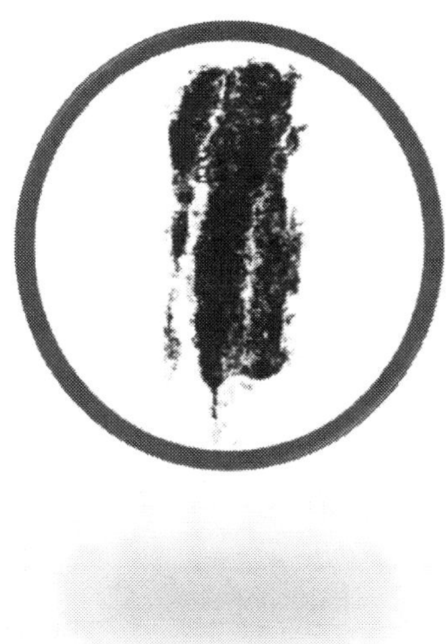

This section of the Trail helped me to understand that not everything is in my control. For example, I couldn't control the things I would encounter along the journey. I just had to accept they were part of the journey no matter how strange they might be. It also reminded me not everything is as it seems, so I need to be careful about assumptions or judgments I make without the facts.

What I can control is how I choose to deal with these experiences and how I choose to accept the reality of a given situation and use it in a positive way. These ideas are powerful insights that apply just as equally on the Trail as they do in the office or in everyday life.

Looking back on this section, I can see that for the first time I was dealt a full hand of my White Blazes and was able to pull knowledge from across this set of experiences. My ability to encounter something in my everyday and then hone that experience into a leadership insight was sharpening and becoming more natural.

As for the naked New York hiker, I'm still trying to *fuhgeddaboudit*.

Section Eight Campfire Conversations

- How do you approach self-care, both physically and mentally, and what areas might need more attention?
- What assumptions are you currently making that could benefit from further examination or testing?
- How do you prepare yourself to handle unexpected challenges that could disrupt your day?
- What aspects of your cultural background or experiences could you tap into more fully to enrich your life or work?

Section Nine

Yellow-Bellied Sapsuckers

Outside my tent, a bird is singing loudly. It's an alarm clock I didn't set, didn't want, and couldn't turn off. I checked my watch; it read 4:45 a.m. I channeled my best Liam Neeson and threatened to hunt the bird down if it didn't hush. Instead, it recruited some of its friends to join in.

This was the start of a long few days' hiking across the forests of southern Pennsylvania and the start of my relationship with the extraordinary and diverse set of birds that call the Appalachian Trail home. Along the Trail live hundreds of distinct species of birds, with year-round residents populating this part of Pennsylvania, such as upside-down birds like the White-breasted Nuthatch who are often seen creeping heads down on tree trunks and the Carolina Chickadee who are often seen hopping and hanging upside down on branches. The Appalachian Mountains also form the western border of the Atlantic Flyway—a flight path for migratory birds. Migratory birds use the mountains as a landmark for their travels and as a temporary vacation home as the seasons change.

Change was something that this section brought into focus for me—change in the way I related to my surroundings, change to the Trail as I moved along it, change as a constant and our response to it.

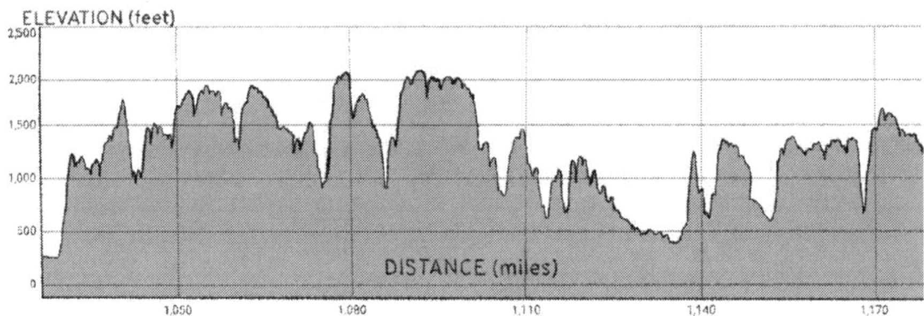

Figure 9 Pen Mar, PA, to Duncannon, PA

The Ghost Towns of Southern Pennsylvania

Change is the only constant.

The forests enveloping the Appalachian Trail in southern Pennsylvania grow dense and thick in these early days of summer. Hidden under the verdant cover is a story of change, of the inevitable march of progress, and of how failing to adapt can have a lasting impact.

Rausch Gap is located roughly one hundred miles northwest of Philadelphia. In 1860, the population peaked at around a thousand industrious people. Fifteen years later only one hundred remained and by 1910 the town lay deserted and abandoned for the forest to reclaim as its own.

Two substantial changes caused this dramatic fall of Rausch Gap, neither of which the town adapted to.

The first change occurred when the coal seams, which were the town's original source of wealth, became depleted. The rising costs to extract the coal and technological advances in both mining and coal use made it uncompetitive against newer coal seams. Second, the railroad company that operated in Rausch Gap was acquired by a competitor. This competitor moved the machine shops and associated jobs to Pine Grove, some fifty miles away. With worthless coal and no jobs, the town faded away. This was a story repeated many times in this part of Pennsylvania.

As I stood in the dense woods, silent and still, I spotted the stone foundations of long-gone buildings and the distant echoes of a failure to adapt. Dark green ivy carpets the vanished floors, and mature trees reached to the sky from inside the outlines of long-forgotten buildings. The pungent aroma of lush vegetation surrounded me in the humid summer afternoon—it too destined to fall and fade away as the seasons change.

Be an innovator.

The world is replete with examples of companies who failed to adapt. In a Fortune article, we find out that as of 2022, only forty-nine companies have been on the Fortune 500 every year since its inaugural list in 1955[40]. Think about that for a moment. Only ten percent of companies adapted successfully across those sixty-seven years. Almost fifty percent of companies in the Fortune 500, as of the year 2000, are gone from the list today. Some were acquired, some failed, and some didn't make the cut anymore. Some wanted to make their money from rewind fees, and late fees, and didn't have enough copies of the latest blockbuster movie on the shelf anyway. You know who you are.

So, what distinguishes surviving companies from those that become irrelevant? I would argue it's leadership's ability to embrace innovation rather than deny it, to create a vision and then take action to realize that future.

Change is never easy, but being prepared to acknowledge change as inevitable, and then showing a path forward, is real leadership. Leadership is not about maintaining the current direction if that's only going to hike you up a mountain into a raging storm; rather, it's about choosing a new trail, and potentially an alternative destination if so needed.

There Is an App for That

Change your perspective.

A couple of days after my early dawn chorus, I experienced the same early morning wake-up call. Except, this time the birdsong sounded slightly different. It was same three flute-like whistles but with a slight additional warble at the end of the third note. "Weird," I thought. "Is that a different bird or the same one?"

A few hours into the day, I crossed paths with an older woman who hiked along wearing a large pair of binoculars. On a hunch, I asked her if she was a birder. I'm not sure if that's a politically correct term for someone whose hobby/passion is going into the woods to search for birds, but it seemed about right.

She was a birder and engaged me in an illuminating conversation about my early morning alarm bird.

Based on my description, and shockingly bad whistling skills, she determined my bird nemesis to be one of the varieties of thrushes. At the time, I thought a suitable foe would be the Spotted Forest Thrush, sometimes called Nightingale Thrush because of its clever vocal abilities. When I asked her about the difference in songs, she told me birds have regional accents, so as I moved along the Trail, the same bird species would have slightly different songs. Boom! How cool is that?

I spent the next few hours in deep thought about pigeons with New Yorker accents and the southern drawl of mockingbirds. It passes the time.

In addition, she told me about an app from the super geniuses at Cornell that could help me identify the bird. The app, called Merlin,[41] identifies a bird from its singing, in real-time. You don't even need to have cell service. The next morning, I used the app to discover that my early morning tormentor was a Wood Thrush.

As I hiked along that day, birdsong captivated my attention, revealing a previously unseen world as if someone had pulled back a curtain. The Ovenbird, Eastern Towhee, Black and White Warbler, and ever-present Red-eyed Vireo sang to me, and the Red-bellied Woodpecker hammered away on the trees as if intent on felling one of them.

This app transformed my relationship with the forest, but it required me to be present while I hiked. To be actively listening for birdsong. I now could *hear* the birdsongs and could readily identify several distinct species. My favorite song, however, was from the bird that sent me down this path. Even Henry David Thoreau became enamored with the flute-like song of the thrush, waxing lyrical with sentences describing the thrush and its song: "There is a liquid coolness of things that are just drawn from the bottom of the springs," "Whenever a man hears it, he is young and Nature is in her spring," and "He sings to make men take higher and truer views of things."[42] Thoreau clearly spent way too much time in the woods.

The thrush creates its mesmerizing vocals as it has two voice boxes and can create two different notes at the same time. This means it can harmonize with itself resulting in a hypnotic flute-like song. Isn't nature utterly remarkable?

Listen to the information around you.

That afternoon, on the Trail, I wondered about the types of information that exist in our everyday business and personal worlds. What information remains unseen or actively ignored on a day-to-day basis? What if we could tune into that information? Could we open ourselves to a rewarding experience? Could there be effective apps that would enable us to be better leaders or help our teams to work more effectively? What if we could see more clearly something all around us that is unseen or unheard?

This could be anything from internal information about what interests our colleagues to ongoing chatter about products or industry trends. Your corporate birdsong if you will. I need to put more thought into this idea, but the concept of opening up existing facets of information that are ignored, and creating knowledge and value from them seems potent.

A great example is the smart ring that I wear. It has given me access to a set of information about myself that was previously out of reach or at best guessed at. Specifically, it helped me to understand that when I go to bed at a regular time, I sleep better and am more prepared to face the day. Sounds obvious, but the cold hard data presented on my app tells me a different story from the one I sometimes tell myself about my ability to top and tail the day.

I didn't realize it at the time, but the Wood Thrush would become my constant companion on the Trail—and its birdsong would become my favorite. Not wanting to go all Thoreau on you, but whenever the thrush sings to me, my step is a little faster, and my pack feels a little lighter.

For the record, my favorite bird's name so far is the Yellow-bellied Sapsucker. This is my go-to insult from now on, so don't cross me.

Celebrate Good Times, C'mon

Take the time to acknowledge milestones.

The remote location of Pine Grove Furnace holds a special place in the hearts of Appalachian Trail thru-hikers, as it sits at the halfway point of the Trail. Its location puts it approximately eleven hundred miles from the southern terminus at Springer Mountain in Georgia, and the northern terminus at Mount Katahdin in Maine. The original furnace at Pine Grove, built in 1764, produced cast iron for over one hundred years. The very cast iron likely used to build armaments for the revolutionary army.

As I'm section-hiking, it's not quite the halfway point based on my miles hiked, but it's still a meaningful day as I drop my pack and stroll into the small general store. Most thru-hikers who make it this far will arrive during early to mid-summer on what will hopefully be a beautiful, hot, summer's day. Over the years, a celebration challenge has taken hold at this halfway point: to eat a half gallon of ice cream.

Thirty-five years ago, when the challenge began, ice cream was sold in a half-gallon tub, but now you have to buy a 1.5-quart tub, and then add a pint of ice cream to get you to the half gallon. Ice cream manufacturers reduced the amount of ice cream in a tub starting around the year 2000. This way they could keep the price the same but give you less product. *Shrinkflation* is an official term to describe this strategy and is common in the food industry. It nicely explains why you think that chocolate bar is smaller than you remember because it actually is.

While a few hikers lounged around outside and dug away at their challenge, I decided on a far more modest vanilla ice cream bar and settled into the shade out of the early afternoon sun. The feel of the wooden stick on my fingers brought back childhood memories of long summer days and the excitement of a distant ice cream truck as its unmissable tune drifted closer. Memories of my own children drifted into view—eating ice pops as if it's the single most important task they have ever been asked to complete. I was content.

Hikers talk about the ice cream challenge almost from day one, and as less than fifty percent of those who start a thru-hike ever make it this far, it's surely worth celebrating.

Celebrate the wins.

You can show empathetic and empowering leadership by building celebrations into your everyday routine. People work hard and, like me, most everyone enjoys a heartfelt celebration. It's meaningful for the person, bonding for the team, and wonderful for morale.

Leaders should cherish opportunities to celebrate and make time for them. Not all celebrations need to be black-tie galas or fancy restaurants, as even a simple acknowledgement of a job well done can hit the spot if delivered effectively. A round of ice cream sure wouldn't hurt either.

Eat the Elephant

Set your sights long-term.

One night I chatted with some hikers around a welcoming campfire. The smoke and the conversation filled the air while the mosquitoes tried their best to participate. The hikers were three friends who, like me, were MYTHs (Multi-Year Thru-Hikers). They were ten years into a twenty-year plan to complete the Appalachian Trail by hiking a hundred miles or so a year. I have met hikers who are six years into a ten-year plan, and ten years into a six-year plan, but this represented the longest plan I had encountered. On their first hike, they were in college, but now they hiked alongside careers, families, and commitments. However, they still made time for The Plan, one week a year, every year.

My MYTH plan is fairly short at four years because I need to raise the funds required to help cure cystic fibrosis sooner rather than later. Completing the Appalachian will allow me to raise both dollars and awareness.

Cystic fibrosis is a disease where time is the enemy. Until recently, it followed a predictable path, gnawing steadily away at patients' lungs and ability to breathe. Repeated infections reduced lung capacity by roughly two to four percent per year until inevitably an especially severe cold, flu, or infection would strike a fatal blow, or require a complex and far from certain lung transplant. Thankfully, innovative classes of drugs like Trikafta from Vertex Pharmaceuticals have slowed this progression, but not for everyone. The new drugs don't work for all genetic variations of cystic fibrosis, and the scourge of antibiotic-resistant bacterial lung infections can still terrify anyone fighting this disease.

Navigate for the long journey.

The ability to execute tactically, while still seeing a long way into the distance, is a remarkable leadership skill. It can be the extraordinary vision of entrepreneurs who can take a blank piece of paper and see a Fortune 500 company, or as we discussed earlier, it could be a leader who takes that same Fortune 500 company and understands what it's going to take to evolve over the next ten or twenty years. Perhaps it's a leader who takes an interest in long-term, complex social issues, planting a flag in the sand to change something for the better. Whatever it is, the longer the goal, the more we must have the patience to *eat the elephant,* one mouthful at a time.

I need to cure cystic fibrosis today, but I know it will take more time. It will require more research and more investment. I know we are on the cusp of gene editing technologies that will drive transformative change in how we treat diseases over the next decade. So, I continue to hike and continue to fund-raise and continue to push myself with every step, until we are done.

The Ballard of the Bear Bag

Choices have consequences.

One evening, while setting up my tent, I watched with amusement as a hiker tried to hang his bear bag for the night. He tried hard to free his rope that, entangled around a branch, showed no signs of becoming loose. The betting was 50/50 on whether he would succeed or injure himself in the process. As I fired up my stove to cook dinner, he struggled on and I hollered out to him that I appreciated the dinner and a show.

Protecting your food from bears and other critters is an essential part of hiking on the Trail. You don't want a bear roaming into camp at night and deciding the delicious smell wafting out from your tent is something worth investigating. Bears have an astonishing sense of smell with black bears able to smell other bears, humans and strong-smelling food from miles away.

Allegedly, their sense of smell is seven times better than that of a bloodhound in part because of something called the Jacobson's organ, which is found above the roof of the bear's mouth. The Jacobson's organ sends signals directly to the hypothalamus, which is responsible for aggression and mating behaviors. If you're going out hiking, you should spend some time with that particular piece of information.

There are three general ways to take care of your food at night. Some campsites will provide bear boxes, a large metal box with a bear-proof latch on it that hikers can place their bear bag into overnight. This is the easy option, but only a few campsites have this luxury.

The second way is to hang your bear bag from a tree at least one hundred yards away from your tent. A bear bag is a lightweight sack that all your food is stored in. You tie it to a rope, attach the other end of the rope to a small bag you weight with a rock, throw that rock over the branch of a tree, and then hoist your bear bag some twenty feet of the ground so bears and other critters can't get to it.

I use a third method: a bear canister. These canisters are made of some magical material bears can't break into, so all you have to do is walk a hundred yards into the woods and place it behind a tree or rock. Hopefully, it's still there in the morning and hasn't rolled into a stream or been whisked away by a marauding mob of squirrels.

The tradeoff between hanging a bear bag and carrying a bear canister is weight (advantage bear bag) versus time and convenience (advantage canister). My canister adds about three pounds to my pack weight, which is a considerable amount in hiking terms. However, I do not have to find a tree or hang the bag at night, saving me a lot of time and annoyance.

Be decisive, explain the why, move on.

Sometimes, decisions lack obvious right or wrong choices. However, given a choice of actions, strong leadership is demonstrated by deciding on a choice, and then transparently articulating the *why* behind the decision.

I was fortunate to see the philanthropist/chef José Andrés give a talk recently. He spoke about decision-making, saying given the options of no decision, wrong decision, and the right decision, the worst of these is no decision. He told a story about how his charity organization, World Central Kitchen (WCK), moving too quickly, made a mistake. They shipped a cargo of breakfast cereals, think cornflakes, to Ukraine rather than shipping the requested bulk cereal such as wheat, maize, and barley. While this was entirely the wrong shipment, they ended up gaining incredible insights into how to expedite aid into a war zone. Objectively, the wrong decision to move fast without all the business processes in place ended up enhancing their overall effectiveness when they corrected course.

As a leader, you might not always make the right decision, but if you can explain why you chose something, and then learn from it if the decision turns out to be the wrong decision, no one can fault you for that.

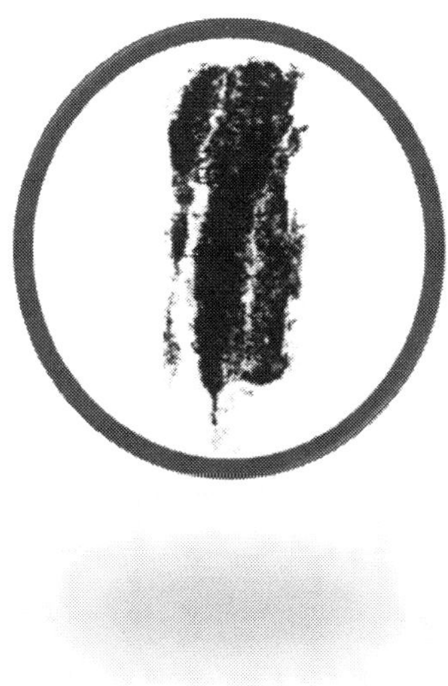

This section of the Trail allowed me to think about change. Change as an inevitable constant in life and business. Change as something that can be harnessed for progress not disruption. Change as a force that will happen to any long-term endeavor and require you to manage new risks, alter expectations, and force you to take new actions.

The more I considered change, the more my Act White Blaze came into focus. I learnt to think about change not from the perspective of what change is taking from me, but rather how must I act to harness that change.

One last note from this section, and this is for anyone who does not change their behavior even when in receipt of compelling information. If you know the fact about the Jacobson's organ being directly connected to the parts of a bear's brain that deal with aggression and mating, and you *still* do not store all your food safely at night, then I would have to question your judgment, you Yellow-bellied Sapsucker.

Section Nine Campfire Conversations

- How do you typically respond to change, and in what ways does it affect your growth or progress?
- How are you effectively leveraging the information available to guide your organization?
- When was the last time you took the time to celebrate a win, and how did it impact you or your team?
- What strategies help you move forward when you find yourself stuck in decision-making?

Section Ten

I Hate Connecticut

I sat alone on a jagged rock halfway up a mountain in the middle of Connecticut. I knew the Trail had defeated me. I did not have it in me to go on. The cold of the rock contrasted against the searing heat of the day, and the yellowish lichen covering it drew my attention away from the decision I struggled to make.

For the first time since starting my Appalachian Trail adventure, I had neither the physical nor mental fortitude to do what I had set out to do. I knew if I called it quits today, I would have to return for a third time to finish off Connecticut, instead of the one-and-done, which was my original plan. Connecticut is not even among the most difficult sections of the Appalachian Trail, so a decision to quit this section right here weighed heavily. My brain tormented me with thoughts about how I could expect to complete my full mission if I couldn't even hike this one section. None of my White Blazes were offering any help as I just couldn't get my head in the right place to consider them at that moment.

Deep down, I knew I would throw in the towel, but the intellectual and emotional sides of me were locked in an epic battle to decide on my course of action.

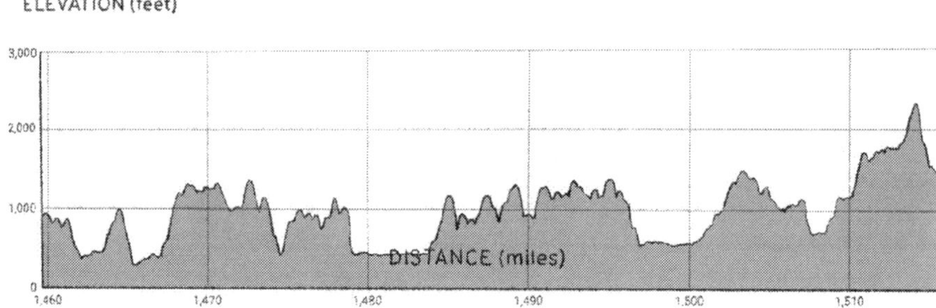

Figure 10 Connecticut

Mr. Patel

Value yourself.

The Hitching Post Country Motel in Cornwall Bridge, Connecticut, is a modest motel. Its single-story, horseshoe-shaped, building is set back from the two-lane road that runs down this side of the Housatonic River Valley. The motel is well maintained, friendly and clean, a short walk to the trailhead, and reasonably priced. I never set out to get frequent-stayer status, but my hiking journey across this section of the Appalachian Trail has meant that over a period of two years,

I've stayed on four separate occasions.

The proprietor, Mr. Patel, is all kinds of awesome. Moving here from India in the mid-90s, he built a life for himself, Mrs. Patel, and their two children. When he talked about the careers of his children, I could see the pride glowing in him. The same pride he and his wife take in running their business.

Mr. Patel does not negotiate on room rates. He knows the value of his offering, and if you're willing to pay for it, he will gladly accept your business. He offers rides to the trailhead for his guests and is accommodating to requests. Mr. Patel knows his business, knows his customers, and puts in the effort to provide a quality offering within the constraints of a small motel building. I liked Mr. Patel.

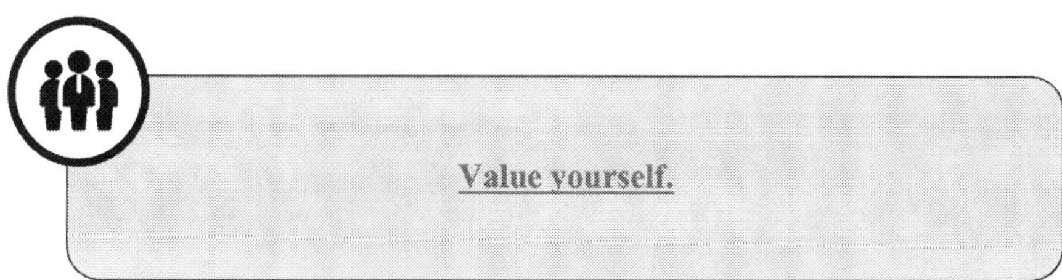

A perceptive leadership skill is understanding your value and the value of those you work with. When I think about key insights the Trail has given me, this is high on the list. It goes hand in hand with believing in yourself. If you understand your value better, perhaps it also allows for you to believe in yourself more. It allows you to stand on your pedestal and not step down from it.

What a motivational leadership skill it is to remind our colleagues of the value they bring to the equation every day. This can be done with a simple thank you: "Thank you for your detailed research." "Thank you for always following up in a timely manner." "Thank you for bringing your deep knowledge on this subject."

Regular progress reviews are a natural opportunity to remind teammates of the value they bring to the team, helping them to better understand that value in themselves. A focus on understanding the value someone brings can be an incredibly important conversation especially when that value is not obvious or is more nuanced. Helping someone to clearly articulate that value can bind teams together with a better understanding of everyone's role in the team's success.

Patience Is a Virtue

Always be learning.

By the time northbound (NOBO) Appalachian Trail thru-hikers have reached Connecticut, they have spent four months or so on the Trail and covered fifteen hundred miles in distance. They will have transformed themselves along this journey, shedding weight and perhaps pre-conceived notions of life. The men will be sporting beards and the women a confidence that is hard-won.

I crossed paths with a few of these hardy NOBOs as I hiked this section south on the Trail. As is customary, I'd spend a few minutes in conversation before we went on our own ways. One question I've taken to asking hikers this far into their journey is, "Can you tell me one thing you have learnt?" It's an unexpected question, and I usually see a few moments of reflection as they ponder their answers. It's possible they are pondering why I use the strange British word "learnt" instead of the typical American "learned." For some reason, it's just one of those Americanisms that I've never been able to acclimatize to.

My favorite response from this section came from a young woman in her late twenties who shared with me that she learnt, "Patience." That, I thought, is an exceptional answer. You can't get this far on the Trail without learning patience, both in other people and in yourself. Too many variables end up being out of your control. It could be weather or physical injury. Perhaps it's equipment failure or the desire to hike with someone who's hiking slower than you are on a given day. A myriad of reasons exist for why patience is something the Trail will teach you.

I thanked her for her answer, and she headed out northbound toward Mount

Katahdin, seven hundred patient miles in the distance.

If you ask a question, listen to the response.

As leaders, it's essential we engage in constant learning and encourage our teams and peers to do the same, too. You can demonstrate a powerful leadership skill when you take the time to ask about someone's learning experiences. That single question, "Can you share with me one thing you learnt from this experience?" can be so enlightening if we take the time to ask it. This could be learning from structured training classes but also from the everyday experience of meetings, team activities, business events, and client interactions.

As I write this, a fond memory comes to me of sitting around the dinner table when my kids were young. Rather than ask, "How was school today?" I would ask, "Tell me one thing you learnt today." Occasionally, this would elicit an informative response and sometimes I would get that "Really Dad?" stare and a deadpan response of "Nothing."

When we give ourselves, and others, the time to reflect on what insights we can take from any activity or life situation, it reveals a wonderful leadership skill. People in the same situation with different perspectives might yield different insights than you. This type of feedback is invaluable and can help us enhance the type of experiences and formal training our teams have access to.

The Land of Steady Habits

Building your brand as a leader.

At the end of a long day of hiking, finding shelter and water just a few steps off the Trail is like winning the lottery. This was not the case with the Limestone Spring Shelter. Located down a steep climb into a valley, almost half a mile off the Trail, it was a losing lottery ticket. If I ever find the person who put the shelter down that particular mountain, we will have words.

For me, it's one of those mental games. When I put everything into getting to a certain point and then someone asks me to do just a little bit more, it seems disproportionally hard. I know the difficulty is in my head. In a weird way, I really enjoy that feeling of realizing that I did, actually, have more to give, being forced to dig deep and find that extra push.

The Finnish have an excellent word to describe this: *sisu*. According to Emilia Lahti in her master's thesis, "Above and Beyond Perseverance: An Exploration of Sisu,"[43] it can be perceived "as a reserve of power, which enables extraordinary action to overcome mentally or physically challenging situations." Much has been written about how to describe the essence of sisu in English. Maybe the right answer is not to translate but to experience.

By the time I had my campsite set up, I was so done with the day that all I had left in me was to crawl into my tent and lay down. I didn't even have the strength left to eat dinner. A first for me and a mistake that would come back to haunt me the next day. I was done, done with Connecticut. In the five minutes before I fell into a deep sleep, I thought about what nickname I would give the State of Connecticut. As I was leaning heavily toward hating on it, I came up with a few choice names, but none are appropriate for publishing.

One of Connecticut's actual state nicknames is "The Land of Steady Habits." It's a cool nickname and came about in the early 1800s to define political stability by repeatedly electing the same officials to top government jobs. The Connecticut State Historian Walter Woodward tells us that Federalists (who were in power) used this phrase to convey wise, steady governance. Of course, their opponents used the same phrase to convey entrenched corruption and backward thinking.[44] Ah politics.

Forge a steady, predictable leadership style.

Steady, predictable habits are a necessary leadership skill. It doesn't matter if it's managing up or down or relating to your peers, a steady and consistent leadership brand will take you a long way.

The research report "Leader Identity as an Antecedent of the Frequency and Consistency of Transformational, Consideration, and Abusive Leadership Behaviors"[45] has exactly the type of unhelpful title you might expect to find in the *Journal of Applied Psychology*. But it does contain some thoughtful research on this topic of consistency, which I will summarize as follows: If you're consistent in transformation or consideration behaviors, people will see you as a leader and be more likely to follow you. If, however, you're consistent in abusive behaviors, you will not be seen as an effective leader. It seems that if you go off the handle occasionally, people can be forgiving, but if you're consistently disagreeable, people figure you out for what you are. Not a leader.

As discussed, being consistent in a positive way about your values, motivation, and other attributes of your day-to-day is important in leadership. Don't get me wrong. While changing over time is possible and sometimes necessary, demonstrating predictability and consistency in the short-term is a well-respected leadership skill.

Bear With Me on This One

No one likes surprises.

I was first out of camp the next morning, hitting my stride as the sun was also hitting its stride. The long rays of the low morning sun streamed through the branches, heavy with summer leaves. I hiked along, immersed in my thoughts, savoring the stillness of the forest and the silence of the morning punctuated only by the occasional birdsong.

So, too, was a large American black bear, catching the same rays atop a mossy boulder only about twenty feet in front of me. Lost in our thoughts, we only spotted each other when we were far too close.

Have you ever seen a startled cat jump up onto its four legs from a sitting position? That is the same move the large American black bear did right in front of me. For the briefest of moments, our eyes locked. I'm sure what the bear saw was a textbook example of human shock on my face, and I'm also certain I can describe what a shocked bear looks like in return. In my head it's David Attenborough's hushed tones saying, "The doughy cheeks of the full-grown Ursus Americanus are raised in what we know as the fight-or-flight grimace." Please feel obliged to try that sentence out with your best British accent.

Thankfully, the bear chose flight and set off running. Seeing that much mass move that quickly in the wild is indeed the legendary stuff of a BBC wildlife documentary.

No one likes surprises.

No one likes surprises. This leadership lesson can be repeated over and over and over. The earlier a client, colleague, team member, or stakeholder can be alerted to something drifting from expectations, the better. This applies to unwelcome and welcome news alike. Reliable and ongoing transparent communication is necessary to develop trust and make real-time adjustments for any anomaly going on.

There's an old adage for this you're likely familiar with: "A stitch in time saves nine." Pick up your needle and take care of what you need to take care of earlier rather than later.

Failure Is an Option

The heart versus the brain.

My pack was super light, as I carried the bare minimum for a single overnight camp, but even so, the Trail in Connecticut proved to be harder on me than I anticipated.

That morning I had already covered twelve miles and had thirteen difficult miles still ahead of me. My schedule was tight, as I needed to be off the Trail by six o'clock at the latest for real-world commitments. As it was still before noon, I felt I had enough time for these remaining miles. The day before, though, had been a rough seventeen miles, and I had to dig deep to commit myself to the afternoons hike.

Pushing onwards, I found myself thirty minutes into a thousand-foot ascent. The sun beat down on me, the temperature rose to 95°F (35°C), and I could sense the early signs of dehydration. I wasn't feeling it. Not at all. I hadn't fueled my body last night, meaning it could not repair itself fully, and in addition, I hadn't fueled adequately for today's effort either.

At this point, I had a choice to make. Turn around and head back down to the base of this mountain where I could get a shuttle to pick me up or push on. I sat on a rock and gave myself fifteen minutes to decide. I said the words aloud, "I hate Connecticut," and then I quit, turned around, and headed back to the road.

Intellectually, I knew I wasn't quitting. I was making the right choice, the safe choice, the choice that would let me come back and finish those remaining thirteen miles another time. It was a choice to stop, not to quit. I understood how dangerous dehydration can be and how it can lead to terrible decision-making the longer it goes on. However, my emotional side screamed at me that I was quitting, something I'd only considered once before in all my hiking. It did not sit well with me.

By the time I reached the road and called for Mr. Patel to come and pick me up, I was good with myself. How did I get there? How did I take *failure* and turn it around in my head?

First, I focused on my *Why*. My *Why* is my two daughters, who fight cystic fibrosis, and their brother, who loves them. It tore at my heart when I watched my daughters deal with the consequences of this disease throughout their childhood and as they've grown into adults. From the medical intervention of repeated hospital stays and surgeries to the personal impact of missed school and the social stigma of being the sick-girl, it tore at my heart. But when I saw the transformation in them as hard-won advances in medicines catapulted them into a world of near normal, my heart lightened its load just to be torn apart again when I spoke to friends for whom these drugs came too late to save their loved ones.

As much as I have wished for it, I can't take the disease from my daughters, so my only choice is to play my part in finding a cure. My mission is to raise the funds that will help to cure this disease by hiking the whole of the Appalachian Trail. My other mission is not to get myself seriously injured while out there.

Next, I thought about the people who would be proud of me for making what they would understand was a tough decision for me. Finally, I focused on the accomplishments that had gotten me to that point: the miles already hiked, the dollars already raised, the first step taken. Well done, me, for all I had already achieved.

Cultivate strength from setbacks.

In a leadership role, we must handle losses, tough situations, and painful outcomes, as no one is immune to these. Focus on the fact you're making the right decision rather than on whatever your emotional instinct is telling you. In this battle between emotion and intellect, it pays dividends to come back to those items I talked about—the why, the who, and our accomplishments. They can act as a bedrock around which to make tough decisions or handle losses. It can also help us get over the natural tendency to dwell on the situation. What if I had played the hand differently or made a different choice?

After the fact I allowed that emotion of failure to stay with me. Not in a negative way though, but rather as a motivator. I allowed it to inform me that there would be tough days and I could get through them. I allowed it to support the decision I made instead of fighting against it. In an excellent research paper, Overcoming Failure in Sport: A Self-Forgiveness Framework[46], published in the *Journal of Human Sport and Exercise*, the authors explore the subject of self-forgiveness in response to failure. They conclude that "through the self-forgiveness process, athletes may be more inclined to engage in an impartial analysis of unsuccessful competitive performances, determine areas in which improvements may be made, and recover more adaptively following failure."

One fixed truth about leadership is you can't change the decisions you made in the past. You can only look to the future, learn from the experience, and try again. Note to self: Always make sure I eat before the end of a hard day's hiking!

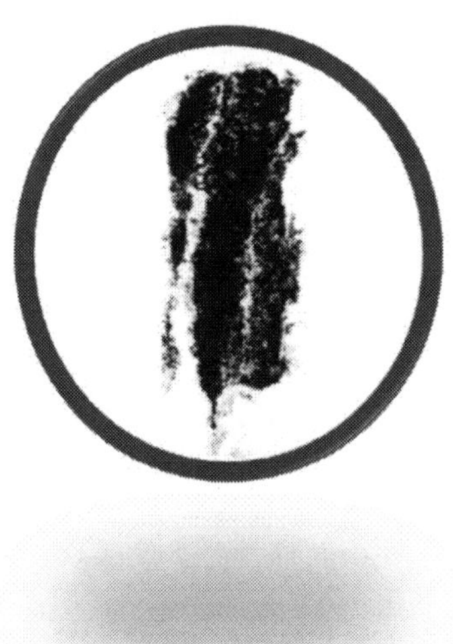

This section of the Trail taught me how to be more comfortable with who I am and to understand my own value and values. Coming to terms with failure and having patience with myself for that experience was deeply inciteful.

In the moment, I not only failed to complete the section, but also failed to lean on my White Blazes. Afterwards, when I had time and energy to contemplate, I pulled out strong insights from these experiences. This in and of itself might be a good White Blaze Leadership insight. Sometimes the spark that comes might not come in the moment but comes later when the experience has had time to ferment.

Of course, I returned to Connecticut and finished those last thirteen miles. I've chosen to forgive Connecticut, which in and of itself is a valuable leadership skill. The Housatonic River Valley is a beautiful part of the country and is well worth a trip to the surrounding area if you get a chance.

Officially, I now no longer hate Connecticut. I'm thankful for these insights it gave me on an intellectual level, but I'm still slightly irked with it on an emotional level. I'll keep working on that.

Section Ten Campfire Conversations

- In what ways do you recognize and value your own worth, and how does it affect your interactions and decisions?
- How do you approach listening in conversations—what helps you focus on truly understanding others?
- What kind of leadership style do you aspire to be known for, and what steps are you taking to embody it?
- Can you share an experience where you navigated a conflict between emotion and intellect, and what you learnt from it?

Section Eleven

1,102 Miles

My logbook reads 1,102 miles of the Appalachian Trail completed, 1,095 miles to go. Halfway. For reference, 1,102 miles could get you from Washington, D.C., to Dallas, Atlanta to Denver, or from London to anywhere in Europe you would care to walk to. From Perth, Australia, you could get to absolutely nowhere else within 1,102 miles. My point is, 1,102 miles is a long way to hike, but I still have half of the Appalachian Trail left to go.

I wanted to capture a few leadership insights from the first half of my journey that I haven't written about before. These include how a shoe accessory and my Value White Blaze taught me a fundamental leadership lesson, and how the power of considered feedback is so valuable.

Furthermore, I want to talk about the importance of recommitting yourself to a long journey, whether that is the physical Trail, a long-term work project, or a personal commitment. Staying the course of this four-year plan is something I had to constantly work on. But it's something that I have figured out how to do. It's a simple technique with powerful consequences and offers an approach we all can apply and use to our advantage.

You Are Going to Do What?

Get to know the unknowns.

Over these 1,102 miles, the Trail has challenged me at every opportunity. It challenged me mentally and physically. It challenged me to consider risk in an intensely tangible and immediate way. It challenged me to trust and believe in myself more. Even when I've gone hungry and thirsty, I've learnt to believe in "The Trail will provide." I've also learnt that the moment we take our eye off the ball or assume the top of the hill is just around the corner, the Trail will remind us who's in charge.

It's brought me closer to nature, and more grateful for the trappings of civilization that are too easily taken for granted. It's taught me less is more, but it must be the right kind of less. It's shown me how to adapt to the variables I can't change, such as weather and terrain, and to own the variables I can change, like my attitude.

The Trail has given me the privilege of meeting people who would never normally fall into my orbit. It's shown me how to judge less, listen more, and be present for every human interaction. I've learnt that we are all on the same trail, it's just that we are hiking our own hikes along the way.

Accept the challenge.

Strong leadership can be demonstrated when we help our friends and colleagues understand how accepting difficult challenges can be rewarding. By definition we know a challenge feels intimidating and perhaps scary. However, the rewards can be tremendous. We can teach that learning to embrace the risk inherent in a challenge will result in valuable new skills and personal growth.

Challenges require us to be a better version of ourselves; otherwise, it's just business as usual. Perhaps a version of ourselves we didn't even know was within us. This is the arc of every hero story—the hero gets a challenge, it all goes horribly wrong, finally wins the day, returns victorious, and is transformed. However, embracing challenges can be as simple as taking the time to learn a new tool or system, or something that requires more courage, such as putting your hat in the ring for an elevated role.

As leaders, we must also understand where people fall in terms of accepting a complex challenge and then provide the right resources to maximize their chances of success. Some, like me, stand on the edge, peering into a challenge, but then almost always jump after a few minutes of contemplation. Others are more cat-like in that they will shout for the door to open, but then need much longer before walking through it, if at all.

If we understand how our colleagues navigate their way into, and then through challenges, we can use that to better understand the type of support, coaching, and monitoring they would respond to during the challenge.

Weathering the Storm

Making smart decisions requires smart data.

The storm front rolled in way faster than I expected. I was thirty minutes away from my off point, with nowhere to hide from this monster. I came out of the trees onto a high ridge and saw the storm front in the distance. The wall of clouds looked as if was straight out of a Steven Spielberg movie. The air shifted, and I could smell the anticipation of the surrounding forest. I needed to get down before the edge of the storm hit and brought dangerous lightning with it. I picked up my pace and headed down to the lowest point I could find. As I neared the low point, the storm let loose. It was epic.

The intensity of the rain and the fierceness of the clouds transformed the afternoon light. All around me that off-yellow, sepia tone colored the forest as if the moment had been captured in a photograph from the 1800s. I flattened myself right up against the biggest tree I could find, struggling to remember if that was a smart move or not. The lightning punched its way into the mountains and the forest trembled when the thunder shouted in response. I was not happy with the fact I'd put myself into this situation. Not happy at all. I should have been paying better attention to the speed of the storm, as I already knew it was imminent.

The rain fell so heavily that I soon realized I had another problem. As I had parked myself at the lowest point, I was now where all that water flowed toward. I needed to move and move quickly in case a flash flood trapped me down here. Stepping out from under the meager safety of the tree, I splashed my way back up the Trail and away from the rapidly forming lake. Thankfully, the storm abated, and I exited the Trail looking like a drowned rat escaping from a ship.

Seek to be an informed leader.

Objective leadership comes from knowing what data you need, how reliable the data is, and when you need that data in order to use it effectively.

In this example, I did not have a single piece of data that would have told me when the storm front would arrive. That information would have changed my actions and would have resulted in a safer and much drier outcome. Data after the fact is still useful, as it informs for the future, but data before the fact is far more powerful.

As I recall this incident, I note I had access to the piece of data I needed but failed to utilize it. First, I have a weather app on my phone that has a radar scanner. Second, I had cell service for some parts of the hike that day, too, but forgot to recheck the progress of the storm, instead relying on my read of the storm's trajectory from earlier that morning.

When I consider that example further, I understood it's not only knowing what data you need but also understanding the temporal nature of that data. Does it change, at what rate does it change, and how much in advance do I need the data to use it to my advantage? Here, my data point was unreliable because I hadn't considered the variability in the storm's speed.

You can coalesce your team around actions by explaining why specific data gives you the information you need to act. This background can strengthen your position as a leader and solidify your standing as someone who does so based on objective facts.

You Won't Know if You Don't Try

Giving the right feedback at the right time.

I was a couple of miles south of the Nantahala Outdoor Center (N.O.C.) in North Carolina. It's 137 miles from the starting point of the Appalachian Trail at Springer Mountain and about two weeks northbound hiking for a freshman class of NOBO thru-hikers. It's also one of those points where people attempting to thru-hike the Trail quit. Two weeks on the Trail feels like it should be enough time to figure out if this is for you. A brutal, technical 3,500-foot climb down to the valley floor to where the N.O.C. is located can test the strongest of hikers, so it's understandable why it can be the last step for some.

I hiked alongside a young man on this section who shared his story with me. He worked at a gas station in the Midwest somewhere. He saved his money, quit his job, and was out here to spend the next six months hiking the Appalachian Trail and finding himself. Except the experience wasn't what he thought it would be, and he was quitting right at the N.O.C. His mom was already en route to pick him up later that afternoon.

My instinct was to smack him over the head and tell him to keep going. There's a saying on the Appalachian Trail that you should "never quit on a bad day." However, it felt to me as if he'd been experiencing bad day after bad day, and I could see in his eyes he was defeated. So, I channeled my trail-name, and instead of berating him for quitting, I coached him.

I told him it was impressive he had tried because if you don't try something, how will you ever know if you could have done it? I encouraged him to keep trying unique experiences so that someday he might find the adventure that becomes his passion, that defines his life. A short while later, I waved goodbye to him, and he headed off to find his mom and try his hand at something else.

Fail fast, move on.

I value the insightful leadership lessons this encounter offered. The first has to do with trying and failing. As leaders, we must be OK with the concept that sometimes we will fail, or our teams will fail. Thomas J. Watson, the iconic founder of IBM, allegedly said, "If you want to succeed, double your failure rate."

Failures can happen for reasons outside our control but sometimes mistakes happen. Our mistakes. Reminding ourselves that success and failure are interwoven is an indispensable leadership skill.

Value honest, authentic, and direct feedback.

The second insight is about providing feedback and knowing what your goal is in providing that feedback. Sometimes we are asked to provide feedback in a structured, formal setting. Think annual review. However, most of the time, we are given opportunities to provide feedback in a more spontaneous manner. It's critical that you take a moment to consider the goal of that feedback. Are the words offered to educate, inspire, or encourage someone? Perhaps they are offered specifically to shock someone into action or a change of behavior.

In the example above, neither of us would have benefitted from me trying to convince him not to quit. That wasn't my job. But I felt like I could provide him with the supportive feedback that trying and failing is how we all learn some of life's most potent lessons. I hope that my coaching made his load a little easier to carry on whatever trail came next for him.

Ice Chainz—Woods Hole Hostel, The Hit Single

It takes all of us.

Ice Chainz is not my rapper name, but if I were a rapper, it would be my first choice. My first hit song would be about the Woods Hole Hostel in southern Virginia. Woods Hole Hostel is a must-stay destination for anyone hiking the Trail. It's the stuff of Trail legend, and Neville Harris, the proprietor, doesn't disappoint. Her grandparents, Roy and Tillie Wood, are Trail royalty, with Tillie Wood being inducted into the Appalachian Trail Hall of Fame in 2017 for her contributions. Woods Hole Hostel stands as a vibrant legacy to the gift the family have given so many hikers over the years.

Neville runs a tight ship, putting anyone who stays at the hostel to work. You can help to prepare dinner and breakfast or perform a myriad of chores that are needed to keep the place functioning.

I was looking forward to a quick weekend hike using this as my base, but the weather conspired against my plans. Within an hour of arriving on a dark, early April night, the snow began falling. What was supposed to be only a few inches became a full-blown blizzard in the morning. Treacherous. Not at all safe hiking weather. I braved a few miles on the forest road but knew trying to hike into the woods and onto the Trail would have been foolish—and dangerous.

Instead, I spent the day listening to Neville tell stories of the founding of the Trail, sharing this experience with the few other hardy hikers cocooned at Woods Hole for the day. Outside, the snow transformed the landscape into a blank canvas upon which the colors of spring would soon be painted.

Sunday morning came with a crisp, cloudless day and a sky that only gets that blue when all the moisture has been removed from the atmosphere. Perfect, I thought, as I had recently bought a set of ice chains (sometimes called ice cleats) for my hiking shoes and couldn't wait to try them. Think the chains people who live in snowy places put on their tires in the winter, except these are for your shoes.

I know it's a little sad to be this excited about a shoe accessory, but one aspect I love about hiking is the *stuff*. I'm not sure wondering aimlessly around REI counts as a hobby, but I'm certain many hikers spend enough time doing just that to make it one. If you're keen on discussing the merits of an MSR Whisperlite stove versus the MSR XGK stove, might I suggest you go hang in the stove aisle. I'm sure someone will happily engage you in that conversation for however long you care to discuss thermal unit burn rates.

Success is a team sport.

The ice chains hold an extremely powerful leadership lesson within them. They work by ensuring multiple points of contact with the ground. Each of these contact points individually is not enough to make a difference, but working together, they provide a firm grip on even the most treacherous ice and snow.

The only way we succeed in life or in a business environment is working together. We can consider this insight and the ability to communicate it as fundamental leadership skills. One of my favorite leadership stories related to this topic is apocryphal about when President John F. Kennedy (JFK) visited NASA in 1962 at the start of the Apollo program and asked a janitor he met what he did for NASA and the janitor replied he was "helping to put a man on the moon."

If we can align everyone on our teams and organizations around the missions we define and if we can make sure everyone knows they are valuable, needed, and trusted, then we can hike across mountains of ice or put a person on the moon.

The Man, the MYTH, the Legend

Recommitting to the Mission.

Section-hiking is a different beast compared to a single, one shot thru-hike. As a MYTH (Multi-Year Thru-Hiker), I must constantly worry about how to get on and off the trail, how to fit the time in between work and personal commitments, and how to stay fit enough between hikes so it's doesn't hurt so much. Trail legs disappear as quickly as they are earned.

The hardest piece, though, is the mental game of staying engaged on this long haul. In my case, it's a four-year plan and here I am, right at the halfway point, and on target to where I wanted to be. Still, I question my commitment to getting this mission accomplished. So how do I motivate myself? How do I keep working on this, especially when the Northern Campaign of the next two years will include some of the hardest, most challenging sections of the Appalachian Trail?

The answer is that I keep returning to my mission, which is to raise the money to buy the science that will cure cystic fibrosis for my daughters and all those fighting this disease. Is motivating myself that easy? It is.

Rediscover the "Why?" of your mission.

From a leadership perspective, we can support ourselves on these long journeys by taking time to pause at critical moments, such as reaching the halfway point of a project or when meeting a product development gate. Using these pauses to focus back on our *why* can strengthen our resolve for the longer journey ahead.

We can also help ourselves recommit by reframing how we consider our accomplishments. For example, I opened this section by saying, "I still have half to go." What if instead I said, "I only have half to go"? I understand this perspective is like asking if the glass is half full or half empty. But the idea I only have one thousand one hundred miles to go makes a meaningful difference in how I think about what is ahead of me. Gosh, it almost makes it feel like those last one thousand one hundred miles are all downhill. If only it was that easy.

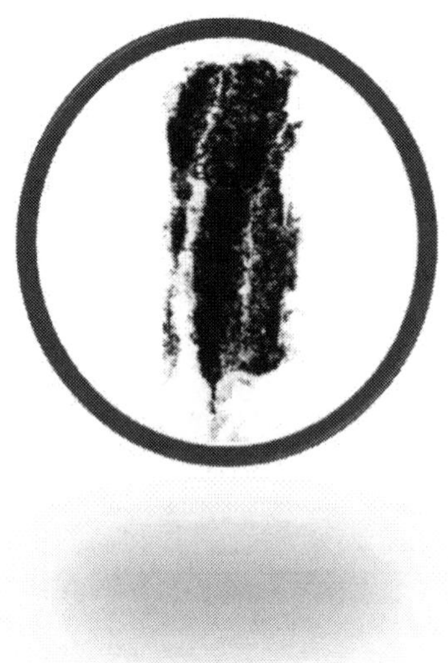

The halfway point of this journey and my mission has given me cause to reflect on all the experiences I could have written about. It also reminds me how much experience we gain in our own lives and how easy it is to forget those memories.

Through these 1,102 miles my experiences solidified into my White Blazes. My Believe White Blaze was shining the most brightly right then. I had to believe in my abilities to complete this journey. I had to believe that I had both the physical and mental fortitude required to get to Mount Katahdin. And I could never waiver from my belief that no matter how small my actions might seem, one day I will be able to say we cured cystic fibrosis.

If there's something you need to recommit to just fall back on your Why. Be proud of everything you've done to this point, put on your ice chains, and let's do this!

Section Eleven Campfire Conversations

- How would you describe your mission—your *why*—and what drives you toward it?
- In what ways do you work to understand the motivations and values of others?
- How do you approach receiving genuine feedback, and what impact does it have on your growth?
- What commitments or goals might benefit from a renewed focus or dedication?

Section Twelve

Alien Abductions and The Erethizon

Aliens abducted Thom Reed on September 1, 1969, near the small town of Sheffield in Berkshire County, Massachusetts. You'll be pleased to know they returned him, unharmed, the same night. I learnt this because the Appalachian Trail runs close to the Covered Bridge location of the incident, and the associated UFO Monument Park piqued my interest. A plaque signed by Massachusetts Governor Charlie Baker was erected in the park in 2019 and commemorates the incident as being "Deemed historically significant and true." So, I guess it must be.

By the time I started my journey north across Massachusetts it was early fall. This was to be my last section hike of the season. I had considered pushing this hike out to spring, as the weather can be variable at this time of the year. However, I had a convincing chat with myself about my mission and my overall timeline, put on my boots, and got myself out onto the Trail.

The trees on the higher elevations prepared to change colors. But where I was down in the flat sections, the same place that had greeted me at the start of the hike, the landscape was all golden corn fields ready for harvest and gentle pastures full of unsuspecting cows waiting to be taken. It was as if Hollywood had requested this exact landscape for the aliens to show themselves.

A few days later, I would experience a chilling close encounter, coming face to face with a creature so bizarre, so clearly alien, that it had to be otherworldly.

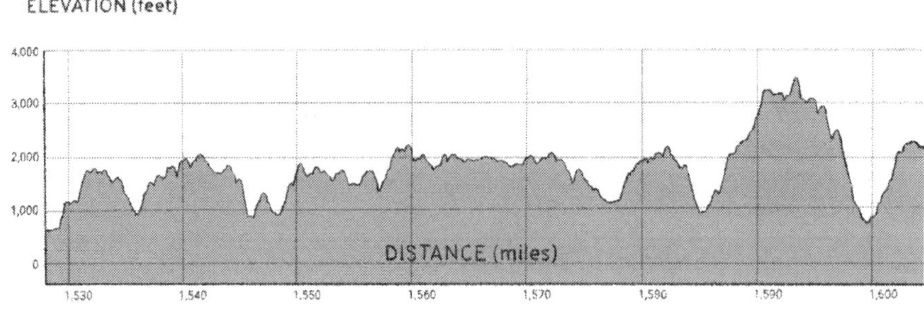

Figure 11 Massachusetts

Lieutenant (Lt.) Dingleberry

You never know when someone will come back around.

I hiked northbound through Massachusetts and several times a day would meet thru-hikers who were on a southbound journey. South Bounders (SOBOs) start their adventure at Mount Katahdin in late June or early July, once the Trail opens. They finish at Springer Mountain in Georgia sometime between Thanksgiving and Christmas, depending on their pace. I stopped to chat with one such hiker when another SOBO came down the Trail. After a few pleasantries, he said to me, "Hey, are you that guy hiking for the Cystic Fibrosis Foundation?"

How did he know? What kind of strange magic was this?

It turns out he was a hiker with the trail name Lt. Dingleberry. He was one of the heroes who came to a fellow hiker's rescue, as written about in Section 6: When Bear S**t Hits the Fan. He had already summited Mount Katahdin but missed an earlier one-hundred-fifty-mile section because of a personal commitment and was back to finish this small section, thereby completing the entire Appalachian Trail.

We stayed and chatted for a short while, recalling the drama and camaraderie of the rescue event until the Trail inevitably tugged on us in opposite directions, and once again, our two paths diverged in the woods.

What goes around will come around.

This is an indispensable leadership lesson everyone needs to remember. At some point in the future, that person in front of you today might come right back into your world unexpectedly. It could be a colleague who becomes a customer or a junior client who's the CEO ten years later. I was on a client call with my team recently, where the client had been an intern with one of my team members fifteen years ago. Their positive interactions from back then set the groundwork for the call we were to have all these years later.

You never know how life will turn out, and as such, being respectful and professional in all your dealings should be a basic tenet of your leadership.

Alien Abductions

Believe and others will too.

It must be an exhilarating experience to be abducted by aliens. I watched a recent episode of *Unsolved Mysteries* called "Berkshires UFOs" (S1.E5)[47] about this area I was hiking through. The show's informative program description reads: "Residents of Berkshire County, Massachusetts, recall their baffling, terrifying experiences with a UFO on the night of Sept. 1, 1969." I was hooked.

Thom Reed, now in his late fifties, is one hundred percent convinced aliens abducted him that night. Thom's belief is so deep, so visceral, he has convinced plenty of other people, too, that this happened to him.

Believe in your mission.

Now you might wonder where I'm going with this and what type of leadership insight can I draw from it? Well, here you go, and it's a powerful lesson.

When you take on a leadership role, you must believe in what you're being a leader for. Belief in something is hard to fake. Sure, conmen and card sharks can be surprisingly capable at that deception, but for most of us, we are not. People are much better at knowing if you believe in what you're saying and doing, rather than knowing if what you believe in is true or not. That last sentence is worth re-reading.

Put another way, as a leader, you must have a genuine belief in your mission or task, and you must express that belief in a manner that will resonate with your audience. They need to feel your passion and commitment. If you can communicate your belief in a compelling enough manner, then that becomes enough for other people to believe in your mission too.

For example, I was fortunate to see Mark Gallagher speak on the topic of winning and belief. Mark is a Formula 1 motor racing executive and author of *The Business of Winning*. In his book he takes you on a journey of "teamwork, innovation and targeting ambitious goals set in an environment of change, transformation and disruption."[48]

Mark spoke about the first day Red Bull owner, Mark Mateschitz, came to speak to the Jaguar Racing team Mateschitz had just bought from Ford in November 2004. Although Jaguar Racing had never achieved success in F1, Mateschitz told the assembled team that the renamed Red Bull Racing team would win the Formula 1 Constructors' Championship within five years.

"Mateschitz believed it that day," Mark Gallagher said, "but no one else did." However, Mateschitz instilled the discipline of belief into the Red Bull Racing team, and they went on to win four back-to-back Formula 1 Championships starting in 2010. That's the power of belief.

Later that night, as I readied myself for sleep, a pitch-dark fall sky filled my vision, and I couldn't but help peer up at the bright stars and the Milky Way and wonder "What if?"

You'll be pleased to know no actual aliens showed up that night, but I had a terrifying encounter with something completely alien to me the very next day.

Getting to the Point

Assumptions make an Erethizon dorsatum out of u and me.

A few yards in front of me, the alien waddled down the Trail. Stopping in its tracks, it turned to inspect me. It was covered in dangerous-looking spikes, and its small, beady eyes shone with intelligence. Definitely not something terrestrial in nature! Okay, so it wasn't an actual alien, just a porcupine; scientific name, *Erethizon dorsatum*. But if its scientific name doesn't sound like the name of a malevolent alien species, then I don't know what does.

This North American porcupine is basically a large rodent covered in quills. The one in front of me was the size of a small dog. Smithsonian's National Zoo and Conservation Biology Institute[49] tells me it can grow to twenty pounds and have thirty thousand quills. I assume thirty thousand quills will give anyone an excess of self-confidence, as this porcupine didn't seem to mind my presence too much. For a minute, we kept on down the Trail like this, with the porcupine looking back at me and then continuing to move along. I was confident he wasn't thru-hiking the Trail, so I was intrigued to see what he would do.

Eventually, he stepped off the Trail and disappeared up a tree. When I say disappeared, he climbed the tree like nothing I expected at all. One moment he was on the ground, and the next, he was fifty feet up, sitting nearly invisibly in the crook of a branch. If I hadn't seen him climb, I would never have known he was there. It turns out North American porcupines are excellent climbers and spend much of their lives in trees.

One final fascinatingly alien fact about porcupines is they have built in antibiotics in their skin. This helps them to heal in case they fall out of a tree and cut themselves with their quills, which must happen a lot for evolution to step in. If you think, "That's me as a porcupine," evolution has you covered.

Strengthen team bonds, ask questions, listen to the answers.

The leadership insight I want to draw here is about assuming the skills someone might have, or rather, not even considering the skills someone might possess. It never occurred to me a porcupine was an excellent climber. I hadn't even considered it, but if I had, I would have assumed that a porcupine wouldn't be an excellent climber considering all those quills on its back.

What if we make the same assumptions about people, or perhaps worse yet, don't even put the effort into assuming anything?

We should take the time to ask about our team's hidden talents and to listen to the answers. This is one we could all do a better job at. There may come a time when we need someone on our team who can climb that tree for us, and it would be useful to know who that is ahead of time.

No "Regrats"

Moving on from mistakes.

After a bruising seventeen-mile day, I hobbled off the Appalachian Trail and onto the half-mile connector path leading to Goose Pond Shelter. It's one of the rare shelters on the Appalachian Trail that has an actual door and an actual caretaker. About halfway down this short stretch heading toward the shelter, I came to a tent site, and my body decided, no more. This was as far as I was going.

When morning came, I woke up early to face a harder eighteen-mile day ahead, and I needed to be on the Trail by six o'clock at the latest. As I tore down my campsite, getting ready to head out, a hiker already leaving the shelter waved at me and shouted, "Blueberry pancakes!"

"Hmmm," I thought as I completed my preparations to leave.

That day on the Trail, almost everyone I met who was traveling southbound asked me how good the blueberry pancakes were at Goose Pond Shelter. Apparently, this is what the shelter is trail-famous for. Delicious and fluffy with that perfect pancake aroma that forces you to have just one more. Doh! Why hadn't I taken an extra couple of minutes and gone to visit the shelter?

The day wore on until all that remained was one more tough peak to climb and four miles left to hike to get to the next shelter. It took me an hour to reach the summit, but the views from the top made the effort worthwhile, so I took ten minutes just to sit and enjoy. In the distance, I could see the hazy peaks of other mountains yet to come and, closer to me, the unending forest that would guide me there. I clambered down the other side of the mountain in about thirty minutes, only to arrive at the same place where I'd started up the mountain over an hour and a half ago. Doh! I'd turned myself around at the top and followed the same white blazes all the way back down again, the way I had just come up.

Now, you might be thinking, "Rookie mistake," but it goes to show you even someone with all my Trail experience can still make a costly mistake, especially when tired. I couldn't take back these two mistakes. Pancake time was over, and I couldn't magic myself back to the summit of the mountain.

Accept your mistakes, learn from them, move on.

Mistakes happen. They happen to other people, and do you know what? Sometimes, they happen to us, too. As leaders, we must own the mistakes we should own. We all need to develop the skill to say, "I will not waste time on what was;" rather, I will learn from it and focus on asking, "What's next?"

I must admit, standing at the bottom of that mountain, wishing I'd eaten pancakes for breakfast, was not my finest moment. I knew better than to dwell on my mistakes, and instead I turned around, put one foot in front of the other, and climbed back up that hill, dreaming of blueberry pancakes every step of the way.

Coyotes

Howl at the moon.

With a full day of hiking behind you, sleep comes as soon as it gets dark. Known as *hiker-midnight*, this was around eight o'clock at this time of year in Massachusetts. It had been another tough hiking day, so after a few minutes of enjoying the star-lit sky, I crawled into my tent and went straight to sleep.

A noise woke me up several hours later. A howling coyote! He was close, unsettlingly close.

It's one thing when you hear coyotes off in the far distance while tucked up in a warm bed, safely hidden behind solid brick walls. However, I want you to picture yourself deep in the woods with nothing between you and a baying pack of coyotes but a thin wall of space-age tent material. Feels a little more dangerous, doesn't it? I made sure my inadequate Swiss Army knife was close at hand and tried to get back to sleep.

Coyotes have successfully adapted to different environments and are now found in every state in the United States except for Hawaii. The twelve thousand coyotes that call Massachusetts home are considered only medium-sized predators. Even so, with a full winter coat, they can be intimidatingly large and sometimes mistaken for wolves.

The rest of the pack soon joined this singular coyote, and it was clear they were having a party. The group howling doesn't necessarily mean some poor deer just took its last few terrified steps, but it's a fair guess that's what happened. Coyotes hunt smaller prey alone, but for larger animals, such as white-tail deer, they will call in the family. They also use this as an opportunity to teach their pups the art of putting dinner on the table as well.

Sometimes coyotes will even form alliances with badgers to hunt specific types of prey in a beneficial alliance for both parties.[50] That night I'm quite sure no badgers received an invitation to the dance.

Sometimes you've just got to howl at the moon.

So, what can coyotes teach us about leadership? Turns out to be a lot.

For example, if you want to win the prize, you must do it as a team. If you want to expand your territory, you must adapt. If you want to grow, you must give the junior members of your team opportunities to learn and grow with you. If you want to go after unique opportunities, you might have to build out-of-the-box alliances.

My favorite coyote lesson? If you're having a fantastic day, howl at the moon.

Cookie Lady & the Trail Stand

Trust: Given or earned?

I was maybe a mile from a road crossing when I passed a woman walking her two golden retrievers. "I'm the Cookie Lady," she said. "My place is just off the Trail in about two miles. Fresh cookies in the cookie box. Help yourself."

I thanked her and wished I'd done a little more research on hiking across Massachusetts before I headed out. The Cookie Lady was indeed trail-famous, and a short while later, I was enjoying a couple of the most excellent chocolate chip cookies you could ever want. "Donations gratefully accepted," said the sign. The table was also full of earrings, necklaces, and other trinkets, and all supported with an honor payment system too. Very cool.

The day before, I'd come across another example of this honor system at the Trail Stand. Sodas were one dollar from the fridge, either cash into the cash pouch, or if electronic payments were your thing, online payment via Venmo. I eagerly drank the soda, left a dollar for the next hiker's sugar hit as a little Trail Magic, and hurried back out onto the Trail. In both these cases, there was a lot of trust in hikers to do the right thing. Most hikers *will* do the right thing.

Be aware of your relationship with trust given, and trust earned.

With little else to do on the Trail that afternoon, I pondered the question: "Is trust given, or is trust earned?" After miles of contemplating, I decided my answer is trust must be reciprocal.

From a leadership insight perspective, I've seen it both ways in my career. I remember a training class where the entire premise was trust was only something you earned. I fundamentally disagreed with that at the time and still do. You can do everything right, but if the other party doesn't have trust in you, it doesn't matter what you do or think you have earned.

We do, however, automatically give trust to people who have formal qualifications or specific roles and titles. For example, a medical doctor, a pilot, or a Certified Information Systems Security Professional (CISSP). It's a shorthand way of saying you can trust me; I've paid my dues. From that perspective, formal qualifications are a highly effective way for professionals to increase the likelihood they will be granted trust. It's also true, though, that trust can be lost far more easily than gained. "Trust me, I got this" is a fine sentiment, but you better deliver on that promise.

Earned trust is only useful if the other side of the relationship is willing to grant trust. When granting trust as a leader, you must be consistent and clear on your criteria. If you choose to withhold trust as a leader, you need to let the other party know what would constitute being trusted.

Trust is a defining quality of a leader. The questions of how you trust, who you trust, and what you do when you don't trust, should offer a worthy opportunity for introspection.

This section of the Trail and the deep, cloudless skies encouraged me to look up toward the heavens. To think about the brief amount of time we have here compared to the stars and ask myself, "What difference do I make?"

Can I trust more, regret less, and on occasion howl at the moon?

The Milky Way shone as brightly as I remembered it from my childhood. It pulled my eyes to the night sky where I could pick out satellites circling high above the earth. Gaze long enough and I would be rewarded with the brief blaze of a meteor as it collided with the atmosphere and burned up—a thin bright line visible for a few seconds its final act.

Perhaps that cosmic event causes you to think about your leadership. About what shining streak of light, however brief, you will leave. Perhaps it will guide your eyes toward your own version of my Inspire White Blaze and ask you to consider how you can build on a simple happenstance in your life and use that to inspire those around you.

If your timing is right, you can even see the International Space Station sailing overhead. At least, that's what I assumed the bright speck of light moving across the sky was. Or maybe, just maybe, it was something else.

As Mulder and Scully said in *The X-Files*, “I want to believe.”

Section Twelve Campfire Conversations

- How would you describe your relationship with trust, and how does it influence your interactions with others?
- What aspects of your mission resonate most deeply with you, and how does that belief shape your actions?
- Can you remember a time when you truly let loose, like howling at the moon? What inspired you in that moment?
- When did you last take a moment to gaze at the Milky Way, and what did that experience mean to you? If you haven't yet, try it!

Section Thirteen

Loss, Faith, and Cwtch

Early into the new year, my mum peacefully passed away. No matter your relationship, or their age, losing a parent is a defining moment in our lives. My mum was a joyous and loving mother, and I understand how fortunate I am for that gift. Still, it raises unsettling questions in me like, "Was I a good enough son?" and "Am I a good enough father?"

I knew I needed to go to the mountains to find answers and peace with her passing. I also needed something from the mountains that is beautifully described by the Welsh word *cwtch* (pronounced like *kootch*).

This might seem like an intensely personal topic when the focus is on leadership, but if the COVID-years taught us anything it's that we need to connect in more honest, more fulfilling ways, both inside and outside the work environment.

So, on a cold January weekend, I headed to the Appalachian Trail in southern Virginia to contemplate and reflect on my mum's life. The Trail did not disappoint.

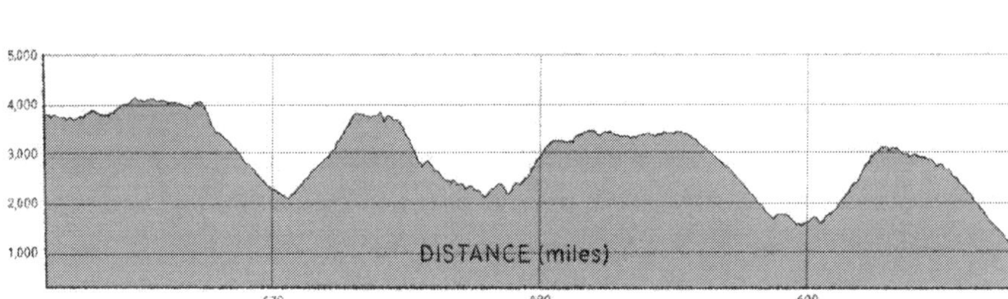

Figure 12 Miller Cove Road, VA, to Wind Rock, VA

Cwtch

There's no place like home.

I grew up near the Eryri (Snowdonia) Mountains of North Wales, so perhaps it's not surprising mountains are in my blood. I spent my childhood in the village of Llansantffraid Glan Conwy, found on the estuary of the river Conwy, where the tidal waters of the Irish Sea clash with the river waters flowing down from the broad range of mountains. You could smell the salt in the air on the days when the sea won that battle. Yr Wyddfa (Mount Snowdon) at three thousand five hundred sixty feet is the highest point in the range, and in Wales and England.

Welsh, the language, is a language of poets and sounds far better when you know it than it does to an untrained ear, or as flat letters on a page. Cwtch is an example of the poetry of the language. It's one of those words that doesn't translate directly into English, although if you search a dictionary, it will inform you cwtch means hug, or cupboard.

An article on a BBC travel site by Australian writer Kate Leaver describes cwtch as "an emotionally significant embrace, an intrinsically Welsh word that evokes a sense of home." She claims that it "makes you feel safe, warm and comforted." I couldn't agree with her more, and think she said it best when she said, "It's in times of fear, danger, distress and melancholy that we most need a cwtch."[51]

I needed a cwtch, badly. The mountains and the Trail always feel like cwtch to me, although "feeling warm" was clearly metaphorical as the temperature had dropped well below freezing.

On my first step on the Trail, I could feel the mountains embrace me, and the tension, sadness, and fog of my grief lifted. On the Trail, I knew what to do: put one foot in front of the other and start climbing the mountain.

Develop your technique to manage stressful situations.

In life and in our careers, it's inevitable we'll encounter times of crisis. In the work environment, these could be events such as losing a critical deal or a teammate leaving for a competitor. It could be personal, such as a colleague being diagnosed with something serious or the death of a teammate or friend. We all went through the crisis of the COVID-years and understand that crises can come in all shapes and sizes.

As a leader, knowing what cwtch looks like for our friends and colleagues can be a critical differentiator in how you respond to a crisis. Not everyone's cwtch is the same, but using your instinct as a leader combined with asking the question can help to calm the waters and weather the storm. In addition, knowing what your cwtch looks like can be a leadership skill that can help to sustain you in challenging times.

We can't always drop everything and head to the hills when life crashes down on us, but we can develop small slices of cwtch that center us. It might be a cup of earl gray tea or five minutes spent listening to Eminem. Prioritize searching for your slice of cwtch. Practice using it when you need to be centered. Then, like an old friend, when you desperately need a cwtch, it will be there for you.

Faith

If you build it, he will come.

Faith is woven into the fabric of the Appalachian Trail. The earliest native Americans, the Catawba, who lived in this region, worshipped many gods, but all with a focus on harmony and balance in the universe. When the settlers came, they brought Christianity, both Catholic and Protestant versions. The Mormons showed up in the late 1880s and must have developed an irresistible pitch because by the early 1900s most of the Catawba converted to Mormonism.

Up and down the Trail I saw abandoned and neglected Baptist and Methodist churches that reflected the tough times rural America has seen. Amongst these sit gleaming houses of worship that also reflect the deep faith still burnt into the people who call this their home today.

Religion never struck a chord with me, so as I hiked up the mountain, I wasn't looking for anything other than to reflect. I thought a lot about my journey to help cure cystic fibrosis for my daughters and how proud my mum was of my commitment and of the progress made in curing this disease for her granddaughters.

I thought about what she would make of the next generation of drugs that are being researched, the mRNA treatments, and the mind-bending science of genetic editing that will lead to a full cure.

Mum would have smiled and said, "I'm proud of you." Then she would have told me a distant story about a doctor in the small Scottish coal mining village of Kelty where she grew up, and how he was related to some relative I don't know, who might have moved to Canada or America or Australia.

I would have smiled and said, "That's nice." And all would have been right with the world.

I also reflected on how much she enjoyed hearing about the accomplishments of my children—Olivia, James, and Sophie—and all eleven of her grandchildren. Her face would light up, the wrinkles a visible reminder of a long life fully experienced. As I hiked, my face lit up, too, with the joy of the memories.

Later, as I neared the first peak, I exited the trees and stepped onto a rocky promontory. Ahead of me, I could see for miles up the narrow, winter-worn valley. When I turned to look the other way back down the valley, a white wall of a snowstorm bloomed in the distance, blowing my way. It was as if someone had painted in the valley with an absence. The storm moved quickly, trees disappearing on the mountains sides as it progressed. I stayed for a few minutes on the rock and waited for it to arrive.

The snow didn't just arrive; it enveloped me. It wrapped itself around me like a physical hug as if the snow itself was giving me a cwtch. My whole body felt on fire, the opposite of what the visual environment told me I should be experiencing. An overwhelming and intense sense of love for my mum consumed me.

It was a moment—a serious "I don't know what just happened" moment. The snow stayed with me for an unmeasurable period and then dissipated as if the whole purpose of the storm had been to give me an opportunity for one last goodbye.

Time on the Trail has a way of pushing us to think about the big questions. About life, death, love, and our deeply held beliefs. I have faith that if you open yourself up, you can find what you need, even if the experience arrives in the most unexpected way.

Everything *was* now right with the world. I smiled, and I laughed myself to the top of the mountain.

Respect peoples' beliefs.

Faith can be a tricky topic to discuss, especially in the workplace. However, strong leadership will always show honest respect for everyone's faith. Take the time to educate yourself on the customs and needs of others. By doing so, you will enhance your reputation as a leader and build more resilient and integrated teams.

When we take that perspective about faith, it's not tricky at all. It's empowering for everyone involved.

Change

I didn't come here to tell you how it will end. I came here to tell you how it will begin.

It's always satisfying to reach a peak, although I should have known this one would be a problem. Fifteen minutes earlier, I had bumped into the only other hiker I'd encountered in two days. We chatted briefly, but before he moved on, he laughed at my Scottish kilt. "That," he said, "is not the best choice today. Once you go over the ridge, the wind is howling, and it's frozen. Good luck."

For me it was the best choice. You see, my mum and dad were always so proud of being Scottish and nothing would have stopped me wearing a kilt on this hike. The tartan (plaid) was a Black Watch pattern. This also held significance as my dad had fought in the Korean war in 1952 as part of that famed Scottish regiment.

Sure enough, as I stepped over the ridgeline, the wind met me with a fierce, in-your-face, up-your-kilt hello.

It was about the coldest I've been on the Trail with the windchill around 0°F (-17°C). I hunkered down behind a large tree to block the wind as I figured out my game plan from here. A random wooden sign attached to the tree read, "Eastern Continental Divide." That made little sense to me. I couldn't Google it since taking off my gloves was out of the question. I doubt I had cell service anyway. So, I arrived at my game plan—suck it up, pick up your pace, and get the torture over with as quickly as possible—and headed back out into the arctic winds.

Later I learnt the location was the dividing point for where water flows, a hydraulic divide, not a geographic one. To the east, where I hiked from, all the water flows into the Atlantic. To the west, where I was going, all the water flows into the Gulf of Mexico.

I thought a lot about that moment when a drop of water falls on the dividing point; two futures lay ahead, one to the Gulf and one to the Atlantic. The raindrop has no agency in this choice. It just happens. The world changes in these small moments with a before and then an afterward. Before, there was my mum, but now only the memory of her remains.

Acknowledge that change is hard.

Just as water is bound to follow the path of least resistance, so to do we find ourselves in situations where we have no choice. The decision is made for us. This can and will happen regardless of your role in an organization. Even the CEO has shareholders that force direction.

These types of situations often force changes in relationships with our colleagues and teams. This could be someone leaving for a competitor, or it could be a downsizing in the workforce or a restructuring of divisions. Your colleagues could be there on Friday but gone from your day-to-day on Monday morning. Just as in our personal lives, business relationship changes can be some of the most stressful experiences we go through.

Change is hard, and it's harder when you feel you have no control. As a compassionate leader you can recognize this and help everyone understand that when you have no control, it's how you respond to the path you must follow that matters.

I'll Be Here All Week

Hello, my name is Inigo Montoya.

My time in the mountains was over for this section and so I returned to the trailhead, where my car was waiting. I drove slowly down the dirt road for miles, lost in my reverie, until I saw an old farmer and his dog, who were crossing from the field back to their farmhouse. I slowed to say good afternoon.

Winding the window down, I said, "It's beautiful out here in this part of the world."

The old farmer pondered my statement for a brief time and, in a well-worn deadpan response, said, "Lots of people tell me that, but I don't see it. So, I guess they must be talking about my face."

I laughed at his dad joke and, waving my goodbye, headed back out into civilization with a smile on my face and my spirits raised.

Be present, listen, and practice your empathy.

You never know what type of day someone is having, what troubles are on their mind, or what is worrying them. A kind word, a simple joke, or a small act such as a friendly smile might be all they need to get them through the next five minutes and to change the arc of their day.

As leaders, we must be empathetic to the people around us, even when we are having bad days. We can't allow our emotions to translate into being gruff, rude, or dismissive. The old farmer knew nothing of my troubles, nothing of the pain I felt for my loss, and yet that small joke made an enormous difference to me as I drove on.

Be Happy

Music? Yes, it's very good, very good for the digestion.

At the small tavern I wolfed down a well-earned hot dinner. The warmth of the room held me tight, and that familiar smell of old beer reminded me of pubs from back in Wales. I remembered nights spent at the Conwy Vale or the Cross Keys where I'd arrive home to a disapproving look from my mum after one-too-many pints.

A folk band filled the noisy room with music from the small stage. They were a bunch of old guys, all talented musicians based on their performance. Their enthusiastic fan club cheered for every lively song while I sat in the corner taking it all in.

One song stuck out to me: a classic released by Rodger Miller in 1965, "You Can't Skate in a Buffalo Herd." It's the type of song they just don't write anymore. Each verse suggests an absurd activity that would be impossible to do. The chorus, however, instructs us that one thing we can do is to choose to be happy.

Now this isn't always true, and plenty of people need professional help to battle mental health issues. However, deciding to be positive about something is a decision many of us do have the power to decide.

From my corner of the room, I was drinking in not just the beer in my hand but also the humanity in the room: The easy patter of the bartender to new customers. The young couple on a date over by the window, their phones turned screen down on the table while they talked. The silent older couple over in the other corner, perhaps everything already said.

I could feel how much fun the band was having as their music washed across the room. For them it clearly wasn't just a gig, rather it was joy. The music is what gave them meaning, and almost certainly the act of playing their instruments was their cwtch.

Life was going on all around me, unaware of my loss. But I was good. I had found what I came to the mountains for. I raised my glass to my mum, told her I loved her, and leaned back into the chair with a smile on my face.

Drive positivism across your sphere of influence.

Most of you may have heard the term "tone from the top" used to convey how leadership sets the direction of the business. It's also leadership's job to set the culture for the organization or your team. Much of this can come from having a positive outlook, from deciding to view the glass as half full, from setting your mind to it. My mum was excellent at that.

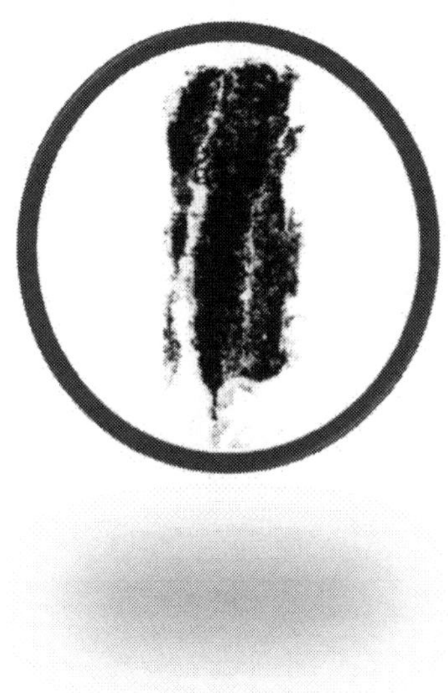

This section of the Trail allowed me to focus on my mental health. To think about how we must do better at recognizing it in ourselves and taking the right actions to address it. To think about how so many of our colleagues struggle with issues on this front; be it from health, faith, relationships, or the constant noise of change in our lives.

My Value White Blaze was probably most forward on this section of the Trail. I thought a lot about my relationship with my mum and how I valued it. In turn, this reflection led me down a path of thinking about how I value everyone in my life that I care for. That's a lot of thinking. In addition, I spent time coming to an understanding of how I valued myself and my needs.

My time in the mountains was the cwtch I needed. It soothed my soul and allowed me to say goodbye to my mum in a personal and meaningful way. If you're having a tough day, week, or year, I hope you can find your cwtch and lean into your faith, whatever that is.

Section Thirteen Campfire Conversations

- What does *cwtch*, a place of comfort or safety, mean to you, and where do you find yours?
- How do you approach the challenge of change, both for yourself and in understanding others' experiences with it?
- What strategies or practices have you developed to manage the unique stresses that come with leadership, especially in times of change?
- In what ways do you demonstrate empathy, and how does it impact your relationships or leadership style?
- How might your teams describe your attitude—do they see you as positive and understanding, and what makes you think so?

Section Fourteen

Virginia Blues

Almost nine million people call the Commonwealth of Virginia home. Over four hard days of hiking on the Appalachian Trail, I met exactly one of them. The rest of the time it was just me, my inner voice, asking me why I was doing this, and the distant whistle of trains hauling whatever freight needed to be moved through southern Virginia to parts unknown.

The one person I did meet was a sweet and hardy older lady who was volunteering as a Trail maintenance worker. She educated me on the *Hepatica americana* wildflower and apologized she had left a tree trunk across the Trail as her chainsaw had run out of gas. I'm fairly certain she was not a representative sample of the rest of Virginia's population, as I've seen no one toting a chainsaw around Reston Town Center or the strip malls of Tysons Corner.

My experiences on the Trail continue to astonish me in ways large and small. In this section, the tiniest of flowers brought forth powerful insights into why we all need to adapt to our environments. The challenge of a mountain climb gave clarity into what goes on inside my head. The history of charcoal drew a compelling picture of why we all need to encourage a diversity of experiences.

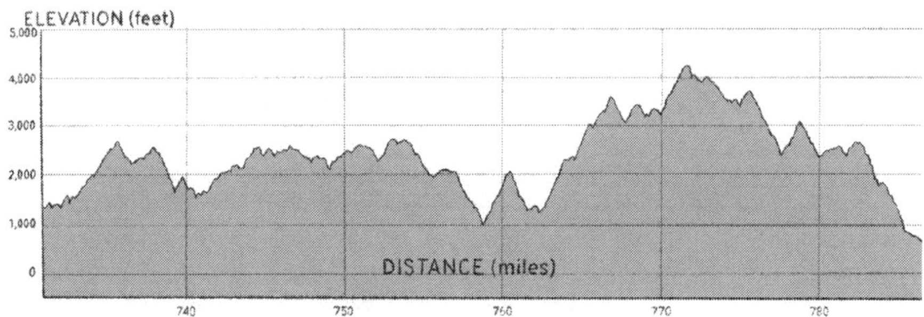

Figure 13 Troutville, VA, to Snowdon, VA

Blue Ridge Parkway

A road less traveled.

This section of the Appalachian Trail located a few miles north of Roanoke, Virginia, runs parallel to the Blue Ridge Parkway for many miles, crisscrossing the actual Parkway frequently. If you have never driven this section of the Parkway, might I suggest you put it on your bucket list? The scenery is breathtaking.

At this time of the year, early spring, the trees are empty of leaves and the roads are empty of traffic. Come summer, and especially in the fall, cars and RVs snake along the Parkway at well under the thirty-five miles per hour speed limit, taking in every astonishing view.

The Parkway runs for 469 miles along the Blue Ridge spine of the Appalachian Mountains all the way from the Great Smoky Mountains in the south up to the Shenandoah National Park in northern Virginia, where it turns into Skyline Drive.

But I was not in a car. I was on foot, struggling up a steep incline with my pack on my back, pondering why anyone would have thought building a road through this pristine wilderness made any sense. The project started under the Roosevelt administration in 1936, with the vast majority completed by 1966. I realized; however, the brilliance of the Blue Ridge Parkway is in the fact it's not a road that's about getting from point A to point B. The Parkway has the complete opposite function of most roads in this respect. The Blue Ridge Parkway is an opportunity for all to experience the majesty of nature and become part of it, even if it's from the comfort of air conditioning and snacks.

It's not the posted thirty-five miles per hour speed limit that slows traffic down; it's the sheer need to take in the views around each turn in the road. Drivers can't help but slow down to experience them. Ample turnoffs give visitors plenty of opportunity to step out and breathe in the fresh air while wondering how vistas this wild and beautiful can be within a few hours' drive from our major cities.

Take the time to smell the pine trees.

An essential leadership skill is knowing when to slow down, when to take the time to step back and take in the view. We can't drive at eighty miles per hour, day in and day out. If we want to perform at our best, we must be honest with ourselves about when we need to take a break. As leaders, we also need to encourage our colleagues and teams to understand this. We need to encourage each other to take our vacations but not take "Responses to email will be delayed" vacations. Rather, we need to see to it that we enjoy a "I'm out for the week with no access to email" vacation. My hiking conditions me to be comfortable with this digital detox, as often I don't even have access to the internet and I'm not likely to use up scarce cell phone power on emails that can most definitely wait until I'm back.

In the *Wall Street Journal* article, "Why Your Team Isn't Taking Time Off,"[52] Deloitte Chief Wellness Officer, Jen Fisher, talks about the always-on society and the badge of busy we try to wear. She highlights the burnout and mental health issues that can come from not taking time off and talks about the disconnect that can end up with employees leaving an organization.

Lead from the front on this one. Take time for yourself outside of work, disconnect when you need to, and encourage those around you to do the same. The work environment will be a better place for everyone if you do.

Hepatica Americana

Adapt and survive.

The wildflowers, which are known as *Hepatica americana*, or round-lobed liverleafs, never even registered in my consciousness as I hiked along. According to people who know these things, they are named liverleafs because the tough leaves are shaped like a liver. The Trail maintenance worker I met was super excited to point them out to me and share their emergence as proof spring had sprung. I felt a little ashamed that I had been focused on my struggles instead of scouring the forest floor for these harbingers of clocks springing forward.

The round-lobed liverleaf has read the book on using evolution to its benefit and has an array of adaptations making it the perfect wildflower for this harsh part-winter and part-spring environment.

Evergreen leaves allow it to photosynthesize during short winter days, so it's poised to come out of the gate as the conditions start to turn favorable. Its flower can close itself during nighttime or during rain. This helps it protect the delicate pollen held within and provides a better chance of finding a stray insect to do what insects do. If no insects are around, the flower has evolved the ability to self-pollinate. About fifteen percent of plants have developed this extraordinary capability.

The seeds held within the round-lobed liverleaf are wrapped up in a protective and nurturing coat of protein and lipids known as an elaiosome. Elaiosome is science talk for ant-Cheetos. Driven by a wild craving for more of this delicious treat, ants will do whatever it takes to get to these tasty morsels. Once they have one in their mandibles, they carry the package to their nest to feed their larvae. Once done consuming the elaiosome, the ants take the seeds to their waste area, which provides the perfect growth medium for future *H. americanas*. This flower-ant symbiosis even has a scrabble-winning name: myrmecochory.

Embrace the skill of adapting to a changing environment.

These tiny little wildflowers hold ample leadership insights for us. If you want to be the first, you must be prepared to come out of the ground ready for whatever the environment will throw at you. Encourage yourself and your teams to think about what changes might come and the adaptations you can make to address them.

The COVID-years were a master class in adaptation. It drove us to embrace novel approaches to work, navigate complex changes in interpersonal relationships, and step out of the business-as-usual mentality. It normalized the ability to think hard about what might come, and it helped prepare us to adapt to changes.

My Question White Blaze was starting to glow with all the questions this idea of adaption was driving. Was I adapting to the new world of post-COVID work? Was I adapting to the emerging world of artificial intelligence and the impact it was sure to have? Was I adapting quickly enough to leverage all I was learning from the Trail?

What I found from embracing my Question White Blaze was that it inevitably led to firing up my other Blazes. This made sense and drove me to further consider my ability to Act, Value, Inspire, and Believe.

Inner Voice

It's coming from inside your head.

The first section hike of the season is always a difficult one, and this one, across remote southern Virginia and its stunningly beautiful landscape, was no exception.

The weather was uncertain, so I carried full winter gear, which makes for a heavy backpack. My fitness level was sub-par coming out of a long holiday season and a schedule not conducive to training. Add in a taxing section of the Trail with some unquestionably aggressive climbs, and this was indeed a recipe for a hard few days, which is how I ended up having to work extra hard to convince myself I could do what I needed to do on my last day of hiking.

The prior evening, I spent the night at the Bryant Ridge Shelter, a large, functional, and well-built shelter. It's the type of space you might think was designed by thirteen-year-old Boy Scouts for thirteen-year-old Boy Scouts.

It was a chilly morning, and I watched my breath float away as I drank my bitter coffee. In my head I ran through all the reasons why I couldn't do what I needed to do that day. Ahead of me lay a nine-mile, 4,500-foot climb with what looked like a relentless uphill battle.

My inner voice is quite creative in inventing excuses for why I should not do this, or couldn't do this: "Come on, Peter, there's a dirt road just a mile away that you could take downhill to get a ride." "Think about it, Peter, you could be sipping on a beer by lunchtime." "This is going to suck, Peter; do you really have that in you?" "It's probably too cold at the top of the mountain, Peter, too dangerous." *Argh*. Once that first doubt crept in there, it's like my mind went into overdrive trying extra hard to make me not do what I knew I needed to do.

In David Goggin's uncompromising book, *Can't Hurt Me: Master Your Mind and Defy the Odds*, he writes about this exact phenomenon calling it the governor. "It's the software that delivers personalized feedback—in the form of pain and exhaustion, but also fear and insecurity, and it uses all of that to encourage us to stop before we risk it all."[53]

So how did I vanquish my governor's narrative, lace up my boots, and head out on the trail?

"Why?" might just be the most critical question you can ask.

I focused back on the fact I knew my mind was playing with me. I wasn't injured and the weather, although cold, wasn't that bad. I've hiked further, and I've hiked in far worse conditions. Objectively, no compelling reason existed for me not to do this. Furthermore, one overriding reason required I do this. That's my unwavering mission: to hike the whole of the Appalachian Trail so that I can raise funds to buy the science that will cure cystic fibrosis for my daughters and the other forty thousand Americans fighting this disease. I've talked about this before, but in tough times, returning to the center, to focus on the why, *your* why, is the answer to taking that first step.

Leadership is focusing yourself and those around you on the why. On those days when outcomes aren't going your way, when external forces strive against you or you're not feeling it, keep returning to your core. What goes along with this return to the core is clarity around your why. Some of the most effective leaders I've had the privilege of meeting are crystal clear about their *why* in any situation. If you aren't clear on your why, perhaps some quality time spent sharpening that particular tool might be time well spent.

Managing the Risk

Make mine a double.

From my reckoning, the most critical piece of equipment on any long-distance hike is the water filter. We can go hungry, but we can't go for long without water. Sure, we can drink unfiltered water out of a stream, but a few days later, this could come back to haunt us if we get a *Giardia* infection.

If you care for more details on the consequences of not filtering your water correctly, might I suggest you google *Giardia*? Warning though, if you're squeamish at all, it's better not to. You might also want to skip this next paragraph.

The description of *Giardia* from the Centers for Disease Control and Prevention (CDC) is, "Giardiasis is a diarrheal disease caused by the microscopic parasite *Giardia duodenalis* (or *Giardia* for short). Once a person or animal has been infected with *Giardia*, the parasite lives in the intestines and is passed in stool (poop). Once outside the body, *Giardia* can sometimes survive for weeks or even months."[54] The CDC makes the parasite sound quite benign. However, having talked to several hikers who have experienced a *Giardia* infection, I can assure you the consequences are far more—how should I politely describe it—explosive.

This was a problem for me, as I had misplaced my water filter. Had I left it on that mossy rock the last time I filled up? Had I put it back in my pack in the wrong place? I couldn't find it, so Plan B became Plan A, which was the spare filter I kept inside my bear canister. I knew where to find that filter and was grateful for my foresight. My mum always told me I'd forget my head if it wasn't screwed on tight, so I think about, and plan for, this type of scenario.

Because I was hiking some even more remote parts of the Trail that year, I upped my risk management game. I carried an extra water filter, lighter, and headlamp as three pieces of essential equipment that the weight-to-risk ratio falls squarely into the just-carry-a-spare column. Also, on the front of my pack, I attached a physical compass and a loud whistle.

For the risk management piece de resistance, I further upped my game with a satellite device that can pinpoint my location to within twenty-five feet of my actual position and has an emergency please-send-the-helicopters button on it. I'm not sure what would actually happen if I pressed that SOS button, and don't want to be in a situation where I have to find out, but it was reassuring to know it was there.

Quantify your risks and react accordingly.

The point here is it's paramount for leaders to not only consider the risks inherent in their activities, but to have contingency plans that are well thought out and match the cost to the risk. Risks come in many forms, and we can't cover everything. But leading with a priority-based approach can help.

An informative Deloitte whitepaper, "The Future of Risk,"[55] looks at how leaders should prepare for a changing risk landscape. It covers such areas as the ability to better understand, control, and mitigate risk through topics such as controls, risk transfer, and risk as a performance enabler.

Most interestingly it also calls out behavioral sciences as a tool to better understand risk perceptions and resulting decision-making. Behavioral science draws on psychology, cognitive science, neuroscience, and social sciences to help us better understand how we assess risk and better understand our cognitive biases in making risk-based decisions.

I previously mentioned how I'm a Pioneer personality type at work. A "Yeah, Let's do this!" first approach type of leader. I'm guilty of uttering the words, "What could possibly go wrong?" on more than one occasion. This phrase acknowledges there's a risk but decides to ignore it anyway. Knowing that's in my behavioral profile, I try hard to remember it about myself when I'm making decisions. It's well worth the time to think about our decision-making biases, how they tie into our personalities, and how they impact our colleagues and teams. After all, none of us want to forget our heads.

Charcoal

Heat makes you burn brighter.

Deep into the forest, I hiked to a flat piece of ground with a random sign stuck right on the edge of the Trail. Despite being weathered and hard to read, the sign served its purpose to inform. It told me that on this very spot, in the late 1700s and early 1800s, there stood a collier's pit used to make charcoal. Some fifty feet in diameter, the flat area was chosen since it lay downhill from the trees that would be burnt and close to the nearby furnaces that would consume the charcoal.

Starting around 1837, innovative techniques using anthracite coal and blast furnaces made this type of charcoal manufacturing obsolete. But in its heyday, charcoal was the only material that could burn hot enough and give off enough carbon monoxide to fuel the iron smelting process in furnaces.

Charcoal is made by heating wood while limiting the amount of oxygen available to it. This removes the water and other volatile components. To do this, the wood is arranged in a conical pile with a central shaft left in the middle. It's then covered in dirt or turf and left to heat for up to five days. By the seventeenth century, a skilled collier might turn sixty percent to ninety percent of the wood into charcoal. What you get at the end is a fuel that will burn at over 2,000°F (1,100°C), compared to wood that burns at about half this temperature.

Encourage your teams to create a broad set of experiences.

The leadership insight I want to draw out here is that certain jobs require you to have the experience of heat before you can burn as hot as you need to. Make sure you're building your set of experiences, taking on expanded responsibilities, and putting your hat in the ring for challenging roles. Draw on the wisdom of others who have been there, seen it, done it.

You can consider all this experience as the heat that will allow you to burn hot when needed. This leans into the need to make sure your teams are also gaining new experiences and broadening their capabilities. It might be as simple as letting someone run a meeting for the first time or asking someone to figure out the answer to a request. A key leadership skill is ensuring the building blocks of experience are put in place.

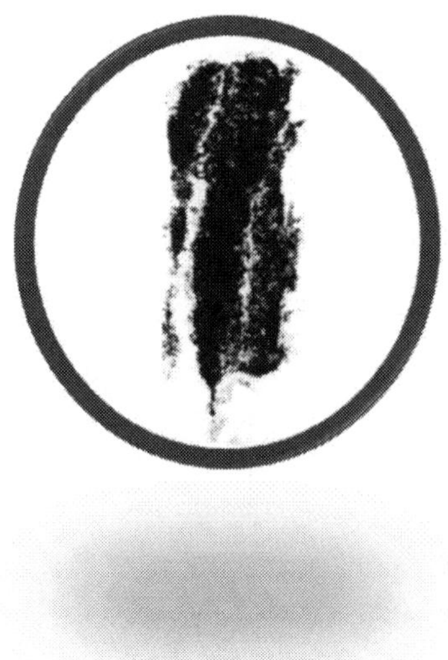

This section of the Trail pushed me to really question what was going on inside my head. To consider if and how I could take control of the doubt that wanted to rule on occasion.

I found that when I slowed down and focused, I could consider my past hiking experience more fully. Then, I could use my experiences to evolve my thought patterns and my motivation.

As I leaned into my Question and Believe White Blazes on this section, I didn't yet realize how much further I had to venture into my own head. I was still lost in the idea that the Trail is fundamentally a physical task. It's not. I would come to find in the thousand miles still ahead of me that the hard part was really inside my head.

I trust the insights from this section of the Trail will help you burn a little brighter, and perhaps when you're considering your next vacation, it's one with more charcoal on the grill and roads less traveled. Make it a vacation where you can tell your inner voice that those emails will just have to wait and that, yes, you *can* do what you know you need to do.

Section Fourteen Campfire Conversations

- How would you assess your organization's ability to adapt to change, and what factors contribute to its adaptability?
- In what ways do you promote openness about mental health within your team, and how does this impact your workplace culture?
- What personal biases might influence your approach to risk, and how do you navigate these in your decision-making?
- How do you encourage diverse experiences and perspectives across your teams, and what benefits have you observed from this diversity?

Section Fifteen

The Priest and Confessions

The Priest rises from the central flatlands of Virginia as a foreboding mass of a mountain. It stands like a solemn guardian watching over the Blue Ridge Mountains and the Appalachian Trail, which of course takes the hardest route possible across it.

At 3,066 feet straight up, The Priest is one of the harder climbs on the Appalachian Trail. This is especially true since on this day I already hiked twelve tough miles southbound across the Three Ridges Wilderness before entering The Priest Wilderness. I stood at the base of The Priest, and it looked back at me as if it was judging my ability to climb the four and a half miles to the summit. I worried that I would be found wanting.

If I could make the climb to the summit, I'd arrive at the trail-famous Priest Shelter. There thru-hikers confessed their trail sins in the shelter logbook. I knew it might make for some interesting reading, and I was already considering my entry carefully.

To get me up that climb, I brought a secret weapon, something that would change my approach to the climb and the rest to follow. It was something that could be applied in any demanding situation and something every leader should fall back on when needed.

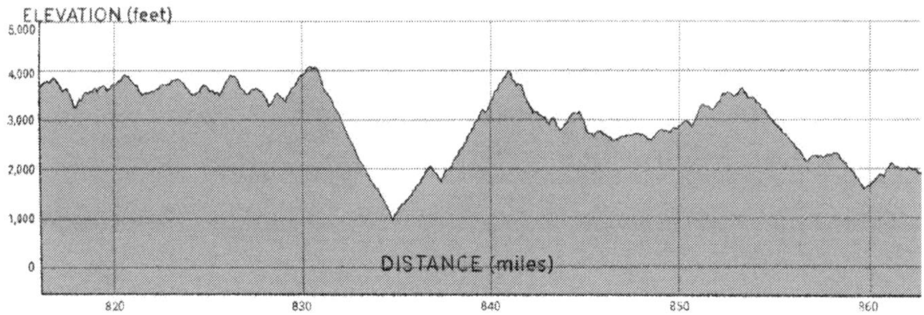

Figure 14 The Priest, VA

Mental Toughness

It's never too late to teach an old dog.

Up to a short while ago, I never even knew such an occupation as a mental toughness coach existed. I discovered the concept of mental toughness as a discipline from my friend, KC White. She is the first person with cystic fibrosis to take on the role as Chair of the National Board of Trustees of the Cystic Fibrosis Foundation, assuming that position in 2022. She is an inspiration to me and to the cystic fibrosis community for her tenacity and leadership.

For so many years cystic fibrosis was a disease of children because most didn't live long enough to grow into adulthood. But thanks to all the advances, more adults are now living with cystic fibrosis than there are children with the disease. Anytime we see an older adult with cystic fibrosis, such as KC, doing extraordinary things with life, their accomplishments serve as a powerful reminder that we can look to the future and not dwell in the past.

KC took her innate skills and honed them into her profession as a mental toughness coach. She now teaches at the University of Pennsylvania's Master of Applied Positive Psychology program, amongst many other accomplishments.

I looked into enrolling in this program, but I rationalized I didn't have the time to take on learning something new at this point. I guess that's an F in positive psychology before I even took a single class. I assumed mental toughness was just me out on the Trail, huffing, puffing, and cussing, until I crawled my way to the top of whatever hill challenged me. I was wrong. Spectacularly wrong.

My organization offered me the opportunity to work with a mental toughness coach through our mental health program. I came into the first session with an open mind but figured, "Hey, what would this guy possibly have to teach me? I'm a tough guy already, right?" It turns out I had much to learn, remember, and sharpen. I've been grateful for the introspection and techniques we've talked about in our coaching time together. Out of these conversations, I drew valuable mental techniques and uncovered the secret weapon I'll talk about shortly.

Be a lifelong learner.

We can and should always refocus on training, enhancing our skills—perhaps unlearning out-of-date skills—and improving ourselves. Even world-class athletes focus on the basics and employ coaches to keep them performing at their highest levels.

It's far too easy to put an opportunity like this off and tell ourselves we are too busy, already know enough, or aren't motivated enough. However, the rewards of creating the time and taking quality training or getting coaching will far outweigh the inconvenience of making the time.

As leaders, we must also encourage our teams and colleagues to do the same. One of the easiest ways to do this is to lead by example. Seek relevant and beneficial training, take the class, engage with the coach or trainer, and then share your experience with everyone. If you don't think you have this in you, perhaps engaging with a mental toughness coach, like I did, might be a reasonable starting point.

The Power of the Positive

It's the climb.

Standing at the bottom of The Priest, looking far away to the summit, I felt excitement at the prospect of the climb. You already know from my journey to this point on the Appalachian Trail that big climbs are my nemesis. My typical technique for getting up one is to put my head down and one foot in front of the other until I can't take another step. Then I'll look up, pick a spot, and force myself to walk there. Sometimes I use the count-to-a-hundred-steps technique because anyone can take a hundred steps. Right? You should see me when I rationalize the next fifty or even the next ten steps. It's not pretty.

This time, though, I packed the secret weapon I'd discussed with my mental toughness coach.

Earlier that morning, with the scent of last night's campfire on my clothes and my coffee mug clasped between my hands, I took the time to visualize the climb. Closing my eyes, I focused not on what *it* would feel like, but rather on what *I* would feel like. What emotions would I experience? How would the mountain feel around me? What immersive expectation lay ahead? Psychologists use the term imagery rather than visualization to convey this inclusion of the emotional and environmental aspects of thinking about a future situation.

That was only the first part of the equation, though. The second part was what I would do about it. What would I do when I experienced the suffering I knew was coming? Sure enough, within thirty minutes of starting the climb, I slowed right down and those old feelings of doubt and "You suck, Peter" swirled around me.

This time, however, I knew what to do. I was ready for this.

Recognizing both the physical and emotional aspects of where I was, I focused on gratitude for the opportunity to experience the mountain and to be hiking, to raise awareness and dollars that would ultimately cure cystic fibrosis, to give my daughters the opportunity to lead full lives, changing their journey forever, allowing them to go wherever they choose to take it, and not dictated by the whims of an indifferent disease.

It was astonishing to see the impact this mental leap had on me. Suddenly, my head tilted up instead of down, and my breathing was measured and easier. Sure, the climb still sucked, everything still hurt, and I still knew I had a long way to go, but my pace was a little quicker and I was smiling. Not once, in the next three hours it took me to climb The Priest, did I have to count out the next set of a hundred steps.

Your mental game is a muscle that needs exercise to develop.

We all find ourselves in situations we don't want to be in but must be for whatever reason. This technique of immersive visualization and imagery is such a powerful tool. If you Google it, you'll find articles such as Christopher Bergland's "Why Vivid Mental Imagery Is like Motivational Rocket Fuel"[56] and Christopher Clarey's "Olympians Use Imagery as Mental Training."[57]

The five minutes I spent with my coffee and my thoughts, focused on what the climb would feel like and how I would respond, paid huge dividends. My response to focus on gratitude was personal to me. You will have your own personal fuel that feeds your movement.

As leaders, we should use this technique to bring this same depth of control and situational understanding into our everyday. This will allow us to respond better in complex or combative situations, show deeper empathy in tough interpersonal interactions, and drive better overall mental health.

Mental toughness isn't about walling off the unwanted situations going on around you; rather, it's about expecting them, recognizing them in the moment, and then being prepared to act accordingly.

Thinking Big

The long game.

South of The Priest Wilderness, I approached the James River Face Wilderness. It's a stunningly beautiful part of Virginia, and as part of the National Wilderness Preservation System (NWPS), its beauty and diversity are preserved for the future. I crossed this wilderness in a single day, coming down from the Blue Ridge Mountains and hiking northbound to finish my day where the Appalachian Trail crosses the James River. It was a rainy day, but the temperatures were good, and I was in my hiking zone as I flowed through the silent wilderness.

Created in 1964, the NWPS now includes 803 separate wildernesses, totaling 4.5 percent of the total land of the United States. Although half of the NWPS acreage is in Alaska, almost every state has at least one wilderness area.

Howard Zahniser, an early environmental activist, wrote the original Wilderness Act. He spent eight years reworking the Act and building the political support to have it signed into law by President Lyndon Johnson. He had the vision to peer into the future, a long way out, and understand change and protection must start *now* to provide us with this experience we are enjoying today. The Act eloquently captured this spirit in its opening declaration: "It is hereby declared to be the policy of the Congress to secure for the American people of present and future generations the benefits of an enduring resource of wilderness."[58]

Howard Zahniser knew he was committing his life to something he would never see the impact of, yet he continued to put all his effort into it. He died in May 1964, a few short months before President Johnson signed the Act into law.

Consider the bigger picture and the responsibility you have to it.

The ability to execute for the long view is an inspiring leadership skill. Knowing that long-term projects will take vision, perseverance, political capital, and the ability to pull people along with you can be daunting. So is knowing you might never see the fruits of the seeds you plant. However, isn't that one reason you're a leader? Because you understand this and still step into the commitment. Be it building a business from scratch or managing your mature business to navigate changing times. Mixing the tactical needs of today with long-term goals is a true demonstration of your leadership skills.

At Deloitte, it's not uncommon to hear leaders talk about the founding of the business by William Welch Deloitte in London in 1845. Decisions being made today are seen as part of an ongoing responsibility to continue that legacy into the future. Decisions made not for short-term gain but rather for long-term health and prosperity for employees who will lead Deloitte thirty or forty years into the future.

I'd also like to touch on businesses' broader societal responsibilities. We see customers and citizens looking to businesses to lead on issues such as equity, diversity, and the environment. These are long-term plays and will require the type of leadership skills we talked about being applied against them.

As for Mr. Zahniser, I'd like to extend a huge thanks to him and tell him how much I value his leadership. The James River Face Wilderness is one of the most breathtaking places I've ever had the good fortunate to visit.

My Head Hurts

Knock, knock, who's there?

One constant of hiking the Appalachian Trail is the sound of woodpeckers doing what woodpeckers do—knocking their heads against trees. This is far too easy a metaphor for your average workday, but I can do better in terms of drawing out a strong leadership lesson from our feathered, head-banging friends.

Woodpeckers drum (the correct term for their head-banging their head against trees) up to twenty times per second for a variety of reasons, ranging from communication to hunting insects in and on trees to excavating nests. I recommend going online and watching a slow-motion video of a woodpecker drumming. You can thank me later.

Each species can be identified by the number of beats in a drum roll, the speed of the drum roll, and the gap between drum rolls. One of the key reasons they have a gap is that if you bang your head against a tree that hard and that fast, your head will heat up. Hence, they need to pause to let the heat dissipate.

A woodpecker's head is an engineering wonderland. It includes thick neck muscles and a super strong bill made up of three layers: bone, keratin, and collagen. Perhaps most extraordinary is a woodpecker's tongue. The tongue has a bone running through the middle of it, the hyoid bone, which passes through a gap in the skull and wraps around the skull. It's so weird, so cool, I want one of those. These features were thought to be designed so the head could absorb the impact shock of repeatedly hammering it against something hard. Or so everyone (who thought about woodpecker things) thought.

Then, in the summer of 2022, in a shock that needed to be absorbed by the broad community of woodpecker specialists, a team of brilliant scientists published a paper[59] upending this long-held belief. By combining high-speed videos, complex computer modeling, and a healthy dash of common sense, they showed woodpeckers take the knocks as they come and do nothing special to absorb the hits. Mostly, it's because woodpeckers have small heads and small brain sizes, and therefore, they can take the impact without damaging their brains. Well done, woodpeckers!

Keep on questioning.

The leadership lesson to draw out of this insight is sometimes we need to go back and re-examine long-held beliefs about why things are the way they are. Plenty of opportunities exist in the workplace to do this. This doesn't need to be a large-scale restructuring of operations but could be small opportunities for change, such as questioning why that meeting happens every Wednesday at four o'clock in the afternoon. or why only one division of your group gets invited to the monthly community call. It could be questioning the approval process for simple office supplies. Why *must* this be routed to Smith for approval?

Five-Whys is a common technique used in engineering for root cause analysis. You can apply the Five-Whys technique in any situation where you need to gain a deeper understanding of why something is the way it is or why something happened the way it did. The technique requires you to keep asking, "Why?" at least five times. It's not a perfect technique by any means, but it's simple, effective, and can help any team uncover information and connections that might otherwise lay hidden. Try it on something that's been on your mind.

As a result of using the five whys, you might rediscover the valid reason for the way something is, thus giving you a deeper appreciation for the complexity of your day-to-day operations. It's also likely if something has been in place for a while, an opportunity may exist to revisit the common wisdom. It could give you the insight needed to make that process better by providing additional value back to the business. Re-examining these processes might even prevent you from having to bang your head against the wall.

Confession Time

Forgive me, for I might have sinned.

The shelter near the top of Priest Mountain has nothing unique to offer in its structure. It's a typical, run-of-the-mill lean-to. Three wooden walls, a sloped roof, and a raised deck. It has a well-used wooden table out front, which is always a welcome addition but nothing special. However, the only item that *does* make this shelter special is the logbook.

Most shelters have logbooks, which can usually be found inside a Ziplock bag to prevent the shelter mice from making nests out of it. Hikers sign their trail names to the log and add any comments or doodles they feel compelled to scribble. These might consist of a few sentences about the weather or how hikers are feeling physically, along with the date and direction of travel. Sometimes, hikers have more on their minds and will pour their souls out onto the pages. In my experience, this is a good indicator that the hiker is close to quitting.

For reasons lost in the past, but most likely to do with the fact there isn't a lot to think about on the Trail, the logbook at the Priest Shelter is the most anticipated on the Trail. Perhaps because of the challenging hike to the summit, hikers often confess their trail sins here, spilling their souls and their deepest Trail secrets onto the pages.

The logbook did indeed make for some fascinating reading. I categorized the entries into three broad categories. The first we'll call "Breaking the Rules Confessions." Here hikers confess to behavior other hikers would shake their heads at. For example, sleeping with food inside your tent, throwing apple cores in the woods, or perhaps the worst sin of all, yellow blazing, which is where you skip a piece of the Trail by using a vehicle. Shame on you!

The second category, "Call of Nature Confessions," has to do with poop and pee, which are a major source of conversation and amusement for thru-hikers. I will save you having to read some examples of the confessions in this category, but know this, they would be mostly unacceptable in real life.

The last category we'll call "I'm Only Human Confessions." All you need to know about this set of confessions is that most of the thru-hikers on the Trail are in their twenties, and well, it can get lonely on the Trail when hikers are out there for months.

Encourage open communication and listen to what you receive.

What could a logbook at the top of a mountain in the middle of nowhere teach us about leadership?

The answer is that if you create an environment that encourages open and honest feedback, people will end up telling you exactly what is on their minds. You get the good, the bad, and the ugly. There are many ways to lead on this topic. I'm sure you have initiatives such as anonymous feedback or open 360-degree feedback programs at work. If you need to, you can always fall back on "My door is always open."

But creating the moment is not enough. Perhaps what is more crucial is what you do with that information. How you respond to the sharing is something that will define you as a leader and become a key part of your brand. Friends and colleagues will share because they want to be heard, sometimes because they are asking for change, and other times because they are reaching out for help. A clear understanding of the motivation behind feedback can help you act effectively in response.

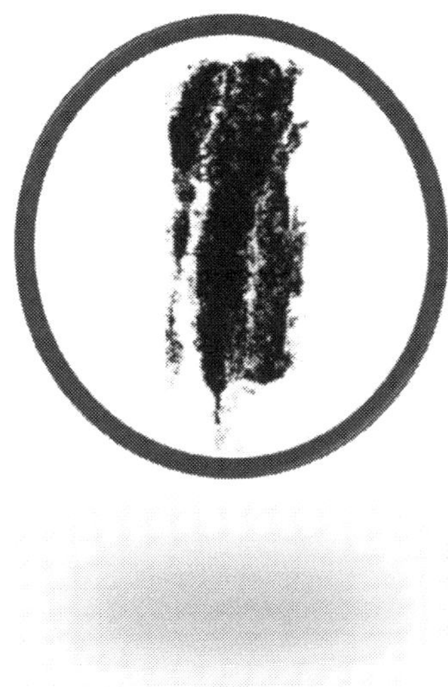

This section of the Trail provided me with the opportunity to pull together so many of the insights I have explored up to this point. They all rolled up into that climb up Priest Mountain. I took control of both my body and my mind and made it to the top without resorting to brute-force methods.

White Blaze Leadership was now almost fully formed as I could instinctively start to consider my White Blazes as direct feedback from my experiences. Moving from recognize to interpret and then to act was becoming second nature to me.

My newfound focus on mental toughness was a game-changer. I firmly believed I had unlocked a door that would ensure I reached Mount Katahdin. My White Blazes are illuminating to me that leadership is as much inward-facing as it is outward-facing. It's a life skill that every leader needs to have at their disposal.

I'm sure you've been curious about what I confessed to The Priest? Well, if you wish to find out, the only way to do that is to climb Priest Mountain and look in the logbook yourself—or use your imagination. Enjoy the climb and stay positive.

Section Fifteen Campfire Conversations

- How would you describe your approach to lifelong learning, and what motivates you to keep growing?
- In what ways does curiosity or questioning play a role in your approach to problem-solving and understanding?
- Can you share an example of how you're leading with a forward-looking vision or by anticipating future trends?
- How might you work on making your communication style more open, especially when giving and receiving feedback?
- What role does coaching play in your personal or professional development, and how do you benefit from it?

Section Sixteen

Good Ideas of Extraordinary Magnitude

The largest Confederate flag I've ever seen is flying lazily in the breeze. It's attached to a giant flagpole set in a field a few miles after I crossed the state line from North Carolina into Virginia on my way to hike more miles on the Appalachian Trail. The bright red background of the flag stood out against the gray morning sky, and the blue diagonal cross with its white stars shrunk and expanded as the flag waved in the wind.

In many small towns I've driven through in this part of the country, there are Confederate flags in yards, flying from trees, and stuck to the bumpers of vehicles on the highways and back roads. A cursory Google search will verify that giant Confederate flags are a thing.

My stomach churned as I spent the rest of the drive trying to reconcile the beauty of this state and the graciousness of the people I have met with the hate and anti-American sentiment the flag signifies to me. I understand that for some, the flag is held out as a symbol of heritage, not hate, honoring ancestors who fought and died on battlegrounds such as Shiloh, Antietam, and Gettysburg.

However, the flag *should also* be a poignant reminder of our history, of a nascent country torn apart, and of a fundamental tenet of what makes us Americans: *we are all created equal*. Yet, there's no question that the Confederate flag serves as a powerful reminder that hate comes in many forms. Even today, some people want to tear our country apart and define modern America to resemble Antebellum times.

The history of Virginia, slavery, and modern-day extremism are inexorably linked to the Appalachian Trail's northeasterly path through the state, from the dense forests of southwestern Virginia to where the Trail spills into Harpers Ferry in West Virginia, a few miles from the state's northern border. As always, the Trail and its story hold powerful insights into what it means to be a leader.

Esse Quam Videri

To be, rather than seem to be.

It's not enough to *talk the talk* when it comes to changing the workplace or the world. To be a genuine leader, we must *walk the walk.* This means taking action. Actions that show we can learn from our past, we can envision a bold future, and we can achieve more equitable and just outcomes for everybody.

Be the change you wish to see, through action.

This insight of walking the walk can best be illustrated by the actions of some extraordinary leaders whose lives have intersected with the Appalachian Trail and who personify the desire to change the arc of history for the common good.

Harriet Tubman

"Every great dream begins with a dreamer."

As I hike steadily north-eastward, across the 544 miles the Appalachian Trail covers in Virginia, the ghost of slavery comes more into focus. The census of 1860 recorded 490,865[60] enslaved people in Virginia. Sit with that fact for a moment. Half a million souls were considered nothing more than property. Half a million. This number represented only one-eighth of the total four million enslaved population of the United States at that time. The "Act Prohibiting Transportation of Slaves"[61] took effect on January 1, 1808. This means, therefore, that these four million people were born into slavery, like their parents before them.

In 1862, one in three people in Virginia were enslaved, and most worked under brutal conditions on the tobacco plantations in the eastern regions of the state. There's no version of this history that is anything but horrific. No version where the plantation owners were benevolent. They were slave owners.

As one moved westward, away from the planter elite of eastern Virginia, the number of enslaved people per county dropped significantly. Perhaps because of their own poor treatment over the centuries, a much stronger anti-slavery sentiment persisted amongst the Scots-Irish populations of Appalachia.

It's not surprising then that one of the primary routes for the Underground Railroad most likely ran along portions of what we now think of as the Appalachian Trail. This was a network of secret routes and safe-houses established to help enslaved people escape to freedom. Its very secrecy means we can't know the exact routes. But without doubt, the Appalachian Mountains were a natural path on their way from the south to the northern free states and cities such as Philadelphia and New York.

Harriet Tubman, herself an escaped enslaved person, was the most celebrated of railroad conductors. She not only guided former enslaved people northward to the free states, but she was also a keen naturalist. In a Smithsonian article from 2022,[62] historian Kate Clifford Larson is quoted as saying about Harriet Tubman, "As a naturalist, she knew the flora and fauna, what to eat and what she couldn't eat, what was dangerous and what wasn't, and how it was going to help her live and survive the next day."

Harriet used her knowledge of the wilds to rescue at least seventy enslaved people, traveling thirteen times into dangerous territory to guide them to freedom. During the Civil War, she served as a scout in the Union Army. Wouldn't it be something to sit down with her today and talk about her experiences?

Her leadership and willingness to act have rightfully made her one of the most prominent civil rights activists in the history of the United States. In 2030, Harriet Tubman will be celebrated on the twenty-dollar bill, replacing the current Andrew Jackson portrait. Every time we pull out a twenty-dollar bill, it will be an opportunity for us to reflect on the fact that only action brings change.

John Brown

"This is a beautiful country."

The northern end of the Appalachian Trail in Virginia drops from the highlands and runs along the border with West Virginia for a few short miles until it reaches Harpers Ferry, where Virginia, Maryland, and West Virginia meet. An iconic location in American history and home to the Appalachian Trail Conservatory and the Harpers Ferry National Historical Park.

It's a quaint tourist town in West Virginia and well worth a visit if you've never been. It's one of only a few in which the Appalachian Trail runs right through the center of town. White blazes on the sidewalk and streetlamps mark the way to where the Shenandoah and Potomac rivers meet.

Here, in October 1859, the abolitionist John Brown led the raid on the federal armory, which many historians believe acted as a precursor to the Civil War that was to follow a year later. When Virginia seceded from the Union in May 1861, most of the western part of the state, known as Trans-Allegheny Virginia, wanted no part of the Confederacy. By October of that year, with the Union Army supplying protection, the area voted to split from Virginia and form the thirty-fifth state. West Virginia officially joined the Union on June 20, 1863.

John Brown's abolitionist views were grounded in his deep faith and in his unwavering belief that "all men are created equal" must mean what it says. He fought against slavery his whole life. In his action on the raid at Harpers Ferry, he hoped to start a slave rebellion that would ignite a full uprising across the South. Quoted in a contemporary work, Brown said, "A few men in the right, and knowing that they are right, can overturn a mighty king. Fifty men, twenty men, in the Alleghenies, would break slavery to pieces in two years."[63]

Even with warnings and help from other extraordinary icons in the abolitionist movement, such as Frederick Douglass and Harriet Tubman, the raid did not go well at all. In the end, two of his sons lay dead, and he, himself, sat in captivity awaiting trial.

John Brown was hung at 11:15 a.m. on December 2, 1859.

John Brown played a meaningful role in moving the nation toward the disastrous conflict to follow. His prediction that slavery would break into pieces in two years was prescient, although not in the way he thought.

Some will still argue the Civil War was about states' rights. And they are correct in this if you accept it was about the right of southern states to be slaveholding states. It was always about slavery. The articles of secession for southern states declare this without ambiguity. The secession document for Virginia, known as the Ordinance of Secession, states: "The Federal Government having perverted said powers, not only to the injury of the people of Virginia, but to the oppression of the southern slaveholding States."[64]

Ordinary and extraordinary men and women across the nation stood up and acted in big and small ways to bring an end to the atrocity of four million enslaved people.

Rahawa Haile

"Did you have fun in town?"

In March 2016, Rahawa Haile began her northbound thru-hike of the Application Trail. Like the thousands who would attempt the journey that year, and the thousands before and after her, including me, she came with not only the weight of her backpack but also the hopes, fears, and dreams hikers carry with them. Rahawa carried extra weight along with these non-tangible items, as she is a self-described "queer black woman."

In April 2017, *Outside Magazine* published a captivating article chronicling her experiences on the Trail. The essay titled "Going It Alone"[65] is now considered one of the best stories they've ever published.

She talks in the essay about seeing the Confederate flag in every state she hiked through and feeling the "tendrils of hate" from Georgia all the way up to northern Maine. She figures out most of the other thru-hikers are woefully unaware of the on-trail experience, where she is *one of us*, versus the in-town experience, where she is subjected to both subtle and overt acts of racism.

As a white man of a certain age, I can attest to not understanding what that experience must be like. How could I? I've never once in my life experienced it. I can intellectualize it; however, having someone tell me they don't see "much of my kind around here," as happened to Rahawa, and trying to feel what emotions that must stir, is beyond me.

Rahawa's writing shines a light on the extra weight she is carrying and gives us a better understanding of what it must be like to stand in her boots. But ultimately, she writes, "The weight I carried as a black woman paled in comparison with the joy I felt daily among my peers in that wilderness."

I'm glad that she felt this way with her fellow hikers and that the Trail, as a great leveler, provided her with the common experience that ties us all together in its simplicity. To paraphrase Martin Luther King Jr., the Trail has no concern for the color of your skin, just the content of your character.

Although her actions might have seemed small to start with, after all, it's merely putting one foot in front of the other, none of us can accurately predict the outcome of our first step. For Rahawa, her first step led to a voice that has touched many and will continue to inspire change.

Heather Heyer

"If you are not outraged, you are not paying attention."

Charlottesville is a beautiful college town situated about twenty miles to the east of the Appalachian Trail at the southern entrance to the Shenandoah National Park. The Blue Ridge Parkway morphs into the Skyline Drive here, offering stunning vistas to tourists as they drive slowly north along its 105-mile winding path.

On the evening of Friday, August 12, 2017, a mob of white supremacists and neo-Nazis descended on Charlottesville. Angry men in balaclavas roamed the streets, the stench of their hate permeating the thick summer air. The next day thousands of residents of Charlottesville spilled into the streets of downtown Charlottesville to protest this invasion of their peaceful town. They had the courage to show this hatred was not welcome and would not be tolerated in their town. Amongst them, Heather Heyer stood tall.

A regular young woman making her way in life, Heather had family and friends and was building herself a better life on a working-class foundation. Her mother, Susan Bro, talked in a Fortune article in 2020[66] about having spent her childhood in the Shenandoah Valley: "Surrounded by mountains. My heritage is coal mining, carved deep from the Appalachian Mountains."

After high school, Heather started waitressing and then took a job at a local law firm as a paralegal. She was putting herself through night school to improve her knowledge of law. Media reports of the day tell how she initially decided to stay away from the rally but felt compelled to go. When Heather arrived downtown at one o'clock on that Saturday afternoon, she was greeted with the sight of antagonists waving confederate flags, KKK symbols, and Nazi salutes. A white supremacist cocktail of hate.

A short while later, Heather lay dead on the street in Charlottesville.

Run over by a hate-filled white supremacist who drove a car right into the crowd of counter-protesters, her life was cut short at thirty-two years of age. Nineteen others suffered injuries they will never forget.

In a powerful article from the *Guardian* newspaper, Heather's mother is quoted as saying, "I think it's a damn shame that a white girl had to die for people to have to pay attention. I think if a black girl had died, or a black man, [the reaction would have been] 'Oh well, another person lost to violent protest.' "[67]

Perhaps the Appalachian Mountains gave her the strength to make a comment like this after losing her daughter to hate. Whatever it was, Susan Bro is much more representative of the hard-working majority of people in Appalachia than those who fly Confederate battle flags.

Good Ideas of Extraordinary Magnitude

Four lives across two hundred years.

Harriet, John, Rahawa, and Heather represent the idea that each of us has a responsibility as leaders to walk the walk. Rahawa finishes her article, "Going It Alone," with the following line: "There is no impossible...only good ideas of extraordinary magnitude." I love that sentence and the sentiment it conveys.

Inspire people to be change agents.

Change might seem impossible, or it might seem like someone else's problem, but it's not. It's mine, it's yours, it's ours.

As leaders we have a responsibility to inspire our teams, colleagues, and communities. We need to be change agents and encourage others to be change agents too.

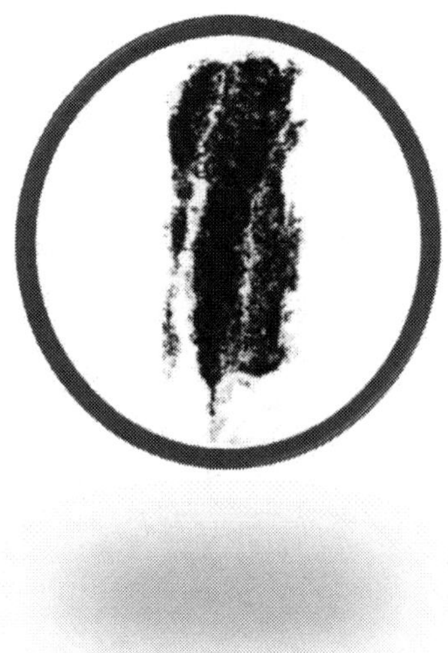

This section of the Trail made me look deep inside myself and consider who I am and what change I want to see happen in the world. I'm grateful for this introspection and for the opportunity to be rather than seem to be.

Every single one of my White Blazes burnt brightly from the insights I received from researching and writing about this topic. Mostly my Act White Blaze. *Esse quam videri*.

Confederate flags will still fly up and down the rural towns that dot the Trail. Some people will still maintain that it's just about heritage. However, I choose to see them now as reminders. Reminders that we have more to do. Reminders that my Black friends and colleagues have a different American experience. Reminders that, as a leader, I need to walk the walk.

Section Sixteen Campfire Conversations

- In what ways do you strive to "walk the walk," and how does this impact those around you?
- What additional actions could you take to lead effectively on diversity issues?
- What change would you most like to see in the world, and how do you envision contributing to it?
- Do you have an idea of extraordinary magnitude? What steps might you take to bring it to life?

Section Seventeen

Lord of the Flies

Vermont threw everything it had at me. Never-ending swarms of gnats, mosquitoes, and black flies. Equipment failure, an end-of-days cult, torturous terrain, below-freezing temperatures, record highs over 90°F (32°C), and moose poop. But mostly the black flies.

If you're not familiar with black flies, let me share. These are not your annoying buzz-buzz house flies. These are actual demon spawn. If Dracula and mosquitoes birthed a lovechild, it would be a New England Black Fly in early summer.

Black flies rip off your skin with their scissor-like mandibles. Then, according to a slew of scientific papers with titles such as “Anticoagulant Activity in Salivary Gland Extracts of Black Flies,”[68] they deploy a pharmaceutical payload of saliva, which includes anticlotting, antiplatelet, vasodilatory, anti-inflammatory, and immunomodulatory components. This keeps my blood flowing and stops me from feeling the horror occurring on my scalp in the short-term. Then they suck up my blood like they are at an all-you-can-eat vampire buffet. “Don’t mind if I do help myself to a little more A-Positive, buzz, buzz.”

Vermont pushed me harder, both physically and mentally, than the Trail has ever pushed me before. It forced me to dig deeper into my mission to raise the dollars to buy the science that will cure cystic fibrosis. But, as usual, along with the suffering came thought-provoking leadership insights.

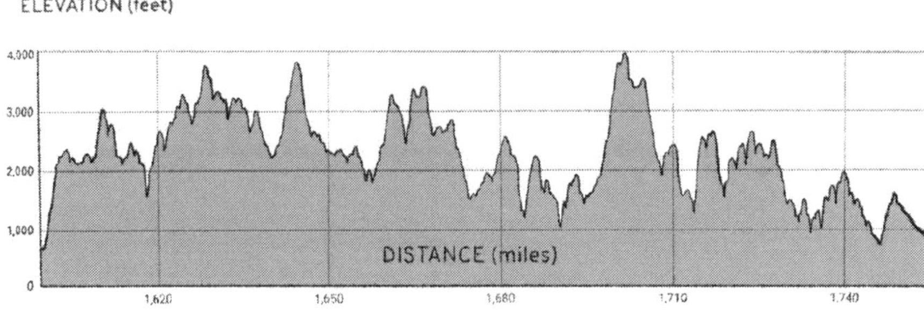

Figure 15 Vermont

Lord of the Flies

“Until the grownups come, we’ll have fun.”

As I spent yet another day fighting off the black flies, my mind wandered to a classic work of literature, *Lord of the Flies*, published in 1954. I read this book in high school because we were told to. As I hiked along, I tried to pull vague memories of what happened in the story. Why was the book titled as such? Was anything in the prose useful to help me gain control of the black swarm that seemed to be hiking the Appalachian Trail with me?

Later, when cell signal became available, I looked it up and read the salient facts around which to frame my thoughts. The author, William Golding, spins a story of a group of preteen boys stranded on a desert island somewhere in the Pacific. In summary, things go horribly wrong, and no one controls the flies. Not really helpful.

The title of the book comes from a pig's head, which the boys put on a stick as an offering to an imagined beast that roams the island. They call this pig's head "Lord of the Flies," presumably because, as it decays, it's always covered in flies.

Golding's novel turns out to hold many insights into the concepts of leadership. Ralph, the main protagonist, is a consensus-building and collaborative leader who initially organizes the boys and wields a conch shell as his symbol of leadership. Later in the book, Jack, the antagonist, usurps his power using pure physical force and fear of the unknown, represented by the alleged beast. Jack's authoritarian leadership style works in the short-term but ultimately leads predicably to dreadful things happening.

The other two leading characters in the book, Piggy and Simon, both end up showing leadership by influence as they leverage their intellectual capabilities and integrator skills to hold the boys together. They do this by exerting influence on Ralph and Jack from behind the scenes. Spoiler alert: Things don't end well for Piggy and Simon.

Recognize different leadership styles.

I took several key insights from going back and re-looking at the story. First, different leadership styles can be applicable at the right time and in the right place. An authoritarian style can work in the short-term, especially when in a crisis. It shortens decision cycles, enhances clarity, and gives no doubt about the required actions, regardless of whether they are right or wrong.

The early Roman Republic leveraged this approach when they created the role of dictator or *praetor maximus*. The praetor maximus was a single man who took charge in order to resolve a specific crisis and then handed back control to the normal government. This worked well for at least 300 years until a certain Julius Caesar decided that making himself a permanent dictator was reasonable. I recommend Mark B. Wilson's book on the evolution of the Roman dictatorship[69] if you're looking to delve deep into this subject.

In the long term, though, democratic, consensus-led leadership can motivate the group and drive the entire team forward around a common goal.

Lord of the Flies illustrated to me how the antagonist, Jack, used the idea of fear of the unknown to undermine Ralph's leadership, breaking the symbolic conch shell to emphasize his control. As a consensus-style leader, I felt this is perhaps something worth noting.

One final piece of leadership information I took from *Lord of the Flies* centered around the idea of adult supervision. In the book, the boys descend into chaos, in part because there's no adult on the island to establish the norms of a civilized society. In business, we often have *adults* in the room with us, such as Legal, Human Resources, or the Board. Their oversight helps us understand right from wrong, informs us of expected norms, and keeps us on track.

It's worthwhile being reminded that we need to embrace those functions, lest we too end up with a broken conch shell.

There'll be Days Like This

Now that song is stuck in your head too.

Deep into a remote wilderness, I was bent double over a rock, throwing up everything I could and then some. The black flies took the opportunity of me removing my bug-net to gnaw at my head, and the sun relentlessly beat down on me, as if enjoying the spectacle. Ugh. How did I even get into this situation?

The day started off well with a big climb to get the heart pumping. The temperatures rose quickly and were soon pushing into the high eighties to low nineties (31°C to 34°C). Record-setting heat for Vermont for this time of year. The section I was crossing had little flowing water, so by midafternoon, I nursed the last of what I carried. I knew I only had about a mile left to get down to Stony Brook, where there would be plenty of water for my evening camp when my path crossed a small but nicely flowing stream. I was well aware I was pushing the boundaries of dehydration, so I took the time to stop and filter water.

Here is where I made a rookie mistake. I dropped an electrolyte tablet into the water to counter the dehydration, and once it dissolved, I chugged the whole liter in one eager go. It didn't take long for my body to reject that much water and electrolytes in such a brief period, which is how I found myself bent over the rocks.

About thirty minutes later, I hiked into camp with that lingering acrid smell of bile stuck in my nose. I was feeling a little sorry for myself but had no choice other than to set about pitching my tent.

The small open patch of ground was strewn with rocks as the nearby stream clearly flooded this ground occasionally. I removed a few of the larger stones and dead tree branches to form a space big enough for my tent. A few days earlier, I had resupplied at a Dollar General store, so dinner for the evening was, ironically enough, a packet of dehydrated potatoes mixed with a packet of tuna. Don't judge me; it was delicious.

As the sun set, I climbed into my tent and lay down exhausted, only to hear the airflow right out of my inflatable sleeping pad. It had developed a leak and was not holding air. What a day.

As I drifted off to a fitful sleep, resting on a pile of river rocks, Van Morrison's song "Days Like This" looped around and around in my head. I couldn't remember most of the lyrics, but the refrain seemed appropriate.

The next morning presented itself with a beautiful sunrise. A deep black sky turned through multiple shades of red until only a blue sky was left in its wake. I was a little sore from sleeping on a bed of rocks, but it was nothing some stretching and a little mediation by the stream couldn't fix. I practiced gratitude for having the experience of yesterday and the beauty of this morning, and then I set out to see what adventures this day would offer me.

Look forward, not backward.

From a leadership perspective, we all will have *days like this,* where no matter what we or our teams have done, the universe will conspire against us. In these cases, leaders can stand tall and remind everyone, including themselves, that these days will come and these days will go. It's an inspiring leadership skill and serves as a powerful learning opportunity for everyone. Showing up the next day and motivating the team to get back on the trail is critical too. Yesterday was yesterday; let it go. Now, let's see what we can do today.

Twelve Tribes and the Yellow Deli

I'll take a pastrami on rye with a side of the rapture to go, please.

The Yellow Deli sandwich shop in the heart of the small town of Rutland in northwestern Vermont serves sandwiches and a slice of radical religion.

The sandwich shop is well-known to hikers, as they also offer a free hostel for hikers to stay in, found right next door. Hikers pay what they can afford to stay, or there are always chores that need to be done. Want to stay a little longer? Well, then, you can go stay on their farm about a thirty-minute drive away. At the farm, you can live off the land for as long as you want, and assuming you're of the gullible persuasion, you can even stay for years as a cult member.

Since the 1830s, Vermont has been a place where counter-culture movements have set up shop. In the mid-1830s, John Noyes created a version of Christianity called Perfectionism. He claimed he was free of sin, and you could be too if you joined his group of "Bible Communists" in Putney, Vermont. He was arrested in 1848 because, apparently, his notions of free love were a little ahead of his time. The strict Calvinist churchgoers were not amused. Noyes then jumped bail and ran off to New York, where he established a new community in Oneida. After Noyes, the community went mainstream and made plates for a living. So, if you have Oneida-brand plates on your table or knives and forks in your drawer, you now have an exceptional story of where they originated.

On October 22, 1844, tens of thousands of Millerites, another counter-culture movement, suffered the brilliantly named "Great Disappointment" when the "Second-Coming" and "End-Of-The-World" didn't happen as prophesied. But they picked themselves up by their ascension robes and rebounded to form multiple branches of Adventist churches that still survive to this day, the end of the world notwithstanding, including the Seventh-day Adventist Church.

Mormons, Fourierists, Garrisonites, and Swedenborgians set up shop in Vermont in the 1800s, leading us inevitably to the arrival of the greatest generation of counter-culturists ever to exist. The Hippies.

The Hippies showed up en masse to Vermont in the mid-1960s. In "What Happened to America's Communes?" in *Forbes* from April 2021[70], Yvonne Daly, author of a book called *Going Up Country: When the Hippies, Dreamers, Freaks, and Rascals Moved to Vermont*, talks about the size of this movement. She says:

Somewhere between two and three thousand communes existed in the United States in the 1960s and '70s with about 75 in the small state of Vermont, making it one of the epicenters of the experiment. It's hard to establish a hard figure as many people lived in group homes but didn't call the arrangement a commune. In a 1970s article for Playboy Magazine, John Pollack estimated that there were 35,800 hippies in Vermont, who accounted for roughly 33 percent of the total 107,527 people in the state between the ages of 18 and 34.

Groovy!

The Twelve Tribes community, which runs the Yellow Deli, established itself in Chattanooga, Tennessee, in the late 1970s. However, the religion proved to be too fundamentalist for the church-going folks of Chattanooga. As a result, the Twelve Tribes ended up moving north to Vermont, whose residents were used to this type of religious expression. Fast forward to today, and the Tribes have about three thousand members spread out across multiple locations. The Yellow Deli sandwich shops they own and operate provide a steady flow of income and new recruits.

I did my homework on the Twelve Tribes prior to getting to Rutland. Their fundamentalist views and some of their beliefs and practices were too outrageously inconsistent with my beliefs for me to part with my hard-earned money. I decided not to visit either the Yellow Deli or the associated hostel. Instead, I took my zero day at the Comfort Inn and ate at the Tap House.

Control your brand and reputation carefully.

So, you might wonder where I'm going with this. As leaders, we need to ensure we are clear about our reputation and brand, which can be severely damaged if we allow ourselves to be associated with third parties that end up being the antipathy of what we believe in, strive for, or have built our hard-earned reputation on.

We have seen this brand crisis happen over and over. Companies get hauled up in the media and court of public opinion for using a supplier in another country that treats their workforce poorly or for associating themselves with an individual who turns out to be far from a role model.

As leaders, it's important to ensure our teams understand why this is crucial. It's also important to learn how to get the appropriate information we need to make informed decisions on this topic. Third-party risk management is a growing concern for many organizations, and rightly so.

To be fair, I did not do my research on the ownership of the Tap House. But given the forty delicious beers on display, I assume their views were a little more aligned with mine than those of the Twelve Tribes.

Grouse

"If it weren't for you, the band would suck."

I traversed three separate wilderness areas during my time crossing Vermont: Peru Peak, Lye Brook, and Glastenbury. In between were long stretches where little to no sign of civilization existed. As the day turned toward evening, several times I heard what sounded like someone trying to start a small engine. I thought perhaps it was a compressor, a small dirt bike, or something else that almost reached the point of turning over, but not quite. I remember being annoyed that the sound traveled all the way deep into the woods and disturbed my peace.

"Do people have no respect for the silence?" I grumbled to myself.

In camp later one evening, sitting on an old log, watching the flames of a well-made fire, I got to chatting with some other hikers. One of the experienced thru-hikers perked up and said, "Do you hear that thumping noise? That's a grouse."

Boom! Mind blown. The nuisance noise wasn't a bad two-stroke engine after all. It was something much more unexpected and captivating.

The ruffed grouse is a drummer and an excellent one at that. The males beat their wings, known as drumming, to create a low-frequency thump, thump, thumping sound that starts out slowly and then speeds up, lasting for about eight to ten seconds. It sounds like a small engine trying to catch.

Although a relatively small bird, typically weighing in at somewhere around a pound, the sound they create can be heard for at least a quarter of a mile, even in the dense woods where they hang out. The drumming is the male's way of proclaiming this piece of the woods, typically six to ten acres, is his.

To make this noise, first he selects a stage on for his performance, typically a log called the drumming log. Once situated, he starts to flap his wings, and with enough practice and patience, out comes the perfect low-pitch thumping sound. The sound is in the 40Hz range, which is so low that owls, his primary predators, can't hear it, but of course female grouses can.

In researching the grouse, I discovered two dominant theories about drumming. The first is that the male grouse builds up shockwaves that drive a sonic boom, and the second is that he creates a vacuum, think thunder-like, that creates the noise. I couldn't find a definitive scientific paper on this, but I went down a rabbit hole of the best drummer ever. *Rolling Stone*[71] tells us that is, of course, John Bonham of Led Zeppelin fame. The rest of their list is suspect, as Dave Grohl only comes in at number twenty-seven, and not a single grouse or woodpecker is on the list.

Leadership is only about what you say and do.

From a leadership perspective, the grouse reinforces a material insight. Leadership isn't about title or rank. It's not about the corner office or the number of people who report to you. Leadership is about using what you have and creating an outsized influence that can be heard across an organization. To motivate people, we have to make them turn their heads to listen and, more importantly, hear what we're saying. To have people turn to look for you and say, "I recognize that. That's leadership." This is your brand, which defines who you are as a leader and how colleagues recognize and respond to your actions.

Two If by Land

It doesn't pay to hold a grudge.

In the vanishingly small town of West Hartford, Vermont, I crossed the White River on a small two-lane bridge and walked along the grass verge of VT14 for about a quarter of a mile. The light rain this morning provided a welcome break from the intense heat of the previous few days. I felt energized as I knew I only had a few more hours of hiking to reach Hanover, a few short miles over the state line into New Hampshire, and the end of this section.

An older man sat out on his porch sipping his morning coffee as I hiked by. We exchanged a few pleasantries, and I learnt his life story in about one minute flat: Fort Bragg, Vietnam, a son, getting sober and finding religion at the gym, another much younger son, turning eighty. It was like reading the jacket of a book, knowing I would have to put it back on the shelf without opening it but wishing I had the time to settle in and enjoy.

After recognizing my British accent, he sent me off with a cheery, "We all love the English."

Right before I disappeared back into the forest again, he pulled up beside me in his pickup truck and offered me a baseball cap because he said, "I noticed you weren't wearing one, and this will make it easier in the rain."

These small acts of kindness—Trail Magic—occur up and down the Trail and are far from the exception. Trail Magic always makes me hold my head a little higher and smile a little brighter. I'm always grateful for any magic provided.

A short while later, I considered his response to my British accent. It was fascinating because, this far north, the echoes of the Civil War have given way to the even more distant gunshots of the Revolutionary War.

In 1770, the Green Mountain Boys were raised as a militia in what later became the Vermont Republic but was called the New Hampshire Grants at the time. This militia took part in several key battles over the following years, including the famed capture of Fort Ticonderoga from the British in 1775. After capturing the Fort, they transported cannons to Boston, which were decisive in lifting the siege and the subsequent signing of the Declaration of Independence a few months later.

The Green Mountain Boys also delivered a total smackdown of the British at the Battle of Bennington in 1777. If you ever get a chance to visit the monument to that battle located in Bennington, Vermont, it's well worth the time. To this day, the Vermont National Guard uses the same flag that the Green Mountain Boys used all those years ago. It has a forest green background with an azure rectangle in the top left containing thirteen five-pointed stars to represent the original thirteen colonies.

The main point I took from this interaction is that Americans, who perhaps should have the most distrust of the English, actually don't. This ability to forgive and move on is an influential leadership trait we could all do with remembering.

Never hold a grudge.

Most of us are surprisingly good at harboring grudges. This skill has zero benefit from a leadership perspective. "I don't want to work with that person because..." "I can't forget that one time they..." "Remember when they..."

It's an easy path to push someone to the side for a real or imagined slight or mistake. The harder path, the one that shows real leadership, is to forgive and to re-engage with someone.

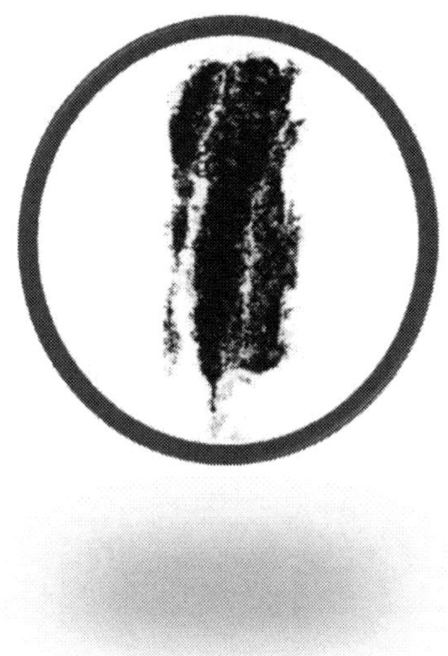

This section of the Trail brought home to me the idea that we can find leadership insights wherever we look. Music, history, nature, and literature are all littered with examples of leadership. To see these insights and learn what they have to teach us just takes time and contemplation. The Appalachian Trail is excellent at providing both.

White Blaze Leadership, with its focus on learning how to recognize, interpret, and then act, is the perfect approach to harness these insights. Perhaps we can consider time and contemplation as the secret ingredients for this recipe.

Vermont pushed me hard, and the black flies followed me the entire way to the end of the trip. But as you can see, the journey also supplied some excellent reminders of what leadership is about. Should you find yourself being pushed extra hard, I suggest a few verses of "Days Like This" to cheer you up.

If that doesn't work, perhaps you can go find a British person to forgive and give them a hug. You'll both feel better for it.

Section Seventeen Campfire Conversations

- How do you approach past conflicts or grievances, and how might they influence your leadership style?
- How do you think your teams would describe your leadership approach, and what characteristics do you believe they would highlight?
- How do you manage your personal brand, and in what ways do you think it affects your leadership and professional relationships?
- What strategies or practices help you navigate and overcome difficult days?

Section Eighteen

At Mile 1776 on the Fourth of July

On the Fourth of July, 2023, I found myself standing at mile 1,776 of the Appalachian Trail. Lambert Ridge is a broad ledge of rock halfway down Smarts Mountain in New Hampshire. The endless view of trees and mountains stretched all the way to the horizon. Overhead, the relentless clouds promised to unleash a torrential downpour, and yet, instead of darting back under the cover of the forest, I paused to savor the moment. I was proud of myself for being right here at this mark, on this date.

As a naturalized American born in the U.K., I dwell on the significance of this date every year when the Fourth of July comes around. The Declaration of Independence is, of course, a remarkable document and represents an inflection point in human history when a ragtag group of farmers, misfits, and merchants stood up to the evil empire.

This David versus Goliath story is the bedrock of countless books and Hollywood movies. Even if your history on the specifics of the American Revolution is hazy, you probably remember the story line to *Star Wars* or *Hunger Games*. Perhaps you may have read George Orwell's *Animal Farm* and *1984* or watched the brilliant TV adaptation of Margaret Atwood's *The Handmaid's Tale.* In all cases, the oppressed underdog rises up, at significant cost, to drive change and make life better for "We the People." Sometimes, it's successful, and sometimes, not so much. That's basically it—only *real* in this case.

I will admit to getting a little emotional standing out on that ledge, contemplating what this date means to me.

I think about the simplicity of the desire for freedom from tyranny and the enduring optimism, philanthropy, and generosity of Americans. These traits are firmly rooted in the struggles the founders faced when they wrote the words: "We mutually pledge to each other our Lives, our Fortunes, and our sacred Honor." I experience the continuing outcome of this pledge firsthand when friends and strangers alike step up to help in our fight to cure cystic fibrosis for my girls.

I think about the sacrifices those who went before us made. I think about the divisiveness and pettiness on which too many are focused today. I think about how we have forgotten that the "unalienable rights" of "Life, Liberty, and the pursuit of Happiness" must apply to all, not just a few.

I had much to think about gazing out from Lambert Ridge, and I could have stayed much longer. But the thunder roared and the hard rain came, forcing me back under the umbrella the trees provided. Hiking this section of the Trail, from Hanover to the Kinsman Notch in New Hampshire, provided me with some remarkable introspection and some excellent insights into leadership.

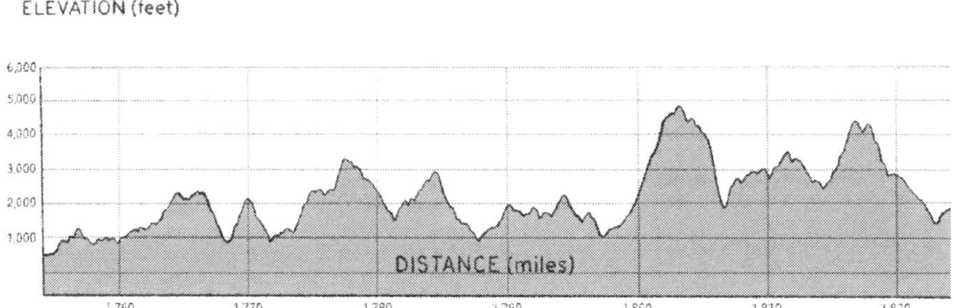

Figure 16 Hanover, NH, to Liberty Springs Trailhead, NH

Terra Infirma—Mud, Sweat, and Tears

Random flame spurts, lightning sand, and rodents of unusual size.

June 2023 was one of the wettest months on record in western New Hampshire, with a full season's worth of rain falling in a few short weeks. Through June and July, hiking in the area was characterized by either extremely slippery rocks or deep and unrelenting mud. If you have never had the pleasure of hiking in this type of mud, let me share with you that it is soul-destroying and sole-destroying. The experience is enough to bring most people to tears. The mud sucks you in, slows you down, and threatens to rip off your shoes with every step. That gritty smell of earth permeates the air, your clothes, and your dreams.

On July 3, 2023, a story appeared on my newsfeed about a Massachusetts woman who, the week before, became stuck in mud for three days. Some passing hikers found her and called the rescue services to get her out. As I trudged along the Appalachian Trail, I sympathized with her plight. That evening, after spending too many hours worrying about the situation, I looked up how to survive getting stuck in the mud.

Daniel Engber published the deeply researched article "Terra Infirma: The Rise and Fall of Quicksand" in Slate in 2010. It provides an in-depth analysis of quicksand and its cultural hold on the psyche of those of a certain age. In one of the best graphics that I've ever seen, the author maps the number of times quicksand appears in a movie against the year the movie was released. This definitively shows us that the 1960s were the heyday of quicksand, with three percent of all movies made during this period having such a scene in them. My favorite, of course, is the scene from *The Princess Bride*, released in 1987, which pays homage to those iconic '60s quicksand scenes.

After reading several scientific articles on getting stuck in mud and quicksand, I'm relieved to find out you can't actually sink to the bottom of a mudhole, leaving your hiker hat floating on the surface. You should be relieved, too. It turns out that while your legs are heavy, your chest cavity provides enough buoyancy to prevent you from getting sucked down any further than your armpits. It takes time to get out of such a situation, but with slow movements and enough time, you can wriggle yourself free.

In a crisis, slow down and take measured, intentful actions.

The technique for getting out of armpit-deep mud offers us a thoughtful leadership insight. To escape, rather than flailing around and using all your strength, slow down and take measured actions intentionally. Less pressure, not more. Controlling yourself and supporting your colleagues in stressful times requires this same skill. It reflects the ability to slow everything down, take the time to assess the situation, communicate the action, and then take small steps, ensuring each action is helpful and not making matters worse.

I'll contrast this to a hair-on-fire situation where action must be immediate and where a certain amount of hand waving is needed, even if it's not necessarily useful. In most work situations, the developing crisis might be uncomfortable, unfortunate, or embarrassing, but you can only sink up to your armpits at the most. In other words, you're not in over your head. As leaders, we can make sure everyone understands the situation and is focused on well-thought-out actions that will get us out of this mess. That ability is a real gift.

In the *Harvard Business Review*, I read Gianpiero Petriglieri's "The Psychology Behind Effective Crisis Leadership," an informative article on the psychology of crisis leadership[72]. Petriglieri talks about the concept of *holding* as an essential leadership skill during a crisis. In the article, he describes holding as "the way another person, often an authority figure, *contains* and *interprets* what's happening in times of uncertainty. Containing refers to the ability to soothe distress and interpreting [refers] to the ability to help others make sense of a confusing predicament." It's a strong concept for leaders to learn and one well worth spending some additional time reading up on.

Moosilauke

That's fun to say, not fun to do.

Mount Moosilauke is the first big mountain in the White Mountain range. It was a taste of things to come as I moved into the most difficult northern section of the Trail. It's a brutal climb of almost four miles straight up as it rises some 3000 feet from Kinsman Notch to a peak of 4,802 feet.

People in New Hampshire love the descriptive term *notch*. It's used to describe a low point in a valley between two mountains. For most of the Appalachian Trail up to this point, these are called *gaps*. For those of you out West, you tend to call them *passes*, presumably because settlers were passing through and not actually settling in those places. In some areas, such as Idaho in the West, they are called *saddles*, which likely comes from the fact that cowboys first named these places.

At least, that's my theory on it.

Many northbound thru-hikers get a shuttle ride around Mount Moosilauke and then slack-pack back over the mountain in a southerly direction. Slack-packing means leaving your heavy pack behind, usually at a hostel, and then hiking a small section of the Trail back to your pack. Thru-hikers do this with Moosilauke because, as brutal as it is going up the north face, trying to come down it with a full pack is flat-out dangerous. Once they reunite with their pack at the end of the day, they take another shuttle back to the point north of Mount Moosilauke where they started their slack-pack hike south and then resume northbound with the full weight of their pack for the rest of the journey.

The climb up is exactly that: a climb. The north face consists of rock, rock, and more rock. The white blazes marking the Trail are painted on large boulders, and I must use my hands and legs to pull myself up and over them. Tree roots form handholds as if the forest knew I would need that help at exactly that place. A beautiful waterfall parallels the Trail for miles, but the water has a far easier time navigating the rocks on its journey downward.

Although New Hampshire is known as the Granite State, most of the rock on Moosilauke is not igneous granite but a type of metamorphic rock called schist. One lesson not taught in geography class is how hard it is to walk over this type of rock. Adding any amount of water on top makes it treacherous—like walking on ice. Try throwing water on your kitchen counter and then walking on it. You'll see.

On this morning, I took the climb slow and easy while the rain fell steadily. I placed each step with precision and did not burden myself with any time pressure. I would get to the top when I got to the top.

Getting to "No" is every bit as important as getting to "Yes."

The key leadership insight I took from my climb is the importance of clearly articulating when the pace of activity is non-negotiable. Regardless of external forces, speeding up won't help. This could involve a quarter-end deadline, a vacation schedule, or a client clamoring for a deliverable. Sometimes, you might find yourself in a situation where trying to accelerate poses too much risk and too much potential for something to go horribly wrong.

One of my favorite business examples of this key leadership insight is the story of the ill-fated video game based on the movie *E.T. the Extra-Terrestrial*. Atari's video game *E.T. the Extra-Terrestrial* was a commercial disaster, according to an NPR interview in 2017. The game designer, Howard Scott Warshaw, said of his work, "I did the E.T. video game, the game that is widely held to be the worst video game of all time."[73]

The reason for this debacle was that Warshaw committed to design and build the game in five weeks so Atari could hit the Christmas market in 1982. For reference, his previous ground-breaking game, *Yars' Revenge*, took ten months to complete. Hubris and Atari's willingness to agree to an unachievable timeline led to E.T.'s place in video game history and also to the eventual downfall of Atari.

We can display exceptional leadership by holding our ground, explaining reasonably why something is a bad idea or has too much risk, and then delivering on what we said we would do. Put another way: Strong leadership is every bit about knowing when to get to "No" as it is pushing to get to "Yes."

River Boundaries

Be careful what you ask for.

The Appalachian Trail crosses over the Connecticut River on the Ledyard Free Bridge from Norwich, Vermont, into Hanover, New Hampshire. Rather than being in the middle of the bridge, the plaque marking the border is surprisingly on the western side of the structure. The two states have been arguing over this 168-mile border since 1664, when King Charles II gave his brother grants to "all the lands from the west side of Connecticut River to the east side of Delaware Bay."[74]

The dispute was only settled 269 years later, in 1933, when the Supreme Court decided the boundary was at the low water mark of the western (Vermont) edge of the river. It further established that every seven years, the Attorneys General of both states must meet at the river in something delightfully called the Perambulation to ensure they are still playing nice with each other. Unfortunately, the law did not specify they must wear early settler costumes, but the thought amuses me.

Vermont Statue Title 1, Chapter 015,[75] codifies this into law with the following: "The boundary line between the State of New Hampshire and the State of Vermont shall be perambulated and markers and bounds renewed wherever necessary once in every seven years forever." Forever is a long time, but hey, laws are laws.

Real-world consequences come from this centuries-old edict passed into law. For example, most of the bridge maintenance and repair costs are borne by New Hampshire. Both states measure how much of the structure is on each side of the boundary line, and that's the percentage paid by each state. The Vilas Bridge at Bellows Falls has remained closed since 2009 since the states couldn't agree on funding for repairs. Here, the bridge is ninety-three percent owned by New Hampshire, a similar percentage to many of the other crossings. After much wrangling, construction work is expected to start in 2028, and New Hampshire has earmarked $17.7 million for the effort. Hopefully, Vermont can find their $1.3 million.

Choose your words carefully.

I see two strong leadership insights in this history. The first is the words we choose to communicate with others will matter. They matter a lot. We must make sure our written communication is clear and unambiguous. For legal documents, leave it to the professionals. Any leader who has spent any time on contracts knows words have specific legal meanings, and the long-term outcomes of using the wrong word can be significant.

Think longer-term.

The second insight involves long-term thinking. Structuring a deal for the now, without regard for the future, is a surefire way to get everyone into a bit of a mess down the road. Consider what changes might occur and how shifts in the economy or regulatory environment could affect agreements long into the future. Then, we can encourage our teams to think about these long-term implications too. This is a challenge that many companies face as the market is relentlessly focused on yielding short-term results. For example, structuring a layoff to address short-term cost challenges could lead to a skills shortage and delay in accelerating growth when the tides shift.

Forest for the Trees

The Wood Wide Web

I'm sure you have heard the saying, "You can't see the forest for the trees." A version of it was initially referenced all the way back in 1546 in a book of proverbs from an English writer John Haywood, entitled "A Dialogue Conteynyng the Number of the Effectuall Prouerbes in the Englishe Tounge"[76] Obviously this was before automated spell checkers were invented. The proverb is captured as: "You cannot see the wood for trees."

As I hiked through this part of New Hampshire, I focused on seeing the forest from a heightened perspective. I had recently finished reading the 2019 Pulitzer Prize-winning novel *The Overstory* by author Richard Powers and had started on *The Hidden Life of Trees: What They Feel, How They Communicate* by author Peter Wohlleben. Both books provided me with a much deeper understanding of the forest than I ever considered. Other books, such as researcher Suzanne Simard's *Finding the Mother Tree: Discovering the Wisdom of the Forest,* also shine a light on this idea of the forest as a cooperative system rather than a kind of place where it's every tree for itself.

I observed the spacing between the trees: Some huddled together like penguins, while others created no-grow zones around themselves. I noticed the differences in the bark of the trees, from the tough and wrinkled skin of the white pine to the smooth surface of the American beech. The trunk of the beech tree feels like wallpaper on a concrete wall. It's almost as if the bark is wrapped too tightly around the tree.

Stepping over the gnarled roots crossing the Trail, I wondered where they were heading and why. Above me, a billion leaves rustled in the wind. I noticed the difference in shapes from one species to another. Each holds the same purpose, to turn sunlight into energy, but each evolved differently across millennia depending on unseen generations of variables—each tree hiking its own hike.

The scientific exploration of the forest ecosystem is still in its early days, with much rigorous work still to be done. And that will take time because forests operate on an entirely different time scale than we do. The oldest tree known to be alive in North America is a bristlecone pine tree in California, which is somewhere around four thousand eight hundred years old. On the East Coast, a bald cypress tree in North Carolina is around two thousand six hundred years old. Oak trees typically can live for six hundred years, and even plain old pine trees have a lifespan of around two hundred years.

As we continue to explore the extraordinary ecosystem of the forest, I'm convinced we'll discover a reality where trees tightly connect with other trees and their surroundings in ways we haven't even begun to appreciate. We'll come to consider the forest and the individual trees within it as a community mutually pledged to each other's lives and fortunes, just as the American revolutionaries were to each other back in 1776.

OK, I know you're thinking Hodge has lost the plot here, but bear with me on this for a moment. Individual trees are only truly healthy when the whole ecosystem of the forest is working in harmony. For example, a healthy forest ecosystem creates its own climate by temperature-regulating the forest floor. Cut down too many trees, and too much sunlight gets through, changing the climate and potentially irrevocably damaging the whole.

Trees that are about to die from old age or infection will push their nutrients back down into the soil and through the connected systems to help nourish younger trees, maybe even their offspring. A tree under attack by insects will release chemicals, alerting other trees to fire up their defenses against those bugs before they spread. Wohlleben refers to all this communication as taking place over the "Wood Wide Web." It's a vast interconnection of trees, underground fungal highways called mycorrhizal networks, insects, and animals working together as a complex, single ecosystem.

Understand your ecosystem.

From a leadership perspective, we must also understand the ecosystem within which we operate and the various roles each of the components plays. This could be within our organizations or across our chosen industries. Understand where resources come from, how and when to compete, and when to cooperate for the common good.

For example, many competitive organizations come together to help drive standards when an imminent threat is affecting their industry. In my domain, cyber security, we see strong networks of competitors sharing valuable cyber threat data through organizations such as the Financial Services Information Sharing and Analysis Center (FS-ISAC). The formation of these organizations created a peer-to-peer network to respond to cyber threats. FS-ISAC, and other similar industry-focused ISACs, now play a critical role across our industry to protect businesses against cyber threats.

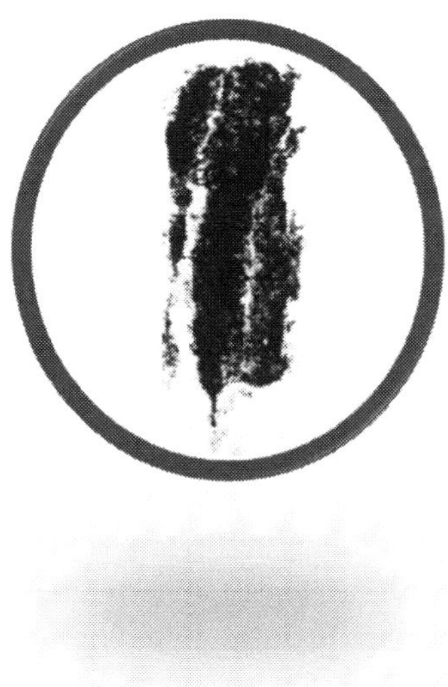

This section of the Trail helped me recognize and appreciate the environment around me in deeper and more meaningful ways, from the mountains and rivers to the deep forest. Every time I hike now, I will take more from what surrounds me.

I feel as if I can use this same appreciation from a leadership perspective when I encourage my colleagues and teams to look around, really observe, and question their surroundings.

My Inspire White Blaze activated this deeper appreciation for the environment. However, it was not about me recognizing an experience I could use to inspire others. Rather, it was about being open to the inspiration my surroundings gave me—an internal focus, not an external focus.

Once I accepted that inspiration, I could apply my Value White Blaze and better understand why it was inspirational. In turn, I hope to share this inspiration outward as I practice my White Blaze Leadership skills.

In New Hampshire, the rest of the White Mountains lay ahead of me, including Mount Washington, which rises to six thousand two hundred feet and is notorious for having some of the worst weather in the world.

I'm happy to share that I've overcome my fear of mud and quicksand. However, the Rodent of Unusual Size (R.O.U.S.) from *The Princess Bride* continues to terrorize my dreams. I'm also glad to share that I haven't hugged any trees yet, but I still reserve the right to do so in the future, probably somewhere near Mount Washington.

Section Eighteen Campfire Conversations

- Can you recall a crisis where a slower, more deliberate response might have been more beneficial? What would that have looked like?
- How do you handle and manage external pressure when it feels unreasonable?
- Are there situations where adopting a longer-term perspective could bring better outcomes? How might you approach those differently?
- How well do you understand the different components of your ecosystem and their interconnections, and how do you use that knowledge in decision-making?

Section Nineteen

Surviving the White Mountains

The sleet blew sideways in fifty to seventy miles per hour winds, and I shivered in what felt like 34°F (1°C). I was soaking wet after three hard days of relentless rain. I had nothing dry left. I peered through the thick fog, trying to pick out the next cairn—a raised pile of rocks marking the way and my only hope of reaching safety.

This is not the Arctic or the Himalayas, but somewhere near the 5,249-foot summit of Mount Lafayette in the White Mountains of New Hampshire. Oh, right, it's also mid-August. Yes, that's not a typo; it's mid-August.

People in this part of the world have two hobbies. The first is hiking in the White Mountains, which the locals and hikers call, "The Whites." The second is talking about hikers who get into trouble hiking in The Whites. The Search and Rescue (SAR) teams who operate in The Whites participate in around eighty rescue missions per year, saving lives and no doubt shaking their heads at the sheer incompetence of some people.

While fighting my way to the summit of Mount Lafayette, I wondered if I, too, was falling into the incompetent bucket. My brain told me I could have been on a beach or a well-manicured golf course somewhere, but instead, I'm deep into another bind of my own making.

The Whites of New Hampshire represent, by far, the hardest hundred-mile section of the Appalachian Trail and are by far the hardest I have pushed myself on this adventure. Mount Lafayette tormented me and brought me to tears, but the experience gave me insights that will stay with me forever.

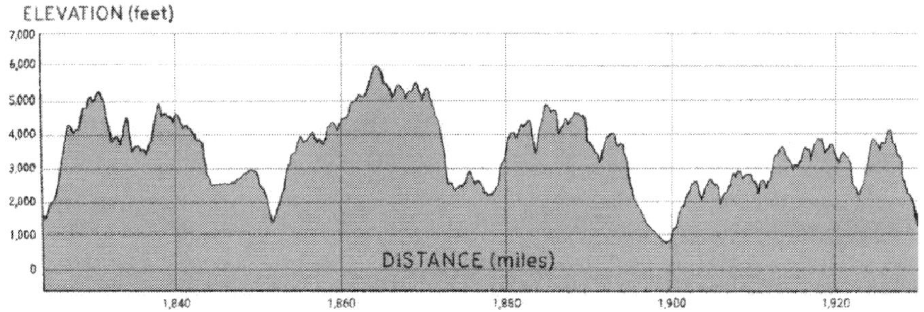

Figure 17 The Whites, NH

The Treeline

And then everything changed.

One of the novel experiences of hiking The Whites is spending an extended period above the treeline for the first time. Here, I hiked right out of the woods into a barren, alien territory that looked like it was cast by Hollywood for a low-budget 1960s sci-fi film. This foreboding landscape above the treeline is a fragile ecosystem known as an alpine zone. In the White Mountains, it sits above the four-thousand-four-hundred-foot mark.

The treeline marks a demarcation point above which trees no longer grow. It's not a hard line. Over a short distance, the forest transforms from fully grown trees to stunted small trees and then to no trees at all. The indicators of this change arrive quickly, and before you know it, it's only rocks and sky.

Scientists do not fully understand treelines and often debate the variables that contribute to this phenomenon. Many researchers identify average summer temperature as the primary factor, while others emphasize rainfall, weather patterns, snowpack, and soil composition. Treelines vary by region, with elevations around eight thousand feet on Mount Shasta in California and ten thousand feet in the Tetons of Wyoming. In contrast, treelines in places like Tibet and Bolivia can reach a remarkable sixteen to seventeen thousand feet.

A 2023 paper published in *Global Change Biology*, titled "Global Distribution and Controls of Natural Mountain treelines,"[77] used remote sensing to show that seventy percent of treelines moved upward by 1.2 meters per year between 2000 and 2010. Its conclusion falls squarely on a global increase in temperatures during this period.

Predictably, the internet is filled with people who deny climate change and refuse to accept that the rise in average temperatures relates to the objectively measurable increase in the average height of the treeline globally. Interestingly, an upward shift in treeline elevation means more trees absorbing carbon dioxide from the atmosphere. It's almost like the Earth is breathing.

Moving up and out of the trees, I encountered a vastly different set of risks and dangers as I became more exposed to the elements. Rain, wind, clouds, dense fog, solar radiation, and electrical storms all became bigger threats and forced me to plan differently while hiking in this zone. For example, the stretch of the Appalachian Trail traversing up and over Mount Washington is around thirteen miles of continuous Trail all above the treeline, which is a long time to be exposed to these risks. No camping is allowed in this alpine zone either; hence, I planned my day with the utmost care and detail.

Recognize change.

The treeline represents a powerful insight into leadership. As leaders, we must be aware when we cross a treeline and know how to respond. In business, treelines might arrive as a merger, an acquisition event, an emergent competitor, or perhaps an innovative technology causing significant disruption in your industry. Think generative AI (GenAI), for example.

Because business treeline changes can come at you quickly, everything can change in a New York minute. Whatever the change is, you must first recognize it—and then get everyone else to recognize it, too. The signs are usually crystal clear, but choosing to ignore them or acting too late can leave you standing out in a raging storm with no plan on how to proceed.

Countless examples exist of businesses that ignored the treeline. Blockbuster danced above the treeline for far too long until it realized it was too late to rewind the clock. Oracle almost missed the Cloud wave, and it took a herculean effort by Larry Ellison to adapt his company to the cloud-first software era and remain the technology powerhouse Oracle is today.

Print and news media companies faced a barrage of business treelines over the last decade as consumers found innovative ways to get their news. Their markets were fragmented, driving rapid digitization and consolidation. This turmoil resulted in many changes in the way the industry works and, ironically enough, a twenty-five percent decline in paper production in the United States from 1999 to 2022.[78] Those who failed to see this treeline for what it was and change their models are no longer in business.

Hopefully, when you encounter a treeline, you will act swiftly and grasp the opportunity it presents to you.

Cairns

I will guide you home.

Cairns dot the exposed sections of the trails in the White Mountains. These piles of rocks sit about six feet high and act as guideposts when visibility becomes challenging.

On the day I set out to climb Mount Lafayette, the fog started out wispy but thickened into a solid, impenetrable butternut squash soup by late afternoon. The cairns offered the only way to follow the Trail. When a small thinning of the fog exposed the next cairn, I fixed my compass in that direction and made a direct line toward it, assuming the Trail lay somewhere in between. Then, I repeated this process over and over. It made for exhausting work in the freezing temperatures.

By the time I reached the summit of Mount Lafayette, I was in full type-2 fun mode and not enjoying myself at all. The cold seeped into my bones, and I knew I needed to make no mistakes as I headed down to the Appalachian Mountain Club (AMC) hut where I would be staying. There was slightly over a mile to hike from this doomscape to my sanctuary.

Cairns have been part of human culture since the dawn of time. In every part of the world, they have been used to mark routes or significant locations, such as burial grounds and tombs of important people. They are common across the U.K., and my favorite cairn lore is about Scottish clans going into battle, where each member would place a stone on a pile, thus creating a cairn. If they survived the fight, they would remove a stone on their way home. In this manner, the remaining cairn constituted a monument to honor the dead, the size of it a measure of the toll paid.

Cairns have become a recent source of controversy, thanks to the Instagram/TikTok generation. Hundreds of wanna-be social media stars have been building impromptu cairns in national parks, creating a backlash in which other Instagrammers film themselves knocking them down. Ah, isn't it fun to live in this era?

The modern-day builders create cairns as either a meditative exercise, artwork, or a fun pastime. The grown-ups in the room, aka park rangers, point out the downsides: It flies in the face of the leave-no-trace policy we should follow when entering a wilderness. Even slight changes can upset the delicate balance of the surrounding ecosystem. Wayward cairns could also lead a hiker away from the actual trail in poor weather, creating a real danger.

Prepare for the storm in advance.

Cairns offer us thoughtful insight into leadership. In sunny weather, they're an interesting feature on the landscape. However, when the going gets tough, the importance of having a well-thought-out set of cairns—highly visible markers that give us a common direction—becomes essential. They're not something we can build after the storm hits.

Do you have cairns built into your organization so that during tough times, everyone has a clear line of sight to what is vital? This could be a clear mission everyone understands, simple repeated messages on priorities, or a set of goals the team or business is working toward, with each one a definable chunk of the tougher whole.

Have you read your disaster or contingency plan recently? Or your cyber breach plan? Do you know what they say? Do they pass the cairn test? Do you have a set of actions and principles serving to guide everyone to the top of the mountain in challenging times, and will they guide them back down and to safety?

It's a critical leadership skill to ensure that in the most challenging times, when the storm is raging, we have something to guide us. Without such a line of sight, it's far too easy to lose our way.

Crying in the Hut

Gimme Shelter—Emotional Rescue.

My destination after leaving the summit of Mount Lafayette was Greenleaf Hut, located a mile ahead through the fog, wind, and fatigue that surrounded me.

Eight of these AMC huts dot the White Mountains, providing shelter and comfort to weary hikers. They can best be described as rustic and functional, having been built originally in the early 1930s. Power is unavailable to guests. There are no showers and, of course, no flush toilets. What hikers are treated to is a hearty family-style dinner served at six o'clock, with lights out at nine o'clock. Sleeping arrangements for the forty or so guests consist of racks of wooden bunks stacked three high, each with a thick foam mattress, a scratchy blanket, and a pillow of sorts. All of which will be reused by the very next guest. In the morning, the delicious scent of a calorie-laden breakfast greeted me promptly at seven o'clock.

For the summer months, each hut has a seasonal management team known as the *Croo*, consisting of around six twenty-somethings. The Croo does everything to keep the huts running, including the wake-up song and the corny skits they perform at breakfast time. They are great fun, hard-working, knowledgeable, and tremendous human beings. In another life I want to be Croo.

Many of the guests who stay in the huts have taken a short four- or five-mile *easy* hike up from the valley floor, just as their families have done for generations. Excitable groups of preteen kids were found in each of the huts I stayed at, enjoying the experience and their first venture into the backcountry of The Whites. Thru-hikers tend not to stay in the huts because they are relatively expensive; however, as they pass by, they can stop in and see if any work-for-stay bunks are available.

I staggered into Greenleaf Hut at about 6:30 p.m. after making the arduous journey down from the summit of Mount Lafayette. I must have looked like a survivor from a shipwreck staggering through the door as I did. All forty guests in the hut were already seated at the shared bench tables for dinner by the time I arrived. They looked warm and rested as if straight out of an L.L. Bean holiday shopping brochure, wearing their fancy designer hiking gear and happy smiles. I stood for a moment in the wave of warmth, soaking wet, disheveled, and a little manic from my experience. Then, I headed to the desk to check in and find my bunk.

When the Croo member at the desk asked for my name, I took a deep breath but instead of speaking, out came a garbled sob. I didn't mean to cry, but it was all I had left in me. It took me a few moments to center myself and get my act together. From the young man's response, it most certainly wasn't the first time he'd seen a grown man cry.

At dinner, I commiserated with another hiker who was in similar shape to me. Both of us were exhausted from being pummeled by the harsh weather and the difficult conditions of the Trail. Our conversation consisted of a barely veiled exercise in holding it together while day-trippers chatted and played board games as if everything was OK with the world. Calories consumed; I headed back to my bunk for the sweet embrace of sleep.

Before falling into a deep sleep, I thought a lot about the raw emotion I experienced. The best way to describe it is to imagine a bag of different colored Play-Doh, where each color stands for an emotion, and then imagine squishing them together, until all you hold in your hand is a muddy-brown colored Play-Doh blob. That's it! The emotion I experienced was *blob*.

Later, when I researched this experience, I discovered that crying at or near the end of endurance events is a fairly common experience. My experience of it being a jumble of different emotions mixed together also turns out to be a reasonable explanation. If you've ever pushed yourself far over your expectations, you may have experienced this too. It's not grief, pride, sadness, happiness, or exhaustion; it's the blob, and it can be massively cathartic.

Gloria Liu's article "I'll Cry If I Want To (and You Can, Too)"[79] in *Outside* magazine explores the science behind this phenomenon. The physiological shift in your body as it moves control from the sympathetic nervous system to your parasympathetic nervous system—from *fight-or-flight* to *rest-or-digest*—causes this need to cry.

If you Google "endurance athletes and crying," you'll find a myriad of articles extolling the virtue of a good cry during a run or at the finish line of a marathon. The perfect example is in the documentary *Where Dreams Go to Die*[80] about an attempt to complete the five loops that make up the Barkley Marathons. This event is one of the most hard-core endurance events in the world. At about forty-six hours into the sixty-hour race, world-class endurance athlete Gary Robbins, aka the GingerRunner, had just come in for a pit stop. At about an hour into the film, he experiences the blob in all its heart-wrenching glory. It's a powerful moment, and I cried just watching this scene as the memory of my experience flooded back into in my head.

Sports psychologists weigh in on the topic with a fevered interest. One of the most thorough scientific papers I read on this topic was "Walking on Thin Ice: Exploring Demands and Means of Coping During an Extreme Expedition."[81]

The authors followed two endurance athletes as they crossed the frozen Baikal Lake in Siberia in opposite directions and charted their emotions and mental states during the twenty-one days they were out in this extreme environment. It's fascinating reading, and while the science is far over my head, the underlying story draws me further into the idea that we can proactively think about our mental states in any situation.

Strengthen your emotional intelligence.

This, in fact, is a key leadership insight. It's critical we learn how to interpret our mental states and understand how they impact the teams and businesses we support. For example, if you have been working untold hours on completing a deliverable, it's likely you too might end up with a blob emotion, which could be triggered by any small catalyst.

It's extremely powerful to recognize what emotions we might carry and how to effectively cope with them or use them to our advantage. It can also be powerful to have a broader perspective when dealing with people. Understanding where they are coming from and what emotions they are experiencing can help you guide a conversation to a more conducive outcome for both parties.

If this sounds to you like I was leading up to the point that inspiring leaders have developed strong emotional intelligence, then I have achieved my objective.

Search and Rescue

The art of good decision-making.

The Whites are serious business, and unfortunately, for some, they can turn deadly. Of the eighty missions SAR teams deploy into the White Mountains every year, some end in fatalities. And it's not only in the winter but year-round. Sadly, a young hiker died in The Whites only the week before I got caught in that awful mid-August weather on Mount Lafayette. Somewhere around six to ten deaths per year occur in the White Mountains. Given the substantial number of visitors to the region, it's surprising the number isn't higher.

I found myself chatting with one of the AMC-hut volunteers and he, of course, regaled me with stories of people who had gotten into trouble out in The Whites. I picked up on an intriguing story he told me about how SAR helicopter crews decide if they will launch on a mission or not. The process takes as much of the ambiguity and personal feelings out of the equation as possible and forces the rescue teams to stick to the facts in deciding their course of action.

I downloaded and read the National SAR Academy Training Manual on helicopter rescue techniques,[82] which makes for some sobering reading, especially from a risk management perspective. The opening paragraph contains the following ominous statement: "As accident investigators repeatedly conclude, 'self-imposed psychological pressure' causes us to make poor decisions when adrenaline clouds our judgment. Poor decision-making is preventable, yet tragically, it's a factor in the vast majority of helicopter rescue accidents."

To counter this, the manual contains a strict set of quantifiable decision points, designed to conclude in a go or no-go decision. It references the United States Coast Guard operational risk model (ORM), called the GAR (Green-Amber-Red) Risk Assessment model, which provides a scoring-based, color-coded model for getting to a go/no-go decision point.

The authors point out what the real value in the process is: "The key ingredient occurs when team members discuss their post-scoring results together, because it generates valuable discussion toward understanding the risks and how the team will manage them. Ultimately, it slows down the operational tempo and forces rescuers to carefully think rather than simply react."

The best risk management decisions take time and perspective.

The leadership insight here is the same. When trying to decide the way forward in a situation involving significant risk, we must first ask the right questions. By building quantifiable consensus around risk with different voices, we can then choose the most appropriate path forward.

Examples might be moving ahead with an acquisition of a company or a large capital expenditure. Momentum can start to drive that decision. "We've invested so much in it to this point." "They are really good people." "I made a commitment to the Board." We should make sure we can objectively make critical decisions and value other perspectives when evaluating risks. It's never too late to make it a no-go.

Pick Your Battles

You can't fight everyone.

The weather in the White Mountains can change in a moment. For example, during the year I hiked The Whites (2023), Mount Washington experienced 8.4 inches of snow in the first ten days of June. Back in 1931, Mount Washington recorded the highest-ever wind speed at 231 miles per hour, which, needless to say, is crazy wild. Based on my direct experience, I know how extreme conditions can get in the summer at higher elevations. I can only imagine what winter storms must be like.

A myriad of books, such as *Not Without Peril: 150 Years of Misadventure on The Presidential Range of New Hampshire*[83] by Nicholas Howe, or the thoroughly enjoyable movie starring Naomi Watts, *Infinite Storm*,[84] bring this unimaginable experience to life.

During my hike across The Whites, I focused a lot of my thinking time on my mission to cure cystic fibrosis. Much like the changeable conditions in these mountains, I've seen this disease raise its ugly head and go from benign to a full-on raging storm overnight. The metaphor is not lost on me, and it fueled me through the hardest parts of this section. One specific memory floated to the surface as I hiked.

I had flown across country and just landed at the Las Vegas airport, on my way to a conference, when my daughter called me. She felt awful and knew that something was very wrong with her. I didn't even leave the airport and instead flew directly to Washington D.C. to pick her up and get her to Johns Hopkins Hospital, where she received her medical care.

The phenomenal cystic fibrosis care team, under the leadership of her doctor, Dr. West, took her in and soon realized she had the flu. For you and me, the flu can be a bad few days in bed, but for someone with cystic fibrosis, it can be devastating. As always, the team at Hopkins brought the skill, experience, and professionalism needed to deal with this serious situation and get my daughter back on her feet. Cystic fibrosis doctors and care teams are exceptional caregivers, toughened by the raging conditions of this disease. My thanks go out to all of them.

I want to illustrate how extreme the weather changes in the White Mountains can be. When I exited the trailhead back down in the valley the day after my Mount Lafayette adventure, the weather was a perfect 75°F (24°C) and sunny. This was jarringly different from my experiences just a few miles hike up into The Whites. Groups of day hikers were excitedly setting out and the forest rangers were doing an admirable job advising those who looked underprepared. Flip-flops are an obvious first indicator, as is someone holding a single eight-ounce water bottle.

One of the rangers engaged a group of four testosterone-laden bros and politely asked them what they were planning to hike that day. One of them spoke up and said they were going to do the loop. "That's great," the ranger said, and then he asked them one simple question. "What are the names of the four trails that make up the loop?"

The bros looked at each other for inspiration, but it was clear they had no idea. Last I saw the ranger, he was leading them over to a map and perhaps a kinder, gentler trail for the day. A large part of a ranger's work at the trailheads is stopping these incidents before they happen.

While section-hiking, I purposely saved the three-day climb up and over Mount Washington for what looked to be a decent break in the weather pattern of heavy rain. Thankfully, the weather gods cooperated. Although it rained during the steep climb to the Madison Hut, the tree canopy protected me from the worst of it. For most of my time above the treeline, it didn't rain; however, a few times, I was buried in a dense cloud layer.

This planning afforded me some of the most spectacular views I have ever seen. As I neared the summit of Mount Washington, I could see so far that I wondered if the flat-earthers were onto something. I spent a solid hour trying to imagine what the view would appear like if the Earth were actually flat. But I couldn't get my head around the physics or optics of such a world, so instead, I spent my time wondering how to survive 231mile per hour winds. You have a lot of time to think on the Trail.

Pick your battles.

Choosing our battles is a wise leadership skill. We don't always have the opportunity to choose, but when we do, careful consideration and a balanced view are required.

An example, based on real-life experience, is over-committing in phase one of a project. This can cause that phase to slip and stakeholders to become disillusioned in the effort. A more careful consideration of the deliverables for a phase one project could yield an easier path to overall success by delivering on some of the easy wins out of the gate.

It's not about waiting for the sunny day, rather, it's actively searching for the set of conditions that are likely to improve your chances of success in any situation.

This section of the Trail forced me to consolidate many of the skills and experiences that I've gained over the last three years and apply them in a targeted manner. The Trail's extreme technical and mental challenges drew on my skills and experience. It feels as if I've been training all along for The Whites.

I spent a lot of time with my Question White Blaze on this section. However, hiding behind questions such as "What am I even doing here?" was, in fact, my Believe White Blaze. The Trail continues to surprise me in its ability to push me deep into my thoughts, and I'm thankful I have developed my Believe White Blaze to help me navigate through those experiences.

Hiking through the White Mountains was exceptional (even the crying bit), and if you've never had the chance, I would recommend staying in one of the AMC huts for the experience. Make sure you book well in advance, though, as they fill up quickly.

As for Mount Lafayette, it's named after General Gilbert du Motier, Marquis de La Fayette. A Frenchman and military hero who fought with Washington during the American Revolutionary War. Perhaps it's somewhat appropriate he is still kicking this British guy's ass almost two hundred fifty years later.

Section Nineteen Campfire Conversations

- What measures, or cairns, have you put in place to guide your business through potential challenges or uncertainty?
- What upcoming challenges are you anticipating, and how do you plan to respond to them?
- How aware are you of your own emotions in different situations, and how do they influence your decisions?
- How do you manage personal feelings in difficult decision-making, and is it always possible or necessary to separate them?

Section Twenty

The Hardest Mile?

Crawling through a damp tunnel on my hands and knees, I swore to myself like a sailor whose shore leave has been canceled. The weight of the giant boulders surrounding me pressed in, making the tunnel feel even narrower than it already was. I don't like enclosed spaces, and while this wasn't a long crawl, it was more than long enough for me. My hands and knees scraped along the stone as I pushed my backpack ahead of me. Somewhere deep below, I heard the rumble of water cascading through an underground cavern. This is the Mahoosuc Notch.

It had been two and a half days since I began crossing the thirty-one miles that make up the Mahoosuc Traverse. I still had another brutal day ahead of me to complete this section. The traverse spans the border between New Hampshire and Maine. It's tough, technical hiking, but the part I was in at the moment, The Mahoosuc Notch, was even more so. Thru-hikers refer to this stretch as the hardest single mile of the 2,197.4 miles that make up the whole of the Appalachian Trail.

I was now two hours into making my way through this hardest single mile, and it would still take another forty-five minutes to reach the end of it.

Yes, it's seriously that hard.

With a pace of only one-third of a mile per hour, you might be thinking Hodge is the worst hiker in the world. Truthfully, however, it's just a measure of how difficult this piece of the Trail is. But despite disliking enclosed spaces, I was thoroughly enjoying the Mahoosuc Notch. My pace was around what I anticipated, and rather than worrying about that, I concentrated on my safety and the overall physical environment around me: the feel of the rocks on my shoes and hands, the likelihood of a chosen route through the next section of rocks being navigable, and the aches and strains in my muscles as I reached, stretched and fought my way across this formidable landscape.

As I wrote about this experience, we were fast approaching another Thanksgiving holiday here in the United States. It's my favorite holiday and one that embodies the spirit of gratitude. On this single mile of the Trail, I lent heavily into my gratitude, as I continued to develop that mental toughness muscle that allowed me to transition from distractive emotions to empowering intent.

The Notch

We can be heroes.

The Mahoosuc Notch is one of the most anticipated and iconic parts of the Appalachian Trail. Descriptions of the Notch run from technical to daunting, but almost all call it *the hardest mile*. For northbound thru-hikers, it acts as a gateway to the final section of the adventure. The White Mountains of New Hampshire are now behind you and only Maine is left to conquer. Get yourself through this notch and it's all downhill from there. Except that's not true, as Maine brings plenty of uphill challenges and tough terrain, as the Trail winds across those last two hundred eighty miles north to Mount Katahdin.

The Mahoosuc Notch itself is buried in a deep ravine with steep fractured rock walls rising to an unobtainable vantage point. If a hiker could look down from up there, they would see a solid jungle gym of large boulders strewn along its floor for exactly one mile.

I stood before another one of these barricades of rocks, rising twenty to forty feet into the clear blue sky. They blocked my view and provided only this challenge to conquer directly in front of me. For the last two hours, I had to decide how to get up, over, around, or under these rock puzzles. The normal Appalachian Trail markers, the white blazes, appeared only a few times to direct me into narrow passages under some giant rocks. It felt like a massive escape room, with the correct answer tailored for each hiker.

The stretches of narrow tunnels below giant rocks pushed me way outside my comfort zone. As I crawled along, I thought about my son telling me a memorable quote from David Bowie, the British music legend, about being out of your comfort zone. In a trailer for the HBO documentary *The Last Five Years*, Bowie said, "If you feel safe in the area you're working in, you're not working in the right area. Always go a little further into the water than you feel you're capable of being in. Go a little bit out of your depth. And when you don't feel that your feet are quite touching the bottom, you're just about in the right place to do something exciting."[85]

Have you ever been there? That place where our feet don't touch the bottom? That's exactly how I felt while crawling through these tunnels deep into the wilderness.

Embrace being out of your depth.

This is, perhaps, an excellent leadership insight. When you push yourself further, whether you feel you're in over your head, or in my case, under a rock, the experience has a way of expanding your horizons.

Like other leadership insights, this one applies to both you and those you lead. The ability to push anyone out of their comfort zone and make them feel good about it is a skill well worth developing. This skill also requires granting trust to someone. The simple act of asking someone to do something new or difficult implies that we trust they have the skills and ability to accomplish the task.

"You've got this" are some of the most powerful words we can ever say to anyone, regardless if we say them aloud or imply them by our actions.

Do the Hard Things

Choose the Moon.

Thru-hikers talk about taking ninety minutes to navigate through the Mahoosuc Notch. As a section-hiker, though, I needed to be realistic about my pace and skills compared to those of a thru-hiker. I took a conservative approach to planning and doubled that time.

I knew hiking this mile would be hard and accepted that fact because, after all, isn't doing hard things the point of this? No one ever told me curing cystic fibrosis would be easy. So, here I was doing harder things than I ever imagined, like hiking the Trail, because I understand it's the hard things that make the biggest difference.

I've spent weeks in Congress advocating for changes in our laws to make life easier for those with cystic fibrosis and felt like all the effort was going nowhere. I've wiped away my tears and told everyone else it would be OK even when I struggled to believe it myself. I've asked for help when I didn't want to ask. I've stood on stage and bared my soul, hugged friends who have lost loved ones to cystic fibrosis, opened the door when all I wanted to do was to stay shut away from the world. I have done hard things.

But none of those challenges can possibly be as hard as waking up every morning with the knowledge that your body is waging a constant internal war. Be it cancer, mental illness, or cystic fibrosis, the truly hard things are within.

Choose to do the hard things.

If leadership is anything, it is this: The ability to clearly define audacious goals—hard things—and then inspire those around us to accomplish these goals. Sometimes, such as with the Mahoosuc Notch, I needed to be inspired. I was the one who needed to dig deep and commit to it. I needed to put myself in a place where I believed this was a challenge I could not postpone and had to conquer.

As leaders, we must inspire those around us and ourselves to achieve hard things. Both words and actions are needed to provide this inspiration. It's as if a purpose in life needs a challenge to make it real—two halves of a whole. By taking the first step and embracing your challenge, you can bring your purpose alive.

One of the most inspiring leadership speeches ever given profoundly illustrates this connection. On September 12, 1962, President John F. Kennedy (JFK) addressed an audience of around forty thousand in the football stadium at Rice University in Houston, Texas. In his speech JFK set out his reasons for why the United States needed to go to the moon, focusing on the specific fact it is a hard thing to do: "We choose to go to the moon in this decade and do the other things, not because they are easy, but because they are hard, because that goal will serve to organize and measure the best of our energies and skills, because that challenge is one that we are willing to accept, one we are unwilling to postpone, and one which we intend to win, and the others, too." [86]

Ted Sorenson wrote this speech for JFK and filled it with powerful imagery every bit as relevant today as it was 1962. It's well worth going back and reading the full text of the speech or watching a video of JFK delivering lines such as, "We meet at a college noted for knowledge, in a city noted for progress, in a State noted for strength, and we stand in need of all three, for we meet in an hour of change and challenge, in a decade of hope and fear, in an age of both knowledge and ignorance. The greater our knowledge increases, the greater our ignorance unfolds."

One year after his speech, on November 22, 1963, the President was assassinated. On a humid day in Houston on July 21, 1969, Neil Armstrong took humankind's first step on the moon, fulfilling the challenge set by JFK seven years earlier.

Just Be You

Won't the real you please stand up?

Is the Mahoosuc Notch the hardest mile on the Appalachian Trail? For me, the answer is a clear *no*. I have had plenty of harder miles on this journey. The mile right before I chose to finish hiking a section in Connecticut is one that sticks out. I had struggled with my decision. While the physical aspects of that day put me in a tough situation, it was the mental aspects I fought with the most. The first mile back on the Trail after my mum passed away was my most emotional mile.

That last mile struggling up Mount Lafayette in horrible weather was the most physically demanding of all the others on the Trail. These were all harder miles for me than the Mahoosuc Notch and all for varied reasons—mental, emotional, and physical.

We should never let others define what hard is for us. The Mahoosuc Notch was the slowest mile of the Appalachian Trail for me, but other than that, I thoroughly enjoyed it. Perhaps it was the perfect weather or the fact that I had spent a few weeks in the White Mountains and was prepared for *hard*. Either way, the hardest mile on the Appalachian Trail brought home to me that one person's definition of hard is not another person's hard.

Bring your authentic self every time.

This led me to think about what being seen as a leader is and how we can sometimes feel someone else's definition of leadership is the one we have to aspire to. Are we letting someone else define leadership for us? Can you be a remarkable leader by being the real you, your authentic self?

I would argue forcefully you can. The skills, traits, and personality you bring will form the shape of your leadership, but you don't need to fit someone else's stereotype in order to lead.

This plays out most often in gender bias toward leadership. A burgeoning field of science examining this area has sprung up. For example, I read an article published in *Frontiers in Psychology* in January 2023 titled, "Gender Stereotypes in Leadership: Analyzing the Content and Evaluation of Stereotypes about Typical, Male, and Female Leaders."[87] It makes for some fascinating, albeit, complex reading. The authors, Manuela Tremmel and Ingrid Wahl, describe how women are ascribed communal characteristics such as "nurturing" and "kind." As a result, they are stereotypically seen as less capable of leadership than men who are ascribed agentic traits such as "ambitious" and "self-confident." This is even more true when the leadership role in question is itself described in masculine terms.

Leadership is not about a set of traits, it's not about being seen as hard pushing or forceful, rather it's about the outcome. Can you coalesce, inspire, and guide people around a common mission? There are many ways to hike the Appalachian Trail, as captured in the saying, *hike your own hike.* And, so too, are there many ways to be a successful leader. This is true for you and for those leaders you have in your orbit.

Perhaps one of the defining characteristics of a world-class leader is that we already understand *being your authentic self* is what makes us successful in this role.

It's Done When It's Done

Be where your feet are.

When I came out of the Mahoosuc Notch I got a genuine sense of accomplishment. "I did it!" I exclaimed. "I completed the hardest mile. I can do anything," and then I tripped over a small rock and ended up sitting in a mud puddle. *Argh!*

This is the way on the Appalachian Trail. If you let go of your concentration for even one second, the smallest rock can trip you up. The smallest piece of moss on a rock can have you hoping you won't break your leg as you fall. That missed blaze can have you hiking thirty minutes in the wrong direction. I have done all of these on my hiking, multiple times, and in each case, a lack of concentration was to blame.

Thankfully, no one was around to see me sheepishly get up and shake off the mud. But the tumble was a solid reminder I wasn't done and still had plenty more hiking to do that day.

Be present.

From a leadership perspective, being present in the moment is a critical skill. By being present, I mean: Are you truly engaged and paying attention to what's right in front of you? To quote a famous Zen saying, "Chop wood, carry water." I love the simplicity of this saying. If a Buddhist monk were to invent a similar saying today, it might be something like, "Walk, don't text," but that might just be me expressing my inner grievances.

If you research *being present*, you'll find many conversations centered around mindfulness, meditation, yoga, well-being, etc. However, for the purpose of this conversation, being present isn't complicated. Simply, "Are you paying attention?" will do. Ironically, the complexity of the mindfulness movement has over-complicated this concept even as it bombards us with messages about simplicity.

Not only do we need to learn how to be present for every call, every meeting, and every personal interaction, but we also need to keep the focus on long-term initiatives. It's too easy to lose intensity and focus as we move deeper into a project, but doesn't the end of a plan require as much commitment as the start?

It's not always easy to be present, especially when we are pulled in multiple different directions. However, with minimal effort, we can learn how to recognize when we're not present and make meaningful choices about what to do. A quote often used by sports coaches, "Be where your feet are," highlights this point. I struggled to track down who originated this quote, but extraordinary coaches from Pat Summitt to Nick Saban have used this principle as a bedrock of their coaching. Don't be thinking about the next shot, next drive, or next tackle. Stay focused on the one right in front of you.

If you're on a call but are responding to emails, instant messaging a couple of colleagues, and checking the weather for the game this weekend, you're clearly not present, even if you believe you are. A fascinating scientific study from the University of Utah shows people who think they are good at multitasking are, in fact, the ones who are least likely to be any good at it. Yes, I'm talking to you.

Ask yourself, "Do I need to be on this call?" because if you do, it's worth giving it your full attention. And if you don't, then go do something else with your time.

If I find myself distracted and not fully present in a meeting, I'll ask someone to give me a minute, finish what I need to do, and then announce, "Right, I'm all yours." This is a meaningful way to remind ourselves and convey to the other person that we are now present. Hopefully, we can avoid tripping over that small rock.

Stay Humble People

Really, stay humble.

What hikers neglect to tell you about the Mahoosuc Notch is that once you finish it, you're not done. Not even close. As soon as I exit the Notch, a brutal, almost vertical climb up a stone mountain face, called the Mahoosuc Arm, presents itself. This is 1,617 feet of tough rock face climb, even tougher considering I had just came out of the Notch.

When I got to the top of the Arm, I was faced with the uncompromising pine bogs. These deep bogs will suck a hiker down and hold them prisoner if they misstep and fail to navigate the wooden planks that sit submerged just under the muddy surface water. Time after time, I had to find the plank with my poles, step where I know it to be, and then repeat. It was exhausting work.

Even though I had completed the Mahoosuc Notch, the Mahoosuc Arm and the pine bogs served as reminders that I could still be humbled by what the Trail had left to throw at me. Tripping over that little rock at the base of the Arm was a fitting example of this. So, too, were the other times the Trail has humbled me any time I thought I was the boss of it.

Stay humble.

I used to have a boss who would weave the following saying into every all-hands meeting: "There are two kinds of people, those who are humble, and those who will be." The Trail has cemented that perspective for me. It would be unwise to go into the Mahoosuc Traverse assuming you're such an accomplished hiker that it won't challenge you. Those who respect the fact the Traverse is challenging—and plan accordingly—will be rewarded by the experience. Those who don't respect it, then the Trail *will* find a way to humble them.

As leaders, we should celebrate the wins, believe we are stronger and more capable, and inspire our teams to be the best they can be. However, making sure you sprinkle some humble dust on top of this is an excellent habit to form.

The famed hardest mile on the Appalachian Trail turned out to be the slowest mile for me and that's how I'll remember it. It helped keep me humble, respectful, and grateful for what the Trail has given me and is yet to show me.

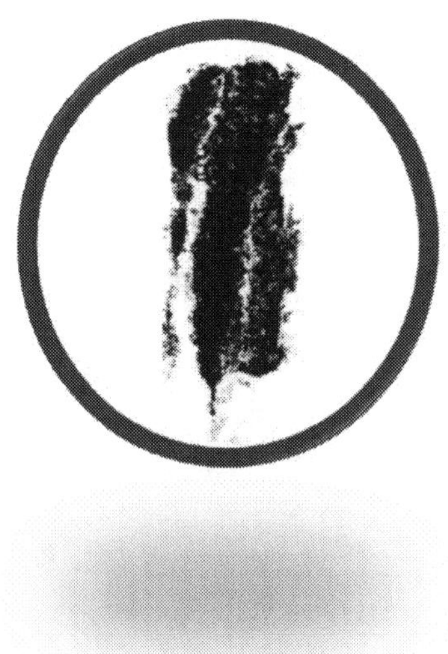

This section of the Trail really brought home to me core ideas about what leadership means. Leadership isn't defined by who we are or where we come from. Rather, it's about how we project ourselves into the world, how we blend the right amount of humility with bravado to tackle the hard things, and how leadership doesn't just happen at the start but is present throughout the whole journey.

This is the core philosophy of White Blaze Leadership, that leadership happens in the everyday, not just in the immediate moments of crisis, drama, and accelerated change. Leadership is recognizing your own set of White Blazes and leveraging those to inspire, act, and believe across the full journey.

Recently, I was back in my home country of Wales for a family wedding and stumbled on a Welsh saying that embodies this spirit of humility and gratitude from a leadership perspective: *Bid Ben, Bid Bont.* This translates to something akin to, "If you aspire to be a leader, you must be a bridge."

In my experience, being a bridge is indeed something we can only do with humility, being present in the moment, and with a healthy dose of gratitude.

Section Twenty Campfire Conversations

- Can you recall a time when you felt completely out of your depth, where your feet didn't touch the bottom? How did you handle it?
- How do you approach challenging tasks, and what motivates you to choose the hard things?
- How do you ensure you're fully present in your interactions with others, and is this something you feel you need to improve?
- In what ways do you work on strengthening your mental toughness, and how do you measure your progress?
- How do you consciously project yourself as a leader, and what kind of impact do you hope that has on others?

Section Twenty-One

Oh,Shenandoah!

The relentless freezing rain had turned my fingers so cold I couldn't feel them. They were useless, numb appendages not really connected to the rest of my body. I pictured them as fish sticks taken straight out of the freezer and grafted to my hands in some kind of weird Frankenstein experiment. A direct result of freezing fingers is that I can't close the clasps on my backpack, and that wasn't even the worst of my problems.

This was my first hike of the season: one hundred fifty miles, southbound from Harpers Ferry, West Virginia. It was supposed to be a breeze.

Sure, it contained the legendary Roller Coaster section of the Trail, but after the White Mountains of New Hampshire last year, nothing could phase me. This section hike completed all five hundred forty-four miles of the Appalachian Trail in Virginia. Crossing it off my list left me only Maine and a few small punch-list hikes to complete the whole of the Appalachian Trail.

Most of this section is the 105 miles the Appalachian Trail runs through the narrow corridor of the Blue Ridge Mountains that contain the Shenandoah National Park. The cool kids call this national park the SNP. The SNP is located just seventy-five miles west of Washington, D.C., and it's known to the thru-hikers as the easiest part of the Trail. If only the SNP had received that memo.

As usual, my time on the Trail was anything but easy. A brutal spring storm system changed what was supposed to be a stroll through the SNP into an exhausting battle against some of the worst weather I've experienced in my whole time out on the Appalachian Trail. It also brought along another set of leadership insights that, in hindsight, were worth the pain, effort, and willpower it took to discover them. Buckle up, hands inside at all times, here we go.

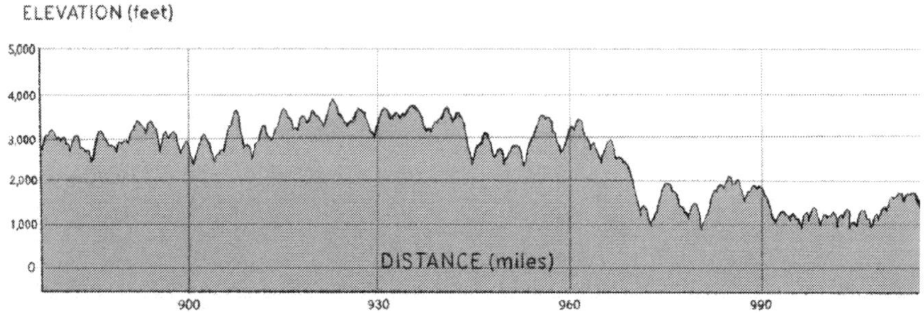

Figure 18 Blackrock Gap, VA, to Harpers Ferry, VA

Riding the Roller Coaster

Put your hands in the air.

South of Harpers Ferry there's a laminated sign attached to a tree right on the edge of the Trail. The plastic cover on the sign is weathered, and the wooden board it's fixed to is rotting away. The sign written in all-caps reads, "HIKER WARNING, YOU ARE ABOUT TO ENTER THE ROLLER COASTER, BUILT AND MAINTAINED BY THE TRAIL BOSS & HIS CREW OF VOLUNTEERS, HAVE A GREAT RIDE!" This is the Appalachian Trail's infamous Roller Coaster section.

Originally, this was a fifteen-mile road-walk section alongside Route 601 from Ashby Gap to Snickers Gap. However, in the 1980s, the park service purchased a sliver of land just wide enough to accommodate a narrow fourteen-mile corridor through the wilderness, and thus, the Roller Coaster was born. It's so-called because, given there was no room for switchbacks, the Trail simply follows the hills up and down, up and down, up and down.

My southbound journey encompassed all thirteen peaks in the Roller Coaster, 3,858 feet of ascent and 4,573 feet of decent. While the Trail itself wasn't technical, it was relentless work. This was especially so as my pack was too heavy, filled as it was with enough supplies for five straight days of hiking.

As a consequence, my pace was slower than I had anticipated and all the self-doubt of the first few days on the Trail flooded back. Thankfully, I was now an expert at dealing with this. I recognized the doubts, took them for what they were, and reminded myself that I was thankful for being out here. I was the one healthy enough to strap on a forty-pound pack and hike in the woods. I was the one still attempting to hike fifteen miles a day. I was the one making a difference in raising funds to cure cystic fibrosis.

Leverage your experience.

This is perhaps a leadership insight that was destined to come at some point on this journey. Now, in my fourth year of this adventure, I can take my experience and use it when and as needed. I have already discovered the tools and techniques; now I just have to apply them. That's why experience matters. That's why it matters for leaders to draw on it, share it, and provide opportunities for others to gain their own experiences.

This is especially true when your world is going through a roller coaster ride. Being able to bring your experience of a longer view of real-world actions and consequences can be critical to navigating intense times of change. I've certainly faced times in my career when I knew the next sharp turn or big drop lay only moments ahead. We have all had to control feelings of uncertainty and doubt in those moments.

Being a leader is being able to help ourselves and our teams enjoy the ride, no matter how terrifying the twists and turns might seem.

Oh, Shenandoah!

Pick your side.

In preparing for my hike through the SNP, I did what any self-respecting hiker would do and sat down with some popcorn to watch the 1965 classic movie *Shenandoah*[88]. If you're not familiar, it's well worth investing an hour and a half to watch it. Rotten Tomatoes lists it at one hundred percent tomatometer approval.

In summary, the protagonist, played by the excellent James Stuart, runs his farm in the Shenandoah Valley alongside his six sons, a daughter, and a daughter-in-law. Set in 1864, the Civil War threatens them from all sides, but Stuart, playing an archetypal frontier maverick, wants no part of other peoples' war.

Of course, things go horribly wrong, much drama ensues, and Stuart unwillingly becomes entangled in the conflict.

From various ledges high on the Blue Mountain Ridge, I peered down into the broad valley, which probably still looks much like it did back during the Civil War. Over three hundred combat actions occurred across the broad, fertile ground during the conflict. One example is the battle of Cedar Creek,[89] where some thirty-one thousand Union troops battled twenty-one thousand Confederate troops. Over a single day, nearly nine thousand casualties occurred, with a thousand men taking in their last sunrise that fateful morning.

It was difficult to imagine what that day must have looked like from my perch high on the ridge. No doubt there were spotters who took in the battle from this vantage point. I wondered what the roar of battle sounded like from up here and how far the smoke from the cannons drifted across the battlefield.

Build an authentic, inclusive work environment.

As leaders, we must be able to balance neutrality against the need to take sides or voice an opinion when appropriate and at the appropriate time. If you try to stay neutral, sometimes the events will overtake you and provide you with no choice. Move too early, or too late, and you might just find yourself on the losing end of the conflict or opportunity.

Polarization of our society along political lines, moral issues, and what seems like even trivial issues is our reality. How we navigate this reality in the workplace requires strong, thoughtful leadership. In a fascinating *Harvard Business Review* paper titled "When Staying Neutral Backfires,"[90] the authors Ike Silver and Alex Shaw lay out a case that voicing opinion can sometimes be a more valuable approach than trying to stay neutral on a topic.

They reason you will come across as more untrustworthy by trying to walk a middle ground. They argue we need to focus on building trust by being able to amicably discuss differences of opinions and beliefs instead. Wouldn't that be something?

I think I agree in part with this philosophy that trying to carry a middle ground can be fraught with issues. It can mask our authentic selves. This authentic leadership is the very quality that makes you who you are. Being able to weave together a team who has diversity in thought and opinions is actually where real strength can come from. If we encourage respect and tolerance of different perspectives and allow everyone on our teams to voice their thoughts, we'll strengthen our reputation as leaders.

Hope

If hope is not a strategy, what is it?

Several days into my hike, the weather shifted. This was all part of an unexpected massive cold front and associated storm that was supposed to stay well west of my location in the SNP according to so-called (air quotes) weather experts.

It started raining mid-morning, and by midday, the squalls were fierce, with the wind blowing hard and the rain stinging through my jacket. I could feel the temperature dropping and the strange sensation of warm wind blowing up one side of the ridge line and cold on the other.

My hope was to make it to the Skyland Lodge by sundown before the worst of the weather arrived. I had been checking the radar and forecast, and while I could see it was bad now, it would deteriorate further through the late afternoon and into the night. The forecast for the next day brought dangerous lightning, along with continued torrential rain and colder temperatures.

Skyland Lodge was the only accommodation open in the SNP at this time of year. The other Lodges in the park would open in early May in anticipation of good weather and the crowds of people who would come to enjoy nature up close and personal. The Lodge was within reach for me provided the weather gave me some breaks and the Trail allowed me to clock a faster time than I had been doing. I knew some elements were out of my control (the weather), some were unknown (state of the Trail), and some were firmly in my control (my effort). Hence, I had hope of a safe, warm bed that night. However, the risk management side of me had also decided on a Plan B if I was unable to make it to the Lodge in time.

As I hiked through the worsening weather, I thought about the concept of hope, what it really is and how it fits into leadership. I had hope on my mind as the 2024 Cystic Fibrosis Foundation annual Volunteer Leadership Conference (VLC) had discussed it as a key theme a few weeks earlier. The conference had a tag line of *Hope in Action*.

An extraordinary volunteer leader, Mike Beatty, spoke about hope in one of the keynote addresses. His impassioned words centered on a key concept that illuminated the power of hope. He said that it wasn't the amazing new drugs that had been developed to fight cystic fibrosis that gave us hope, but rather, it was our hope that had given us these amazing new drugs.

As the rain pelted my body, I thought about how Mike had framed the power of hope and how he had turned the conversation on its head, using hope to inspire me in such a meaningful way.

I had hope of reaching my goal of shelter for the night, and I have hope for a cure for cystic fibrosis.

Hope is a powerful tool for an informed leader.

As leaders, I think we can and should use hope as a powerful tool. Leaders must be inspirational as well as aspirational, and hope can provide a means to communicate both. Hope allows us to discuss the actions that are required in order to reach any aspiration in an objective and believable way.

Rick Page's 2001 iconic sales book *Hope Is Not a Strategy*[91] is an excellent book; however, too many people have picked up on the title alone and the word *hope* has become somewhat maligned in the business world as being a weak, ineffective word.

While I agree wholeheartedly that hope is not a strategy, that does not mean that it has no place in business. Hope is simply a measure and acknowledgment of doubt. Used as a noun, hope is a powerful descriptor, for instance, I have hope in our ability to deliver this project. At this point on the Trail, I had hope that I would reach the lodge. But used as a verb, hope is weak: I hope we can deliver this project. I hope I can reach the lodge.

When we use hope to express a measure of doubt, we also imply that if we address the risk or those things that have uncertainty, then we can further increase our chances of success and win the day—we will prevail.

My hope of reaching Skyland Lodge that evening was dashed on the slippery rocks of the Shenandoah Valley. The weather worsened, my pace slowed, and the afternoon progressed into early evening. I was only three miles from Skyland, but it was already getting dark, and the weather was awful. The temperatures had fallen steadily, the rain beat down, making the path dangerous, and the wind bent the trees as it came up over the ridgeline.

I knew that the safe option, Plan B, was going to be to find a spot to camp and get myself set up before darkness fell across the forest.

Bring in 'da Noise

Bring in 'da funk.

The rain was still falling steadily as I prepared my campsite for the night. I had found a stealth site near the top of a mountain that looked to be about as good a spot as I was going to get before dark arrived. I moved a few recently fallen twigs and branches from the flat piece of ground and then inspected the terrain with my risk background on full display.

First, I checked the trees above for dead branches. The wind was already blowing hard, and I didn't want one crashing down on me in the middle of the night. This is considered good practice for any camping spot regardless of the weather. Next, I checked the drainage as I knew it was going to rain heavily all night, and I didn't want to wake up with water pouring into my tent. Finally, I thought about which way around to pitch my tent so that it would have the least resistance to the wind.

Pitching the tent when it's raining is a juggling act as you try to keep as much rain out of the tent as you can before you get to secure the flysheet over it. I managed to do a pretty good job considering the rainfall, and soon everything was stowed and covered. Dinner was mac and cheese and my usual chamomile tea. After braving the rain and wind one last time to walk my bear canister into the woods, I was now ready for hiker midnight and a well-earned rest.

Several hours later, I woke to an unsettling sound. In my groggy state, I couldn't quite figure out why I was hearing the sounds of squealing tires on a racetrack. Half awake, I listened to repeated cars peeling away, imagining the smoke rising from the tarmac and that acrid smell of burning rubber in the air. Part of my brain knew this couldn't be true, but the sound was so convincing, so visceral. As I listened, the noise shifted into wild screams of ghouls terrorizing my tent. I had to force my mind to wake up and rationalize what I was hearing. The sound ebbed and flowed, and I was now awake enough to ascribe the noise to the wind. No drag cars. No dementors from Harry Potter trying to steal me off to Azkaban. Just the wind.

There is, of course, a scientific explanation for what I was hearing. When air moves through or over an object, it produces Aeolian sounds, named after Aeolus, the

Greek god of winds. Both the shape of the object and the velocity of the wind play a role in determining the resulting tone. Imagine each leaf or tree branch creating its own vortex in the wind. All these vortices then combine, oscillating at just the right frequency to create these extraordinary sounds. In the end, though, it's still just noise.

Know when something is just noise.

A leader can clearly articulate when something is just noise, when it's just the wind blowing, and not anything that can really impact what you're doing. This could be a simple internal re-organization. It could be messaging from a competitor or someone throwing around vague threats. Sometimes, it could feel like the dementors are coming for you, but you know that's really not the case.

I can remember a time when we were deep into a proposal to a customer and found out that a competitor, one we had never heard of, was going around telling everyone who would listen that they were a shoo-in for the project. Is it noise or something to be concerned about? Rather than react, we took the time to understand the answer to that question. We revalidated that our position was strong and that we had all our bases covered. We did our homework on the competitor and decided that this was, in fact, just noise. That is indeed what it turned out to be.

I will contrast this with another similar occasion when we didn't take the time to answer the question, "Just noise?" and lost an important deal as a result. The competitor brought an innovative approach to the table, and our client became enamored with this new solution. If we had inspected the noise to a greater degree, we likely would have recognized it and could have countered it. It was a frustrating loss knowing that we heard the metaphorical winds blowing but did nothing about it.

To be outstanding leaders, we must discern what is noise from what actually needs attention. Then we can communicate that across our teams and colleagues, resulting in a refocusing of energies on the activities that have real impact and consequences.

Trust

Of course, I trust you.

The next morning, the rain was not only torrential, it was cold. Somewhere around 34°F (1°C). It was close to being freezing rain. This is where the problem with my fingers developed. I had gloves with me, but not wet weather gloves, and I desperately wanted to keep my gloves dry. So, with bare hands, I set to work tearing down my camp. I can fully pack up in thirty minutes if need be.

My fingers would get numb quickly, and then I'd need to stop and warm my hands inside my dry gloves under my rain jacket. This continual process slowed me down significantly, especially as packing up requires some fine finger work to close clasps and adjust pull down ties. A miserable hour later, I was finally ready to leave. My pack was even heavier now, as much of what I carried was soaked through. This added several pounds of water weight to my load.

The first mile on the Trail was straight down, and while it was treacherous in the slippery mud, I was glad this part of the Trail was not full of rocks. Reaching the low point, I saw a sign for a pull-off that was on Skyline Drive. Day visitors could park for a few minutes here and walk the short distance up to a viewing point. I knew I was far behind schedule. The weather was ghastly, and the next two miles up to the pinnacle would be daunting. So, I headed to the road and see if there was anyone there who would give me a ride to the Lodge.

I made a plan that if no one drove by or stopped to pick me up in the next twenty minutes, then I would have no choice but to go back under the cover of the trees and ride out the storm right there.

There was one truck in the pull-off, but no one was around and there was no traffic on Skyline Drive. Trees bent over hard in the wind and the rain was so intense I couldn't see more than twenty feet. Suddenly, a guy came out of the forest with his young daughter. I assumed they had attempted to go to the viewing spot before turning around in the weather. I asked in my most polite British accent if there was any chance he could give me a ride up to the Lodge. Hurrying to his truck, his response was that he didn't think he had enough room.

I understood. It wasn't about room in the truck; it was about trust. He had his young daughter with him, and I was, as best as he could tell, a crazy homeless man, wandering around in a storm, in the middle of a wilderness. I wouldn't give me a ride either.

A minute later, his wife and son showed up, and they all hopped into the warm, safe truck. I stood by the side of the road doing my best job to look as miserable and harmless as I possibly good. I didn't need to try that hard. There's a great hiking term for this called "To Yogi Bear something." It's where thru-hikers try to get pity from others, usually so they will give us picnic food.

After a few minutes, the guy got back out of the truck and came back over to size me up. Obviously, they discussed the situation in the truck and decided that I might be worth the risk. Could they trust me? A brief conversation later, my pack was in the back of the truck and I was in the safety of the front passenger seat, explaining my adventures to the family. They were on spring break taking in some national parks and would now have a great story to take back home about the day they recused a hiker. I was grateful for the trust they showed in giving me the ride.

A short while later, I was safely in my spartan Skyline Lodge room while the storm unleashed its full force at the top of the mountain. As I lay on a soft, dry bed and listened to the thunder, I couldn't help but think about trust and the interconnectivity it has with hope.

Be a trusted leader.

Being a leader requires a keen understanding of all facets of trust. With our world's continued ability to manipulate perceptions of truth, it's becoming more of a societal issue as well.

Francis Frei, a Harvard Business School professor gave an excellent TED talk: *How to Build (and Rebuild) Trust.*[92] She breaks down trust as having three components—empathy, logic, authenticity. I thought about how my rescuers must have worked through those three components until they arrived at a decision to offer me a ride. Clearly empathy was an easy one as I must have looked miserable. Having spent time with them after the fact they were authentically kind and generous people. So that leaves logic as the component that they had to work through. Balancing the risk of giving a stranger a ride against the benefits of teaching their children a valuable lesson about helping someone in need.

But what does it mean to be a trusted leader?

If you research this topic, you will find a list that suits any attention span. It ranges from blog posts like "4 Things Trusted Leaders Do" to books by *Wall Street Journal* bestselling authors, such as David Horsager, who wrote *Trusted Leader: 8 Pillars That Drive Results.*[93]

Stephen Covey has a couple of books on this subject. *The Speed of Trust: The One Thing That Changes Everything*[94] takes a compelling perspective that trust is a fundamental differentiator and is something that you, as a leader, can learn and amplify throughout an organization. Like my comment on hope earlier, Covey inspects trust as a verb (something you create) versus trust as a noun (something you feel) and puts the focus on you as a leader clearly on the verb. *Trust & Inspire: How Truly Great Leaders Unleash Greatness in Others*[95] builds on this earlier work. The book takes the perspective that we must redefine leadership away from command and control and to one where a trusted leader is someone who trusts their colleagues and inspires their best as a result.

Hope and trust are intimately entwined, as trust also serves as a measure of doubt. "I trust in my team to deliver that project" is something that is based on experience and relationships. It's knowing that the team has what it's going to take to deliver the project based on objective data points. We have the right skills; we've done this before. It's a quantification of risk and doubt. If I have trust, then I have high hopes. If I have no trust, then I have little hope.

We all should aspire to be trusted leaders. As you grow as a leader, you can develop and hone this quality, even though it's grounded in intangible skills.

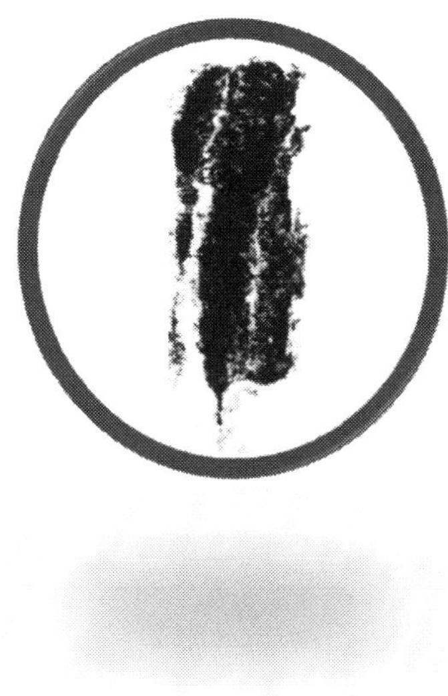

This section of the Trail presented me with some exceptional insights into leadership, hope, and trust. It forced me to consider how I trust, relate to hope, and the consequences for both. It also gave me the time to consider how I can leverage both as part of being a leader.

Hope and trust are blended into all of my White Blazes. How can we believe if we don't have trust? How can we take that first step if we don't have hope? Sometimes a Question White Blaze will force us to consider both trust and hope in a very immediate way. Do I trust this person standing right in front of me? Those are the everyday experiences that give us the opportunity to apply White Blaze Leadership.

The SNP is a stunning location that is easily accessible to so many in the mid-Atlantic region of the United States. I highly encourage you to add a trip along the Skyline Drive to your bucket list. I'd even be fine if you took your car along with you for the journey. Double-check the weather before heading out, though, and I trust that you will enjoy your adventure.

Section Twenty-One Campfire Conversations

- How would you describe your relationship with hope and trust, and how do they influence your decisions and actions?
- What experiences do you rely on when facing challenges, and how do they shape your approach?
- How do others perceive you as a leader, and what factors contribute to whether or not you are seen as trusted?
- In what ways might you be concealing your authentic self, and what impact do you think that has on your leadership or personal life?
- What is happening right now that you think might just be noise, and how do you distinguish between noise and what truly matters?

Section Twenty-Two

The Maine Event

Death by lightning or death by bear? I carefully weighed my options, knowing full well that this was not my finest hiking moment.

I crouched in the mouth of a small cave, somewhat concerned that a bear might live here. In front of me was a curtain of rain and the booming violence of thunder while the sudden summer storm unleashed its worst on this remote Maine mountain top. Behind me, my backpack blocked the tunnel that lead further into the darkness. It was my lame attempt to buy a few seconds should a beast actually live in there.

The fully developed storm appeared over the ridge of the mountain exactly as I ascended the final difficult climb to the summit. As happens during the summer, the morning forecast gave no warning except for the obligatory *scattered storms*. I'd had no cell service to that point, but I had now climbed high enough such that just as the storm appeared so did cell signal. My phone beeped urgently at me. "Find Shelter Immediately!" warned my weather app.

"No kidding," I thought as the rain moved in and the first bolts of lightning cracked down. This is how I found myself hiding in a damp, confined bear cave.

As the Appalachian Trail winds its way north-eastwards through western Maine, it does not give up the miles easily. In return for enduring challenging terrain, big climbs, hordes of black flies, difficult river crossings, and moose poop, I was gifted extraordinary wilderness views the likes of which I had not seen in all my hiking.

The Trail is so far north at this point that the summer days are long. It starts to get light around 4:30 a.m. and is still light past nine o'clock in the evening. This allows for long hiking days, which is just as well since the tough terrain makes for slow going.

Maine brought some hard-earned leadership insights, and obviously, neither bears nor lightning prevented me from completing this section.

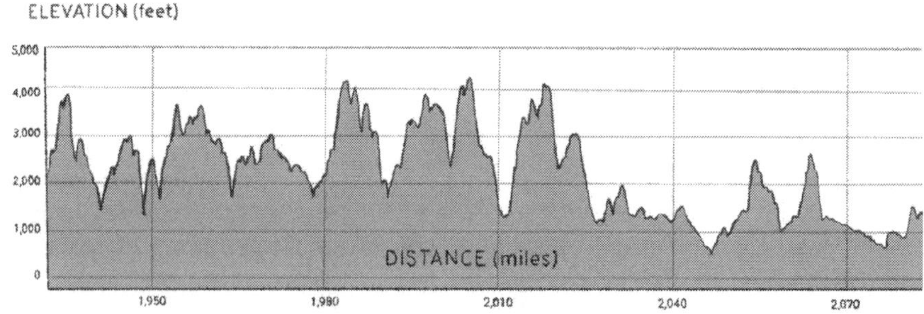

Figure 19 Grafton Notch, ME, to Monson, ME

Me Versus Carnivorous Plants

Feed Me.

As the shuttle driver pulled away from the trailhead, he shouted out the window, "Oh, make sure to look out for the carnivorous plants." Then, he was gone.

The dust rose from his tires and he disappeared down the remote logging road. I stood there for a moment, trying to reconcile his statement with what I knew about the dangers of hiking in Maine. Bear, Moose, Wolf, Lynx, and Cougar clearly make the dangerous list. Black flies claimed the top spot on the super annoying list. But I don't have a list of hungry plants that eat hikers.

While I spent a solid few hours lost in thought about this particular peril while trudging up the next mountain, it turned out that I didn't need to worry so much.

The purple pitcher plant (*Sarracenia purpurpea*) is carnivorous but thankfully grows to be only about a foot tall at the most, according to the United States Forest Service.[96] I found some beautiful specimens in the bogs, which are regular features of this part of Maine and often located further up the mountain than one might expect. It's exactly because the pitcher plant grows in these wetlands that it has evolved to catch insects. Typically, plants pull nutrients from the soil, but in these wetlands, that's not an option, hence the carnivorous approach.

The pitcher-shaped leaves collect rainwater, and because the bristles inside face downward, insects have an exceedingly difficult time getting out once they get in. After struggling, the insect will meet its doom when it falls into the water at the base of the pitcher and becomes part of the circle of life.

Keep on questioning.

As leaders, we must remember there's always someone who's intent on ruining our day. New businesses and business models evolve all the time with the express purpose of taking our hard-won market share. In my profession, cyber security, bad actors are everywhere, continuously creating new and innovative mayhem. They want to steal our data or shake us down for Bitcoin after a ransomware attack. The business equivalent of carnivorous plants abounds all around us.

It's imperative we, as leaders, never allow ourselves or our teams to become complacent to this reality. Continuing to question what competition and risks we face, what new threats might be emerging, and how to shift out of harm's way is an important part of leadership.

Crossing the River

No bridge too far.

I've waded across a few small streams during my Appalachian Trail adventures, but Maine elevates the game. Rivers, streams, brooks, and ponds all need to be crossed or forded without the aid of a bridge. There are over twenty crossings on the Trail in Maine that are more than thirty feet wide. The water levels on this section ranged from rock-hopping to waist-deep, and consequently, my feet stayed wet for hours at a time.

As you might imagine, the water levels highly depend on recent rainfall and accumulated rain totals. In 2023, there was so much rain that many of the river crossings became too dangerous, forcing hikers to find alternative routes around them. Now, in 2024, some crossings challenged my resolve but thankfully none felt overly dangerous or required me to find an alternative path.

At the small town of Caratunk, the crossing is always considered dangerous because of water releases from an upstream hydroelectric dam. The ATC came up with a unique solution. Here, during hiking season, a crossing service is provided with a guide who ferries hikers and their backpacks across the river in a canoe. A white blaze is painted on the canoe, making it an official part of the Appalachian Trail.

River crossings can be dangerous no matter how deep the water is. Much of this has to do with the properties of water and physics. According to a highly informative article on the website of the Pacific Crest Trails Association (PCTA), "Water weighs 62.4 pounds per cubic foot, and the pressure exerted by moving water increases with the square of its velocity."[97] I went down a bit of a rabbit hole trying to validate that, but sadly, my math skills just weren't up to it.

The point is that it's easy to lose your footing and have the weight of the water push you down into the stream or river. Combine the weight of the water with the weight of your backpack, and it's a recipe for disaster.

A few golden rules exist for a river crossing. Firstly, face the water and lean into the flow. This prevents the force of the water from pushing you over if you slip on a rock. Secondly, ensure that you have a grounded position with two firm foot placements and your hiking poles before taking another step. If you have other hikers with you, then techniques such as crossing as a triangle or in a wedge can help reduce the risk, especially for the weakest hikers. Finally, unclip the straps of your backpack. In this way if you do end up underwater, you should be able to wriggle free from your pack and surface.

Lean into challenges.

There are some far too obvious lessons here for what it means to be a leader.

The first might just be about knowing what to do in a given situation and preparing for it. Everyone knows that eventually we might find ourselves in a situation where the economy downturns, an unsavory incident happens in the workplace, or our organization is breached in a cyber-attack. But how many of us take the time to educate ourselves on what to do in those situations ahead of time? Educating ourselves is the first step.

Leaning into the problem is also another great leadership lesson. If we turn your back on a problem, as if ignoring it will make it go away, we're far more likely to suffer the consequences. Leaning into a problem, inspecting it, understanding what is happening and then using what we have to our advantage to counter it is great leadership.

The term *leaning into something* was popularized by ex-Meta COO Sheryl Sandberg in her 2013 book *Lean In: Women, Work and the Will to Lead*.[98] Her organization, LeanIn.org, says, "The book challenges us to change the conversation from what women can't do to what we can do, and serves as a rallying cry for us to work together to create a more equal world." She advocates for women to physically lean in at the table to be heard and project confidence, power, leadership. Sandberg's book created a firestorm of conversation around how women navigate work-life balance and, hopefully, will continue to stir discussion as we all lean in on this issue.

Finally, the power of working as a team can reduce the risk for everyone as long as we know how to pull our resources and work together.

Applying these insights from a leadership perspective might just get you, and your colleagues, safely to the other side of any river you choose to cross.

From Here to There

You can't get there, from here.

It's not only the Trail that is hard in Maine. The logistics of getting on and off the Trail are harder in Maine too. Trying to plan my sections, hiking days, resupply, and zero days all proved to be complex and something I had to rework as soon as I got up there.

I first heard this quintessential Maine saying from a shuttle driver I had called about a ride to a trailhead: "You can't get there from here." It's a great saying and one that is used to express how difficult it can be to drive to places that are deceptively close as the crow flies.

I experienced this firsthand when even a short thirty-five-mile section of the Trail would equate to double that distance by car to get from one trailhead to the other. Lakes, rivers, mountains, and a lack of roads all conspired against me to chew up time and money.

Know when to change how you get from here to there.

From a leadership perspective, this phrase holds a lot of power. We must be able to look at situations and know if we can "get there, from here." If *there* turns out to be an impossible task, then that's a point where a leader must coalesce everyone around them and form a plan to do something different.

I've seen this play out in our research to cure cystic fibrosis. The extraordinary advances in harnessing small molecules and new medicines have been a miracle for most of those fighting this disease—including my daughters. However, for the ten percent of people for whom these drugs don't work, there's no incremental improvement or next-gen version that will fix the problem. It's impossible to get there from here.

That's why the Cystic Fibrosis Foundation launched a $500 million program called "Path to a Cure,"[99] which drives research in cutting-edge biotech like gene editing and gene transfer. The Foundation knew we couldn't get *there from here*, so the leaders formulated a new plan to find a path forward that was achievable.

The conversation about not being able to get there from here is undoubtedly one of those hard conversations. It brings pride of ownership, fear of change, and uncertainty to the forefront. However, as leaders, it's our job to recognize these situations and do the hard things. If we do these hard things and have these hard conversations, then we can forge a path to *there*.

Zero-Days

A body at rest.

After five straight days of tough hiking, it was time for a zero day. A zero-day is one where you hike zero miles, usually staying at a hostel or at a budget motel in a trail town. If you only hike a few miles in a day, that is called a near-zero day or nero.

The frequency of zero days varies depending on the weather, hiking speed, available funds for accommodation, and the tramily one hikes with. On average, thru-hikers probably take a zero day every ten days. However, section hikers like me tend to need more frequent zero days as our legs aren't in the same condition as thru-hikers.

The primary purpose of zero days is to give the body a chance to rest and repair itself. An insane desire to eat anything and everything that a hiker can find usually accompanies these days. A whole large pizza? Bring it on. This is the fuel the body needs to activate and support the healing.

The fascinating Whoop blog article "Feels vs. Facts: Why You Still Need a Rest Day, Even When You're Feeling Good"[100] by David Roche & Megan Roche, M.D. explores the science behind rest days. The authors discuss the significant impact overtraining can have on the endocrine system. For example, missing rest days can lead to an excess of the hormone cortisol, or a decline in testosterone levels in men.

They warn that most injuries start well before we even notice them. Athletes who added downtime, often without even perceiving any injuries, experienced a significant improvement in running economy, which is the amount of oxygen a body needs to run at certain speeds. Using a large data set from users of Whoop, a health-tracking device, the authors conclude that taking rest days is a critical part of being a high-performing athlete.

Know when to take a zero day.

The leadership insight I'm going to highlight here might be obvious to you. We need to make sure that we build rest time into schedules and those of our teams. In the long-term, this will make everyone a better "athlete."

What rest looks like for you and your colleagues will vary greatly depending on the variables in your environment, just as it does for hikers. It could be short hours on Fridays before the busy season starts or as simple as taking everyone out to lunch. Ensuring that health and wellness training is available to everyone also goes a long way in helping us understand the power of rest as a way to improve our performance both in and outside of the workplace.

Three Days

Rest the mind.

I've always found the first few days back on the Trail to be tough hiking days. It's not just due to the physical nature of the Trail but also because of what is going on inside my head.

Usually, I'm carrying a lot of "noise" up there, and it takes a few days to settle down. I'm hiking along thinking about that report that I didn't finish, the important call I'm going to be missing, or something in my personal life that I'm going to need to get to as soon as I get off-trail. Noise.

However, by day three, I've always found that this noise dissipates. My surroundings seem to become crisper, and my thoughts, more even and measured, have quietened. The topics I tend to think about are either simple, like when will I stop to eat, or deeper and far more expansive than normal. For those bigger thoughts, it's as if I have better control of the process and can sift through ideas that had never even occurred to me previously.

The REI blog article "The Nature Fix: The Three-Day Effect"[101] cites compelling scientific research that confirms my suspicions this isn't just me making it up. It's an actual thing. Author Florence Williams draws on research from scientists who were studying Attention Restoration Theory (ART). ART proposes the restoration of higher-function prefrontal cortex-mediated executive processes through exposure to nature. These are processes such as selective attention, problem-solving, inhibition, and multi-tasking.

With an experiment designed with wilderness backpackers, the researchers showed that these unplugged hikers achieved nearly a fifty percent improvement in creative thinking and insight problem-solving. Further research showed that this effect occurred only in people who genuinely unplugged. Taking a vacation where you're on your phone all the time or binge-watching the latest must-see show in your hotel room won't help your creativity.

The article concludes that when we put ourselves in an environment that minimizes attention disruption and multi-tasking, our sensory perception, empathy, and productive day-dreaming step in to use those processing cycles.

Resting the mind is as important as resting the body.

As leaders, we need to set the example for how to take vacation time and learn how to do that properly ourselves. I'm fortunate to work for an organization that actively encourages everyone to disconnect when they take vacation time. If you struggle to remember your password when you get back, that's probably a good sign that you have had strong restorative time.

I also think the need to decouple ourselves from technology is critical when we're looking for true rest and relaxation. Sitting on the beach doom-scrolling isn't going to give our brains the chance they need to reset. Instead, read a book or just stare out at the waves.

Imagine coming back from a long weekend after being fully unplugged and having a fifty percent increase in your problem-solving and creativity. That would be worth every penny of the time you just took off.

Four Years

Olympiad.

As I was preparing for this section of the Trail, every news channel was ramping up its coverage of the upcoming Olympic Games to be held in Paris. It's the thirty-third Olympiad of the modern period and the seven hundredth since the Greeks got bored and decided some friendly competition between the city-states would be an excellent day out.

In ancient Greece, the word Olympiad was used as a measure of time—four years. Specifically, the Olympiad was the period between the games. The reason why the games were every four years is lost in antiquity, but today, all major global sporting events, from the Olympics to the World Cup, take place on a four-year cycle.

I spent a good deal of my time on this section thinking about my journey along the whole Appalachian Trail, as this fourth year of my plan will see me hike my final section and complete the full length of the Trail. At some point I got to wondering if four years spent doing something might carry a certain human significance.

High school is four years, as is college. From the Middle Ages up to today, apprenticeships also take around four years.

As I hiked through the dense forest of western Maine, I pondered if four years is the amount of time it takes for someone to go from immature to mature in all these endeavors. If you have natural talent, four years of training in a sport could get you into the Olympics. Four years in high school takes you through the cycle of "no clue, think you know, actually do know, got it, and ready to do something else."

This is perhaps the same cycle I have gone through over these last four years with my hiking. I look back at my early days and realize how much I had to learn, but now, with just one more major section hike later this year, I'm ready to stand at the top of Mount Katahdin and be done.

Practice patience.

We live in a world that is accelerating and one where we normalize instant gratification. When Amazon doesn't deliver that essential to you the same day, it's a disaster. The pace of technological change is running faster than we can, and artificial intelligence is only increasing that pace. But our ability to learn, mature, and become competent in our chosen domains does not accelerate at the same speed. Certainly, tools can help us learn faster, and access to ubiquitous information can help us become more knowledgeable, but nothing replaces experience.

Impatience might be one of the biggest aspects of the workplace that leaders have to contend with today. Not all impatience is unwarranted. There are times when we or our colleagues should be impatient. If our business is moving too slowly to adapt to changes, then it makes sense that team members might feel slowed down and become impatient.

What doesn't change, though, is real experience. You can't have experience unless you've failed. Unless you sat in that meeting or had to solve a hard problem. You can't have experience if you haven't built your network and learnt from people who have been there and done that. You can't have experience if you try to shorten the time to get to promotions and responsibility. Some things just take time.

Impatience is easy. We are all good at that. Leadership, though, is about finding the right balance between patience and impatience and helping colleagues understand when, why, and how to apply patience.

In the informative *Harvard Business Review* article "Becoming a More Patient

Leader,"[102] David Sluss found that the benefits of a patient leader were reflected in a thirteen percent increase in productivity and a sixteen percent increase in creativity and collaboration compared to a leader who was not considered patient. That's a significant impact on a business if you can find the right balance.

I'd like to think that I've become more patient as I've aged. It's something that I still need to work on, but I do try to be more intentional about my responses when things aren't going exactly how I would like them to go. Finding that balance comes down to really understanding the impact of being impatient versus patient.

There were times when dealing with my daughters' issues related to cystic fibrosis that I was impatient with good reason, and almost certainly times when I was impatient in situations where a little patience would have better served my daughters. I'm grateful to all the people who were patient with me in those situations.

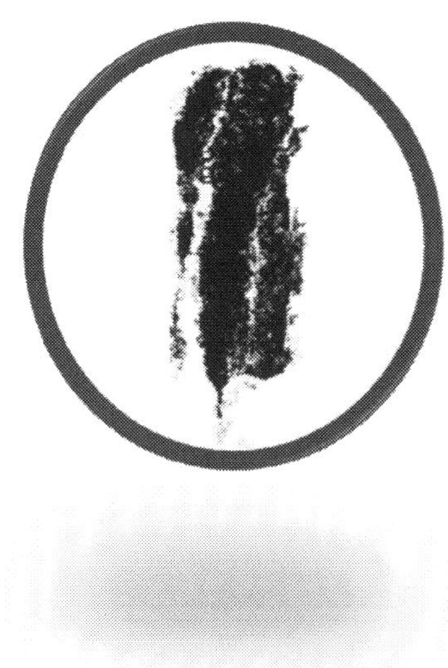

This section of the Trail provided a strong reminder that just because we're near the end of a journey doesn't mean it gets easier. Keeping the intensity, the desire to deal with new challenges, and the mindset to get to completion were all brought to the forefront. It was perhaps my thinking about patience that helped me to realize that patience is indeed a strong foundation for dealing with these aspects of the hike and of my professional career.

I previously mentioned that contemplation and the time required to contemplate might be the secret ingredients of White Blaze Leadership. Certainly, the more you practice, the more natural recognition of your White Blazes come, allowing insights from your day-to-day to flow. Finding the time can be difficult for all of us, but ultimately, time is in our control. Be it zero days or four-year plans, which of your White Blazes can you use to find the time and think about your leadership?

The remote wilderness of western Maine is humbling in its scale. The small towns that dot the landscape are few and far between, but as always, the people I met both on the Trail and in the small towns were warm and welcoming.

Remember how I was hiding in the bear cave? Well, thankfully, if there was a beast in there, it chose not to come out. I patiently waited for the storm to pass, gathered my belongings, gathered myself, and scrambled up to the top of the mountain, keeping one eye over my shoulder just in case the bear had woken from its slumber. With the storm now dissipated, the view from on top was exceptional.

Sometimes, patience really does pay dividends.

Section Twenty-Two Campfire Conversations

- How deeply do you understand your competition, and in what ways do you use that understanding to inform your strategies?
- How do you approach the challenges—the rivers you must cross—and do you lean into them fully, or do you resist?
- Are there problems you're facing where the current approach feels blocked, and how might you rethink or reassess the situation to move forward?
- How do you intentionally rest and recharge both your mind and body, and what makes that time meaningful for you?
- How do you balance patience and impatience, and what guides you in knowing when to wait and when to take action?

Section Twenty-Three

The 100 Mile Wilderness

Like any good video game, the Appalachian Trail throws one of its biggest, baddest boss levels at you right before the big ending. In this case, it's the 100 Mile Wilderness in remote northern Maine. Get through this next one hundred miles and all that's left to conquer is Mount Katahdin.

The warning sign helpfully posted at the start of the hundred miles implores me not to head onwards unless I have "a minimum of 10 days supplies and are fully equipped." It doubles down on this by also stating, "Its difficulty should not be underestimated." It doesn't specify what fully equipped means, but I suspect it includes enough calories, enough ibuprofen, and a healthy dose of courage.

The Trail has taught me well, and there's no way I would underestimate this next one-hundred-mile section. The sheer scale of it, its remoteness, and its reputation all weighed heavily on me, as did my pack. As always, the weather would be a determining factor in how much pain the Trail was about to inflict.

At this time of the year, mid-September, I knew the weather could vary between perfect 62°F (17°C) hiking weather and miserable rainy days of 40°F (4°C). Even though I felt like the Trail owed me good weather for everything it's put me through, I still packed my cold weather gear and rain gear as I knew the Trail was indifferent to my suffering.

As it turned out, the Trail took pity on me and provided perfect hiking weather and an extraordinary week navigating this breathtaking wilderness.

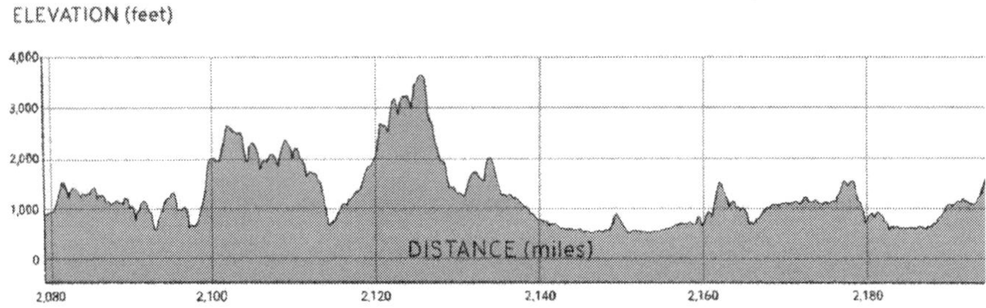

Figure 20 The One Hundred Mile Wilderness, ME

Great Branding

100 Mile Wilderness? That sounds scary!

Most people will think you're a little bit crazy if you tell them you're off to hike the

100 Mile Wilderness. They aren't completely wrong about that, but the reality is that it isn't the hardest, or the most dangerous, part of the Appalachian Trail. It just has really great branding.

For my part, I acquiesced to not hiking solo for this section, so my good friend, trail name Fixer, agreed to accompany me. He had never overnight backpacked before, so the 100 Mile Wilderness definitely sounded scary to him, his friends, and family.

Like me, Fixer has two children with cystic fibrosis. His daughter, Jena, lost her battle with this awful disease when she was just thirteen years of age. Over the last thirty years, Fixer has been a leader in raising the funds required to buy the science that will one day cure cystic fibrosis. Fixer joining me for one more fund-raising mission was deeply meaningful to both of us.

The 100 Mile Wilderness essentially divides into two parts. The first forty-two miles from Monson, Maine, to the top of White Cap Mountain has some big, hard technical climbing. Classic Trail punishment. The last fifty-eight miles are mostly Appalachian Trail flattish miles with beautiful lakes and stunning views as Mount Katahdin comes closer and closer. Don't let the word *flattish* deceive you. Trust me, the majority of those last fifty-eight miles aren't easy. Tree roots carpet those miles and will trip you up in an instant if you let your attention drift.

Hikers can get a food drop at the thirty-mile and sixty-mile markers. Hostels like Shaws use remote logging roads to bring fresh supplies to weary hikers. This means you can manage your pack weight over the arduous first part and then pick up bigger miles in the second half.

The 100 Mile Wilderness is indeed a challenge and shouldn't be underestimated. It demands and requires the right preparation. It inspires you to succeed but will remind us who the boss is if it's not given due respect. However, I would maintain that the given title of 100 Mile Wilderness is more brand marketing than a warning for experienced hikers.

Align your brand and your values.

Building your own brand is one of the most important aspects of leadership. Not all leadership styles are the same and not all leaders are cut from the same cloth. This is a good thing. We don't live in the 1960s corporate cookie-cutter ideal of leadership any longer. We live in a world where anyone can aspire to leadership, and everyone should have that opportunity.

You play a central role in shaping your brand. What matters is not only what you say and do but also what you say you do and say. The closer those two things align, the greater your team's belief in your leadership.

Have you ever written down your leadership brand? Can you? Does it match the reality of your day-to-day? Writing down that brand can actually help anchor your actions closer to your ideal brand on an ongoing basis.

Your brand needs to be succinct but also align with who you are. A representation of your value. If you want to be known as the most innovative leader, build your brand around that. If you want to be known as the most knowledgeable about your industry, go for it. The attributes of your leadership brand are totally within your control. Aspire to it, own it, live it.

Rebellion

Stand Tall.

Most people will tell you that a tax on tea sparked the Revolutionary War. However, I'm now in the group that will tell you it was the eastern pine trees of northern Maine that led to the Rebellion and the Declaration of Independence.

As I traveled further along the 100 Mile Wilderness, the forest became filled with these majestic trees. Known as the Sequoias of the Northeast, they can stand over two hundred feet tall and grow dead straight into the sky. Their presence drew me in as if they had a gravity all of their own and, living for hundreds of years, a story of their own to tell me, too.

In the mid-1600s, these trees drove the new world economy as the demand for ship masts was a critical issue for England. Across Britain, oak trees were depleted, with most of the mast-sized trees already felled or standing in enemy territory across Europe. The British Navy needed these trees to make masts so it could continue its domination of the high seas. Britain literally stamped its mark, known as the Kings Broad Arrow, on the largest of the eastern pines. Three vertical cuts with an axe in the shape of an arrowhead on the tree trunks told colonists that the trees didn't belong to them—they belonged to the Crown.

Needless to say, and quite predictably, the colonists weren't down with this dominion, which led to the Pine Tree Riot of 1772.[103] The excellently named Ebenezer Mudgett led a riot against the British after they raided his sawmill and arrested him for cutting down Kings Broad Arrow marked trees. Mudgett's act of defiance showed that the British were vulnerable, and his action led directly to the actions of the Boston Tea Party a year later. The eastern white pine was the emblem chosen to be part of the first colonial flag, clearly demonstrating its importance to the founding of the United States.

It's unlikely that any trees marked with the King's Broad Arrow still exist. Extensive logging in the nineteenth and twentieth centuries has left little of the old-growth forest. The Appalachian Trail runs through the Hermitage National Natural Landmark in the 100 Mile Wilderness, which contains some of the oldest eastern pines. I can't help but peer up and into the dense woods and wonder if just maybe.

Small acts can have great consequences.

Even small acts of leadership hold the potential for significant change. I'm sure Ebenezer couldn't even imagine that his leadership would result in the formation of the United States of America. I often think about this aspect of leadership when I'm raising dollars to buy the science that will cure cystic fibrosis.

Small donations can have the biggest impact. It could be the twenty US dollars that buys a test tube that holds the eventual cure. You just don't know. I love the following saying: "You know how many seeds are inside an apple, but you have no idea how many apples are inside a seed."

That is leadership. Cultivating seeds. Understanding that every action has its consequences, and it's your job as a leader to set the direction for those consequences even if you can't see all the way out.

New Tricks

You Can Teach an Old Moose New Tricks.

It turns out that I had been using my hiking poles incorrectly since the very first time I grasped a pair and headed into the woods. Normally, I would just hold them by the handles and hike along, using them to provide stability and support my efforts. However, my hiking partner for this section, Fixer, decided he would educate me on the errors of my ways.

The right way to use poles, he informed me, is to lace your hand up through the loop and then bring it back down so that the meaty bottom part of your palm rests on the strap. In this way, you can relax your grip on the handle and the poles will still do their work. In addition, if the pole gets stuck in a rock gap or mud, it stays attached to you. Simply tug up with your hand, and the pole will be free again.

I listened carefully to Fixer explain all this to me and then considered my options. I could ignore his advice because, after all, I'm an experienced hiker. What does he even know? Or I could actually try his advice.

Taking the mature route, I agreed to test out his method. "It will take a little getting used to," he advised, "but once you get it, you will understand." Sure enough, it took me a day of having to think about how I was looping the straps on my hands, and by the second day, it had become just the way I did it. Every time the technique paid dividends, Fixer would give me an encouraging nod as if to say, "Good job for learning something new."

Always be open to learning new things.

It can be difficult for leaders to admit that they don't know everything and that there's room to grow, learn, and change. This bias toward inertia in learning can be powerful. Leaders need to be intent on making the time to reflect on new ideas and how those ideas might impact their leadership and the teams they lead.

The Irish playwright George Bernard Shaw famously stated, "Progress is impossible without change, and those who cannot change their minds cannot change anything." It's worth thinking about that statement and asking yourself the question, "Am I open to new ideas?"

A 2021 article in the *HCA Healthcare Journal of Medicine on Leading Organizational Learning* concludes with the following:

The global, competitive environment in which organizations compete requires leaders who are adaptive, highly communicative and have a high acumen for continuous, in situ learning. Leaders who possess these attributes and the capability to serve as a positive role model for organizational members create foundational elements for their organizations to manage the myriad of forces slowing successful progress.[104]

Being a leader who values learning, whether that means digging into the impact of GenAI, the latest in regulatory laws, or any number of new technology opportunities, can only add value to you and your organization.

White Cap

A view that is earned.

White Cap Mountain is the highest point in the 100 Mile Wilderness at 3,644 feet. It's a challenging climb, but the Maine Appalachian Trail Club (MATC) has done an incredible job of maintaining the Trail, making it far from the hardest ascent I've done.

Once I reached the top, I was rewarded with some of the most extraordinary views on the whole Trail. On a clear day, like it was, I could see south almost all the way to the New Hampshire border, where Old Speck Mountain reaches four thousand one hundred forty feet. I easily picked out the peaks of the Bigelows, even though they are one hundred miles south from this point.

Walking over to the viewing point looking north from White Cap, I took in an awe-inspiring view of Mount Katahdin, seventy-three miles away. Mount Katahdin stood on its own, rising from the broad, tree-filled plain that sat between me and that final challenge. From up here, I was greeted with nothing but the immense forest and the distant peaks of other mountains dotting the horizon.

The immensity of the wilderness caught me by surprise, and the sight of Mount Katahdin brought forth unexpected tears as I thought about completing this four-year journey and the bigger mission to cure cystic fibrosis that had inspired the first step.

Look for value in the moment.

Sometimes, the view you get as a leader is worth everything you put into achieving that role. It could be seeing a colleague get promoted or receiving the gratitude of a client for a job well done. Perhaps it's Board approval for a new strategy or as simple as a thank you from a team member.

Whatever that moment is, learn to embrace it and accept it with the gratitude that it deserves.

Succession

Nothing lasts forever.

As I headed into the wilderness for this final major section of the Appalachian Trail, I was acutely aware that my equipment and my body were both showing signs of wear and tear from this four-year journey.

The bag that straps to the back of my pack and carries my tent poles had a huge hole in it. This required some serious MacGyvering to secure the poles and make sure they didn't just fall out on the Trail. An essential clasp on my pack had gotten smashed on a rock along the way and was unusable. My dirty water bag had a few pinhole leaks, and the tent had a rip in the roof fabric, which was letting in bugs at night. Nothing serious, just the consequences of quality products being well used.

I knew going in that my calf muscle could be a problem. Recently, I had been studiously ignoring the nagging pain from it as I hiked along. It was nothing that a healthy dose of ibuprofen, tiger balm, and my ability to ignore it couldn't deal with. Overall, I had been injury-free for most of the four years, except for one dance with COVID, which put me out of hiking commission for a month. However, I really could feel those years starting to catch up with me.

Believe in the next generation.

As leaders, we should all have one eye on succession planning. It's not something that we can do at the last minute and requires us to think about the future. At some point in time, we simply won't be in the leadership position we are in now. Hopefully, we are on to different challenges with new opportunities to lead that match our skills and desires.

However, it's incumbent on us to leave the new leadership team in a strong position to pick up the reins. This means developing talent, providing opportunities to gain experience, and engaging with sage advice when things don't go as planned. It also means providing encouragement even when a new leader's brand or direction isn't the same as yours.

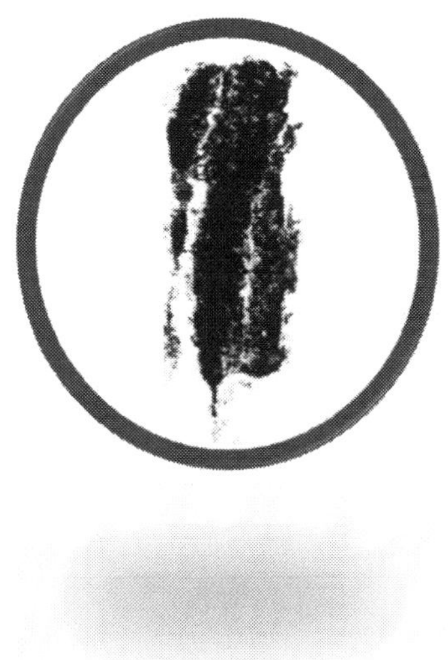

The 100 Mile Wilderness turned out to be not so scary after all. The scale of the forest and the majesty of the eastern pines felt like home. The eerie sound of the loons echoing off the broad lakes overnight and the incessant chittering of the red squirrels laid down a soundtrack that soothed my soul. Hiking with Fixer allowed me to talk out some of the emotions of this final section and our shared mission to cure cystic fibrosis, not just in a manly men-hiking-the-100-Mile-Wilderness-in-kilts kind of way, but in a meaningful life-is-amazing kind of way.

When I finally stepped out of the woods, it was a brief walk to Abol Bridge. From there, I got an unrestricted view of Mount Katahdin. No longer distant, it felt so close it seemed like I could reach out and touch it. That 4,179-foot climb to the summit, the sheer rock walls, the voices in my head—that's all I have to face to complete the Appalachian Trail. Mount Katahdin stands there, daring me to climb it: "I dare you. I double dog dare you."

Section Twenty-Three Campfire Conversations

- How would you describe your leadership brand, and what key qualities do you want it to reflect?
- Is there an idea or opportunity you have that holds great potential, but you haven't yet acted on? How might you begin to plant that seed?
- How have you approached long-term succession planning, and what steps are you taking to ensure a strong future for your team or organization?
- What bold challenge or risk—a "double-dog dare"—is pushing you right now, and how do you plan to face it?

Section Twenty-Four

Mount Katahdin

Just after five o'clock in the morning, as I headed to the trailhead to start my final day on the Appalachian Trail, I saw for the first time a moose. The sky was still dark, and the early morning fog danced around the thick trees. In front of me, the moose, standing broad and tall like some mythical creature, seemed to acknowledge me with a tilt of his head. He moved slowly in the trailhead's direction as if to say, "This way."

He walked ahead and, looking back at me one last time, disappeared into the trees, lost in the enveloping darkness. I took the magical moose as an omen that the forest approved.

"I'm ready."

Seven hours and an arduous 4,200-foot climb later, I stood atop the 5,267-foot summit of Mount Katahdin—the finishing point for my odyssey on the Appalachian Trail.

Behind me was five miles of unrelenting ascent, including a mile of mostly steep rock climbing. At times, that climb felt as dangerous as it probably was, but I crushed it. I was living in the zone. I channeled my four years of Trail experience and my four years of toughening my mind to deliver a worthy trail-ending performance, if I do say so myself.

Summitting Katahdin did not turn out to be a singular defining moment. There was no sudden feeling that everything was different or that somehow a new door had been opened or even one closed. I had spent time with my mental toughness coach discussing how to deal with moments of failure, but never about moments of success. And here I was in one of my greatest moments of triumph, completing the Appalachian Trail, and I hadn't prepared myself mentally.

After taking the required photos, I didn't know what to do, what to say, or what to think. I hadn't even considered that ahead of me I had an arduous descent back down the mountain.

So, I did what I had done many times on this journey, I found myself a perfect rock to sit on and contemplate. From high atop Mount Katahdin, I could see forever out across the forests of Maine. I closed my eyes and peered into my memories of the Trail.

Inspire, Believe

Choose the hard things.

I could see back along the thick forests of Maine all the way to the White Mountains of New Hampshire. The howling gale on top of Mount Lafayette was as fresh in my mind on the final day as it was on that brutal day in August 2023 when it tortured me. I witnessed the Appalachian Trail as it dropped into the flatlands of southern New Hampshire, and I recalled the torrential rain and endless blackflies I endured hiking through there and Vermont in the summer of 2023.

I looked further south as the Trail wound through ninety miles of Massachusetts wilderness and into my nemesis, the state of Connecticut. There, the short fifty-two miles took me far too long to hike and almost had me quitting my mission. Southbound from there, it was an extraordinary hike through New York and New Jersey in the summer of 2022, replete with bear encounters and violent storms.

Pennsylvania took two full hiking seasons, 2021 and 2022, to complete. Its 229 miles tormented me with more rocks than I ever cared to see again, and I sometimes wondered if my bones would ever recover.

A short hop through Maryland and West Virginia, and then further south to Virginia with its 544 miles. Virginia was the only state I hiked through in all four years. I became enamored with the unspoiled beauty of southern Virginia and the Blue Ridge sections of the Trail. The memory of my mum's passing and my healing time on the Trail in Virginia was brought front and center again. I know she would be so proud of this accomplishment.

North Carolina and Tennessee seemed so far away now, both in distance and time hiked, but with my eyes closed tight, the Great Smoky Mountains shone with all their brilliance. The rugged mountains gave way to the final section of Georgia and the Appalachian Trail's starting point at Springer Mountain, 2,197.4 miles away.

I held it all in my mind for a few fleeting moments and then opened my eyes. The Trail was gone, and in front of me, I witnessed a stunning vista of Maine's endless forests from my perch atop Mt. Katahdin.

I thought about the deep-rooted leadership lesson of doing the hard things and seeing them through. One of the main takeaways from the journey is that leadership is choosing to do the hard things. It's choosing integrity over convenience. It's choosing to stand up and step onto the path. Leadership is about believing in yourself and using your actions to inspire others to believe in themselves.

Value, Question

Make a positive difference.

I closed my eyes again and focused on my mission—my *why* for being out here. I thought about all those who came before me in the fight to cure cystic fibrosis—legends in this battle like Mary Weiss, Doris Tulcin, Frank Deford, and Bob Beall. These are just a few of the giants upon whose shoulders we stand.

I thought about the thousands of young lives lost across the years, like Jena, and the families who fought, grieved, and continue to fight to cure this disease. I reveled in our miraculous progress and how my daughters now have a bright future ahead of them.

The dedication of so many scientists, caregivers, volunteers, and Cystic Fibrosis Foundation staff has made this future our reality—each devoting their life's work to the same mission of curing this disease. These are the people who have questioned what is possible, valued every single life, and pushed the boundaries of modern medicine. They have made the impossible possible.

Then I thought about those still without an effective treatment, those who have endured a lung transplant, and those whose outlook remains uncertain. This part of my journey, my time on the Appalachian Trail, is done. However, the bigger mission to cure cystic fibrosis still casts another trail ahead, one with new challenges and bigger mountains yet to be summited. It's a trail we must embark on if we are to reach the finish line of a cure.

Lastly, I thought about leadership from the perspective of our responsibility to give back and to make a difference in society. You have everything it takes to make an impact on whatever scale you choose to make it. Choose your trail magic and go deliver it.

Another one of my main takeaways from the journey is to choose to make a positive difference in someone else's life. That is leadership.

Act, Lead

Lead in the quiet moments of the everyday.

I opened my eyes again and became aware of other hikers at the summit of Mount Katahdin—thru-hikers who had completed their own journeys at the same point in time as me. I wondered about their missions, their pasts, and their futures.

I contemplated how the history of the United States is woven into the fabric of the Appalachian Trail. Katahdin (*Greatest Mountain*) is sacred to the Penobscot tribe, who believe the mythical thunderbirds live inside the mountain and protect us. America's indigenous peoples had an entire history with the Appalachian Trail before we thrust the Revolutionary War upon it, before we tore it apart with the Civil War, before we tore down its ancient forest to build our cities and homes, before we destroyed six billion chestnut trees with our imported diseases, and before acid rain and climate change altered the very fabric of the forests.

I felt immense gratitude for the extraordinary wonder of the Appalachian Trail and the thousands of volunteers and professionals who work on our behalf to preserve it for future generations. I remained hopeful that we can, and will, bring the forests of the East Coast back to their healthy state.

And I was grateful for the extraordinary gift the Trail had given me over my four-year journey, offering me opportunities to consider leadership and what it means to be a leader. The Appalachian Trail has forged me into a better man and a better leader.

The biggest message I want to share from this journey is that leadership is not about hubris or the loudest voice. It's not about corner offices, how many people work for you, or our titles. It's about leading in the everyday—in the quiet moments of our day-to-day life.

Seizing opportunities to lead in these quiet moments requires us first to recognize the moment when it appears and then to interpret what it's telling us, perhaps in ways we might never have imagined. Finally, to truly seize the opportunity to lead, this moment requires us to take action to show that leadership.

Even if the action seems inconsequential in the moment, or even if we're deep in a forest, these are the actions that define each of us as leaders.

Choose to lead in the quiet everyday moments, and then leadership in the big moments will come naturally. This is White Blaze Leadership: Recognize. Interpret. Lead.

This journey started with a simple step onto the Appalachian Trail on the morning of April 2, 2021. Four years later, I look out from the summit of Mount Katahdin, and at just after noon, September 15, 2024, I take the first step into my next adventure.

Acknowledgements

I did not define gratitude as one of my White Blazes but rather as foundational across all my White Blazes. However, here is a moment to pull it to the forefront and to be genuinely grateful for everyone who helped me on the journey and in the creation of this book.

For everyone I met on the trail and especially for those I hiked some of the miles with thank you for that shared experience. The memories of those miles stay with me, from relentless climbs and bear encounters, to bog traverses, stream crossings, crazy weather, remote shelters, and mosquito madness. I trust that you will continue to walk well, find clean water, and discover flat ground on which to pitch your tent. I apologize for any torture I might have inflicted upon you (especially you Sting.)

There can never be enough thank yous for the women and men who dedicate themselves to maintaining the Trail. I thank you for your mostly unseen work. Please know I saw it and my gratitude is deeper for knowing that you are out there.

"The Trail will provide" is a saying that is fulfilled by the trail angels, hostel keepers, and shuttle drivers who make the logistics of section hiking the Trail almost bearable. Thank you for being there exactly when needed.

To my family, friends, and colleagues who supported me in ways big and small, please know that you took every step with me in our shared mission to cure cystic fibrosis. I couldn't have done it without you. Especially you, Stuart, my #inthistogether crew, my XtremeHike family, and Greg, whose mental toughness coaching was essential.

Can I thank the Appalachian Trail? Sure I can. It is a truly remarkable wonder of the world. We live in an extraordinary time with the technology and capacity to protect and ensure the Trail is there for generations to come. We must find the will power to make sure that happens.

Writing and then creating a book out of that writing turns out to be a hard journey in its own right. For those of you who read early versions of the book or my LinkedIn posts and provided feedback I thank you.

I could not be more grateful that I had the incredible Mathews sisters to guide and support me through the process. Angie, your mastery of commas is only second to your endless enthusiasm for me and for the mission to cure cystic fibrosis. Val (at valmathews.com), your ability to shape and edit the ramblings of a hiker into an actual "real book" is extraordinary. I'm just going to keep you two on the long trail with me.

And finally, I'll come back to my mission, my why, which is to find a cure for cystic fibrosis. Thank you, Olivia, James, and Sophie for being my inspiration. Thank you to everyone searching for a cure. Thank you to everyone who has donated or helped us move further down the trail towards a cure in any capacity. Please know that I will remain out here, on the long trail, until we can say that there is a cure for each and every person with cystic fibrosis.

Equipment and Provisions

I am often asked about the equipment and provisions I used for my four-year journey on the Appalachian Trail. The following is not a full list, just a list of my primary and favorite ones. No sponsorships were provided for my hike.

Equipment

Boots: Merrell Moabs 2 and 3 (non-waterproof). Over the four years I went through about twelve pairs including training and Trail time. I can't say enough about these shoes. Never once had an issue with my feet. That might sound like a lot of pairs, but what you wear on your feet is the most fundamental equipment choice you can make. I get around four hundred miles per pair. Less if the weather made them so disgusting, I had to discard them. There are wonderful shoe choices out there, but I chose to stick with the mantra "if it ain't broke don't fix it" for all four years. Merrell people, thank you, you are awesome.

Socks: Darn Tough Hiker Micro Crew cushion socks are designed to last. They might seem expensive for a sock, but they come with a lifetime guarantee and compliment the notion that what you wear on your feet is the most fundamental equipment choice you can make. My biggest problem was losing individual socks, so I ended up buying the same pattern every time I bought a pair. That's solid sock risk management strategy.

Crocs: Tie-Dyed Crocs. (Thanks, Sting). My favorite overall piece of equipment. This stylish pair of tie-dyed Crocs would hang outside my pack and the first thing I would do as I got into camp is take off my boots and put these on. They were an oasis for my tired, bruised, smelly, swollen feet.

Location Device: Garmin InReach Mini GPS Satellite communicator. This satellite tracker provided peace of mind for the more remote parts of the Trail. It could pinpoint my location and had an emergency SOS button that allowed for two-way communication with an emergency response team.

Kilt: SportKilt.com. Hiking kilts are comfortable, lightweight, versatile, quick drying and of course make you the most stylish guy out on the Trail. I own four hiking kilts and have Trail tested them to the max. It might seem a little eccentric to an outsider, but kilts are a thing on the Appalachian Trail and an engaging conversation piece with other hikers. I will admit that I wore a pair of shorts into town on most occasions.

Outer Jacket: Patagonia Nano Puff Jacket. Weighing less than twelve ounces my first thought was that no way this could keep me warm. I can't fathom how the team at Patagonia made this jacket, but it did indeed keep me warm even on the coldest days and my jacket survived all four years of hard Trail wear.

Gloves: I could not find a pair of gloves that would keep my fingers warm on cold days. I went through about three pairs per hiking season trying to find something that would work. I use a silk liner and those hand warmer pouches, paired with gloves that advertised keeping me warm no matter how cold it is. They did not. Gloves were also a close second in their lose-ability to socks. I did manage to hold onto a pair of Outdoor Research gloves that got close to doing the job.

Pack: Osprey Atmos AG 65. I don't know what material they make this from, but I subjected it to heavy Trail abuse for four years and the pack never once let me down. We should make everything to this level of durability. There are lighter packs for the ultralight hiking crew, but I enjoyed the sturdiness of my pack versus the ultra-lights. Like that movie with Tom Hanks where he makes friends with Wilson the basketball, I will admit that I have a strong relationship with my pack. My only gripe with my pack is that written on its back it says in big letters *anti-gravity*. Loaded to capacity with fresh supplies and winter gear it most certainly does not have anti-gravity.

Poles: Trekology. I also don't know how they engineer these collapsible poles to be so resilient. I broke my first pair descending a sheer rock wall in the White Mountains after giving them years of hard Trail suffering. It felt as if the pole sacrificed itself to save me from a terrible injury. I ordered a new pair as soon as I got internet service. Hiking poles might seem a little awkward at first but trust me on this, they are essential equipment, especially on the downhills.

Tent: Nemo Hornet 2P. It's stunning how light these tents are and how small they pack down to. At two pounds and five ounces it was the perfect tent for me and big enough to accommodate myself and my pack for those nights with heavy rain.

Cold Weather Sleeping Bag: My Nemo 15 Disco sleeping bag was comfortable, but more importantly kept me warm in dangerously cold temperatures. Rated down to 15°F (-9°C) I paired this with a Sea to Summit Thermolite Rector

Extreme Sleeping Bag Liner that provided another fifteen degrees of warmth for those nights that were colder than 15°F.

Stove: MSR PocketRocket 2. At 2.6 ounces in weight, this thing packs a heating punch that made sure my morning coffee was ready to go in no time. It sounds like the afterburner on a fighter jet when you crank it up.

Water Filter & Bag: Sawyer Squeeze Water Filter System. I carried this light weight and easy to use filter along with a mini version of the same for a backup. I paired this with a one liter Cnoc water bag as my dirty-water bag. Filtering water out of a stream was the most grounding of activities for me on the Trail. Knowing that this filter protected me every time was comforting.

Bear Cannister: Garcia Backpackers Cache. I could just about fit five days' worth of food inside it. It doubled as an excellent seat and with brightly colored duct tape wrapped around it acted as a handy MacGyver tent repair kit. One day, when the torrential rain would not stop, I even used it as a water barrel to collect the rain so I didn't have to hike to a stream. One final use was as somewhere to put the Trail stickers I picked up at various locations along the way. Later into the trip as the terrain became even harder and I needed to lower the weight of my pack I moved to an Ursack and shaved off two pounds.

Meals

Breakfast: Oatmeal, peanut butter, and coffee (medium roast premium instant).

Lunch: Tortilla, Peanut butter, Tuna Packet.

Dinner: (favorite) Backpackers Pantry Pad Thai. I would save this for after the hardest day of a section. Decaf Chamomile Tea.

Snack: Homemade trail mix of Sour Patch Kids (original flavor), dry roasted salted peanuts and white yogurt raisins. Don't judge me.

Drink: Nuun electrolytes were an essential part of my provisions, and I would make a point to use one tablet a day. Dr. Pepper was the craving whenever I got back into civilization.

Reading List

Endurance: Shackleton's Incredible Voyage by Alfred Lansing. Leadership and survival.

Breath from Salt: A Deadly Genetic Disease, a New Era in Science, and the Patients and Families Who Changed Medicine Forever by Bijal P. Trivedi. A history of the race to cure cystic fibrosis.

Can't Hurt Me: Master Your Mind and Defy the Odds by David G[illegible]s. A manual for mental toughness.

The Business of Winning: Insights in Transformation from F1 by Mark Gallagher. How to win.

Lord of the Flies by William Golding. Terrific book on leadership not so good on pest control.

Dictator: The Evolution of the Roman Dictatorship by Mark B. Wilson. No leadership reading book list is complete without something about the Romans.

The Overstory by Richard Powers. A complex, powerful read. It will make you want to hug a tree.

The Hidden Life of Trees by Peter Wohlleben. It will make you want to hug another one.

Finding the Mother Tree: Discovering the Wisdom of the Forest by Suzanne Simard. You are now a tree hugger.

Not Without Peril: 150 Years of Misadventure on The Presidential Range of New Hampshire by Nicholas Howe. The title tells you everything you need to know.

Business Chemistry: Practical Magic for Crafting Powerful Work Relationships by Kim Christfort and Suzanne Vickberg. A secret business advantage.

Breath: The New Science of a Lost Art by James Nestor. Making us think about something we take for granted.

The Impossible First: From Fire to Ice——Crossing Antarctica Alone by Colin O'Brady. Make impossible, possible.

Mad, Bad, and Dangerous to Know by Ranulph Fiennes. More impossible made possible.

References

1. The actual total distance of the Appalachian Trail varies slightly year to year depending on trail maintenance work, re-routing of sections for environmental protection purposes, and weather events all of which can change portions of the Trail. The Appalachian Trail Conservatory figure for the full length for 2024 is 2,197.4 miles.

2. Ware, Andy and Jon Bergdoll. "Americans Gave a Record $471 Billion to Charity in 2020, Amid Concerns About the Coronavirus Pandemic, Job Losses and Racial Justice." Lilly Family School of Philanthropy, IU Indianapolis, June 16, 2021. https://blog.philanthropy.iupui.edu/2021/06/16/americans-gave-a-record-471-billion-to-charity-in-2020-amid-concerns-about-the-coronavirus-pandemic-job-losses-and-racial-justice/.

3. "Explore the A.T." *Learn* More, Appalachian Trail Conservatory, https://appalachiantrail.org/explore/.

4. Thoreau, Henry D. Walden; or, Life in the Woods. Ticknor and Fields, August 9, 1854. Project Gutenberg, August 1, 2008. https://www.gutenberg.org/files/205/205-h/205-h.htm#chap01.

5. Surden, Esther. "Privacy Laws May Usher In Defensive DP: Hopper." Computerworld, January 26, 1976.

6. "CF Foundation Estimates Increase in CF Population." Cystic Fibrosis Foundation, July 28, [illegible]. https://www.cff.org/news/2022-07/cf-foundation-estimates-[illegible] opulation.

7. Michels, David, Kevin Murphy, and Karthik Venkataraman. "How Investing in DEI Helps Companies Become More Adaptable." *Harvard Business Review*, May 5, 2023. https://hbr.org/2023/05/how-investing-in-dei-helps-companies-become-more-adaptable.

8. "Never Doubt That a Small Group of Thoughtful, Committed Citizens Can Change the World; Indeed, It's the Only Thing That Ever Has." Quote Investigator, November 12, 2017. www.quoteinvestigator.com/2017/11/12/change-world.

9. "Fortune favors the bold. – Virgil." Visual Paradigm Online. https://online.visual-paradigm.com/flipbook-maker/templates/quotes/fortune-favors-the-bold-virgil/

10. "Clingmans Dome Tower Great Smoky Mountains National Park." National Park Service. https://www.nps.gov/places/clingmans-dome-tower.htm.

11. "Extra-Terrestrials and Other Stranger Things: Four-in-Five Canadians Believe." Angus Reid Institute, August 24, 2016. https://angusreid.org/wp-content/uploads/2016/08/2016.08.17-Conspiracies.pdf.

12. Hardison, Ayesha K. "Why Maya Angelou Partnered with Hallmark." *Humanities Magazine* 42, no. 1, Winter 2021, National Endowment for the Humanities. https://www.neh.gov/article/why-maya-angelou-partnered-hallmark.

13. Chang, Yen-Ping, Yi-Cheng Lin, and Lung Chen. "Pay It Forward: Gratitude in Social Networks." *Journal of Happiness Studies* 13, no. 5, October 2012, 761–781. https://ideas.repec.org/a/spr/jhappi/v13y2012i5p761-781.html.

14. Sacks, Oliver. "My Own Life." The New York Times, February 19, 2015. https://www.nytimes.com/2015/02/19/opinion/oliver-sacks-on-learning-he-has-terminal-cancer.html.

15. Schltz, Colin. "Shackleton Probably Never Took Out an Ad Seeking Men for a Hazardous Journey: The Famous Tale of how Ernest Shackleton Put Together His Antarctic Expedition Is Probably a Myth." *Smithsonian Magazine*, September 10, 2013. https://www.smithsonianmag.com/smart-news/shackleton-probably-never-took-out-an-ad-seeking-men-for-a-hazardous-journey-5552379/.

16. Lansing, Alfred. Endurance: Shackleton's Incredible Voyage. 2nd ed. Carroll & Graf Publishers, 1999.

17. Carroll, Patrick, Pablo Briñol, Richard E. Petty, and Jed Ketcham. "Feeling Prepared Increases Confidence in Any Accessible Thoughts Affecting Evaluation Unrelated to the Original Domain of Preparation." Journal of Experimental Social Psychology 89, July 2020, 0022–1031. https://www.sciencedirect.com/science/article/abs/pii/S0022103119304780.

18. "To Cut Down a Tree in Five Minutes, Spend Three Minutes Sharpening You Axe." Quote Investigator, March 29, 2014. https://www.quoteinvestigator.com/2014/03/29/sharp-axe/.

19. "Relishing Change." GE Annual Report 2000, February 9, 2000. https://www.annualreports.com/HostedData/AnnualReportArchive/g/NYSE_GE_2000.pdf.

20. Specifications of Signalling System No. 7. Q.700 ed. ITU-T, March 1993. https://www.itu.int/rec/T-REC-Q.700-199303-I/en.

21. Fletcher, Ashley. "Jack Daniel's and Uncle Nearest Announce First Selections for the Nearest & Jack Advancement Initiative Leadership Acceleration Program and Business Incubation Program." Jack Daniel's Press Room, September 24, 2020. https://pressroom.jackdaniels.com/jack-daniels-and-uncle-nearest-announce-first-selections-for-the-nearest-jack-advancement-initiative-leadership-acceleration-program-and-business-incubation-program/.

22. Rogers, William P. "Report to the President by the Presidential Commission on the Space Shuttle Challenger Accident." Presidential Commission, June 16, 1986. https://sma.nasa.gov/SignificantIncidents/assets/rogers_commission_report.pdf.

23. Kuster, M., G. A. Wood, S. Sakurai, and G. Blatter. "Downhill Walking: A Stressful Task for the Anterior Cruciate Ligament? A biomechanical Study with Clinical Implications." *Knee Surgery, Sports Traumatology, Arthroscopy* 2, March 1994, 2–7. https://link.springer.com/article/10.1007/BF01552646.

24. "Academic Outcomes" United States Air Force Academy, 2024. https://www.usafa.edu/academics/outcomes/.

25. Stilwell, Blake. "Here's what NASA Says Is the Perfect Length for a Power Nap." *Business Insider*, August 26, 2021. www.businessinsider.com/nasa-research-found-the-perfect-length-for-a-power-nap-2019-3#.

26. "Spinach." State of New Jersey Department of Agriculture, https://www.nj.gov/agriculture/farmtoschool/documents/seasonality-chart/F2S%20Spinach.pdf.

27. Dewi, Nani Asna, Krisna Yetti, and Tuti Nuraini. "Nurses' Critical Thinking and Clinical Decision-Making Abilities Are Correlated with the Quality of Nursing Handover." *Enfermería Clínica* 31, no. S2, April 2021, S271-75. https://www.sciencedirect.com/science/article/abs/pii/S1130862120306033?via%3Dihub.

28. Ragasa, Ephraim V., and Phillip E. Kaufman. "Common Name: Mosquito, Scientific Name: *Psorophora ciliata*." University of Florida, Entomology and Nematology Department, October 2012, Last Updated: August 1, 2018. https://entnemdept.ufl.edu/creatures/AQUATIC/Ps_ciliata.htm.

29. Simpson, Eleanor H., and Peter D. Balsam. "The Behavioral Neuroscience of Motivation: An Overview of Concepts, Measures, and Translational Applications." *Current Topics in Behavioral Neurosciences*, 27, Springer Cham, November 25, 2015, 1–12. https://pubmed.ncbi.nlm.nih.gov/26602246/.

30. Trivedi, Bijal P. *Breath from Salt: A Deadly Genetic Disease, a New Era in Science, and the Patients and Families Who Changed Medicine Forever*. BenBella Books, Inc., September 8, 2020.

31. Christfort, Kim, and Suzanne Vickberg. Business Chemistry: Practical Magic for Crafting Powerful Work Relationships. Wiley, May 2018.

32. Lewis, Abbey. "Good Leadership? It All Starts with Trust." Harvard Business Publishing: Corporate Learning, October 26, 2022. https://www.harvardbusiness.org/good-leadership-it-all-starts-with-trust/.

33. Hugo, Victor. Quotable Quote, Good Reads. https://www.goodreads.com/quotes/16020-each-man-should-frame-life-so-that-at-some-future.

34. Slepian, Maggie. "Least Favorite Sections on the Appalachian Trail." The Trek, March 15, 2017. https://thetrek.co/appalachian-trail/least-favorite-sections-appalachian-trail.

35. "If You're Going Through Hell, Keep Going." Quote Investigator, September 14, 2014. https://www.quoteinvestigator.com/2014/09/14/keep-going/.

36. "Palmerton Zinc Pile Palmerton, PA: Redevelopment." United States Environmental Protection Agency, https://cumulis.epa.gov/supercpad/SiteProfiles/index.cfm?fuseaction=second.redevelop&id=0300624

37. Steele, Lauren. "Happy Nude Hiking Day! Here's How to (Legally) Make the Most of It." Mens Journal, December 4, 2017. https://www.mensjournal.com/adventure/happy-nude-hiking-day-heres-how-to-legally-make-the-most-of-it-w489096.

38. Buchanan, Gordon. "The Polar Bear Family and Me." BBC, January 7, 2013. Video Series 1–3. https://www.bbc.co.uk/programmes/b01pyql5.

39. Shakespeare, William. *The Tragedy of Julius Caesar*. Barbara Mowat, Paul Werstine, Michael Poston, and Rebecca Niles, eds. Folger Shakespeare Library. Washington, DC: Folger Shakespeare Library. https://www.folger.edu/explore/shakespeares-works/julius-caesar/read/4/3.

40. Bove, Tristan. "These 49 Companies Have Been on the Fortune 500 Every Year since 1955. Here's Who They Are." *Fortune*, May 24, 2022. https://fortune.com/2022/05/24/fortune-500-companies-list-every-year-exxonmobil-chevron-pfizer.

41. Merlin. The Cornell Lab of Ornithology, Land Trust Bird Conservation Initiative. https://www.birds.cornell.edu/landtrust/merlin/.

42. Torrey, Bradford. The Writings of Henry David Thoreau in Twenty Volumes, Volume VII, (of 20) Journal 1, 1837-1846. Houghton Mifflin and Company, 1906; Project Gutenberg, June 25, 2018. https://www.gutenberg.org/files/57393/57393-h/57393-h.htm.

43. Lahti, Emilia. "Above and Beyond Perseverance: An Exploration of Sisu." Master's thesis, University of Pennsylvania, January 2013. https://repository.upenn.edu/entities/publication/4fba8cd3-6488-44f2-ab70-559db9bdd58b.

44. Woodward, Walter W. "The Unsteady Meaning of 'The Land of Steady Habits.' " Connecticut History, March 25, 2022. https://connecticuthistory.org/the-unsteady-meaning-of-the-land-of-steady-habits/.

45. Johnson, R. E., M. Venus, K. Lanaj, C. Mao, and C. H. Chang. "Leader Identity as an Antecedent of the Frequency and Consistency of Transformational, Consideration, and Abusive Leadership Behaviors." Journal of Applied Psychology 7, no. 6, 2012, 1262–1272. https://doi.org/10.1037/a0029043.

46. Cowden, Richard Gregory., and Everett L. Worthington. "Overcoming Failure in Sport: A Self-forgiveness Framework." Journal of Human Sport and Exercise 14, no. 2, 2019, 254–264. https://doi.org/10.14198/jhse.2019.142.01.

47. Clarke, Marcus A. "Berkshires UFO." *Unsolved Mysteries* S1.E5, Netflix, July 1, 2020. https://www.imdb.com/title/tt11229146.

48. Gallagher, Mark. *The Business of Winning*. Mark G[illegible]r. https://www.mark-gallagher.com.

49. "North American Porcupine: *Erethizon dorsatum*." Smithsonian's National Zoo and Conservation biology Institute, May 27, 2022. https://nationalzoo.si.edu/animals/north-american-porcupine.

50. Dell'Amore, Christine. "Why This Coyote and Badger 'Friendship' Has Excited Scientists." National Geographic. February 5, 2020. Video. https://www.nationalgeographic.com/animals/article/coyote-badger-video-behavior-friends.

51. Leaver, Kate. " 'Cwtch': The Hug Invented by the Welsh." BBC, June 25, 2018. https://www.bbc.com/travel/article/20180624-cwtch-the-hug-invented-by-the-welsh.

52. Fisher, Jen, and Michael Stephen. "Why Your Team Isn't Taking Time Off." The Wall Street Journal, March 29, 2021. https://deloitte.wsj.com/cmo/why-your-team-isnt-taking-time-off-01617044529.

53. Goggin, David. Can't Hurt Me: Master Your Mind and Defy the Odds. Lioncrest Publishing, November 2018.

54. "Giardia: About *Giardia* Infections." Center for Disease Control (CDC), May 3, 2024. https://www.cdc.gov/giardia/about/?CDC_AAref_Val=https://www.cdc.gov/parasites/giardia/.

55. Albinson, Nancy, Andrew Blau, and Yang Chu. "The Future of Risk: New Game, New Rules." Deloitte. https://www2.deloitte.com/us/en/pages/risk/articles/future-of-risk-ten-trends.html.

56. Bergland, Christopher. "Why Vivid Mental Imagery Is Like Motivational Rocket Fuel: Functional imagery training boosts motivation via personalized visualizations." Psychology Today, August 29, 2021. https://www.psychologytoday.com/us/blog/the-athletes-way/202108/why-vivid-mental-imagery-is-motivational-rocket-fuel.

57. Clarey, Christopher. "Olympians Use Imagery as Mental Training." New York Times, February 22, 2014. http://www.nytimes.com/2014/02/23/sports/olympics/olympians-use-imagery-as-mental-training.html.

58. "S. 4 (88th): An Act to establish a National Wilderness Preservation System for the permanent good of the whole people, and for other purposes." *Public Law* 88-577, Sept. 3, 1964.

59. Wassenbergh, Sam V., Erica J. Ortlieb, Maja Mielke, Christine Böhmer, and Robert E. Shadwick. "Woodpeckers Minimize Cranial Absorption of Shocks." Current Biology 32, no. 14, July 25, 2022, 3189-3194. https://doi.org/10.1016/j.cub.2022.05.052.

60. "State of Virginia Table No 2. - Population by Color and Condition." United States Census Bureau, Population of the United States in 1860: Virginia, p. 518, https://www2.census.gov/library/publications/decennial/1860/population/1860a-36.pdf.

61. "The Slave Trade." National Archives. Last modified on January 7, 2022. https://www.archives.gov/education/lessons/slave-trade.html#toc-the-act-prohibiting-the-importation-of-slaves-1808.

62. Weisstuch, Lisa. "Harriet Tubman Is Famous for Being an Abolitionist and Political Activist, but She Was Also a Naturalist." *Smithsonian Magazine*, March 10, 2022. https://www.smithsonianmag.com/history/harriet-tubman-is-famous-for-being-an-abolitionist-and-political-activist-but-she-was-also-a-naturalist-180979689.

63. Hinton, Richard J. *John Brown and His Men; with Some Account of the Roads They Traveled to Reach Harper's Ferry*. Funk and Wagnalls, 1894. In the digital collection *Making of America Books*. University of Michigan Library Digital Collections. https://quod.lib.umich.edu/m/moa/ack4822.0001.001/3?q1=Declaration+of+independence.

64. Virginia Convention of 1861. "Virginia Ordinance of Secession (April 17, 1861)." *Encyclopedia Virginia*. Virginia Humanities, December 7, 2020. https://encyclopediavirginia.org/entries/virginia-ordinance-of-secession-april-17-1861.

65. Halle, Rahawa. "Going It Alone." Outside Magazine, April 11, 2017. Updated Feb 5, 2023. https://www.outsideonline.com/culture/opinion/solo-hiking-appalachian-trail-queer-black-woman.

66. Bro, Susan. "My Daughter Heather Heyer's Death Taught Me How to Grieve. We All Need to Know How Today." *Fortune*, 12 August 2020. https://fortune.com/2020/08/12/heather-heyer-charlottesville-anniversary-grief.

67. Beckett, Lois. " 'A White Girl Had to Die for People to Pay Attention': Heather Heyer's Mother on Hate in the US." *The Guardian*, October 1, 2017. https://www.theguardian.com/us-news/2017/oct/01/heather-heyers-mother-on-hate-in-the-us-were-not-going-to-hug-it-out-but-we-can-listen-to-each-other.

68. Abebe, M, M. S. Cupp, F. B. Ramberg, and E. W. Cupp. "Anticoagulant Activity in Salivary Gland Extracts of Black Flies (Diptera: Simuliidae)." *Journal of Medical Entomology* 31, no. 6, November 1994, 908-11. https://pubmed.ncbi.nlm.nih.gov/7815406/.

69. Wilson, Mark B. 2021. *Dictator: The Evolution of the Roman Dictatorship*. University of Michigan Press eBook Collection, 2021 https://doi.org/10.3998/mpub.10150936.

70. Flannery, Russell. "What Happened to America's Communes?" *Forbes*, April 11, 2021. https://www.forbes.com/sites/russellflannery/2021/04/11/what-happened-to-americas-communes.

71. Weingarten, Chris R., et al, "100 Greatest Drummers of All Time." *Rolling Stone*, March 31, 2016. https://www.rollingstone.com/music/music-lists/100-greatest-drummers-of-all-time-77933/.

72. Petriglieri, Gianpiero. "The Psychology Behind Effective Crisis Leadership." *Harvard Business Review*, April 22, 2020. https://hbr.org/2020/04/the-psychology-behind-effective-crisis-leadership.

73. Brumfeil, Geoff. "Total Failure: The World's Worst Video Game." National Public Radio (NPR), May 31, 2017. https://www.npr.org/2017/05/31/530235165/total-failure-the-worlds-worst-video-game.

74. Stone, Harlan Fiske, and Supreme Court of The United States. *U.S. Reports: Vermont v. New Hampshire, 289 U.S. 593 (1933).* 1932. Periodical. https://www.loc.gov/item/usrep289593.

75. "Chapter 15: New Hampshire-Vermont Boundary" in *Title 1: General Provisions*. The Vermont Statues Online, Vermont General Assembly. https://legislature.vermont.gov/statutes/fullchapter/01/015.

76. Heywood, John. 1546. *A Dialogue Conteinyng the Nomber in Effect of All the Prouerbes in the Englishe Tongue*. London: Fletestrete by Thomas Berthelet, 1564. In the digital collection *Early English Books Online*. University of Michigan Library Digital Collections. https://quod.lib.umich.edu/e/eebo/A03168.0001.001?view=toc.

77. He, Xinyue, Xin Jiang, Dominick V. Spracklen, Joseph Holden, Eryuan Liang, Hongyan Liu, Chongyang Xu, Jiahui Du, Kai Zhu, Paul R. Elsen, and Zhenzhong Zeng. "Global Distribution and Climatic Controls of Natural Mountain Treelines." *Global Change Biology* 29, no. 24, July 21, 2023. https://doi.org/10.1111/gcb.16885.

78. "United States Pulp and Paper Industry: Statistics & Facts." Statista Research Department, September 19, 2024. https://www.statista.com/topics/5268/us-pulp-and-paper-industry/#topicOverview.

79. Liu, Gloria. "I'll Cry if I Want To (and You Can, Too)." *Outside Magazine*, October 8, 2022, Updated Jan 30, 2023. https://www.outsideonline.com/culture/essays-culture/cry-sports-adventure-science.

80. Newberry, Ethan. *Where Dreams Go to Die: Gary Robbins and the Barkley Marathons*. August 1, 2018. Video. https://wheredreamsgotodie.com.

81. Devonport, Tracey J., Carla Meijen, and Juliette Lloyd. "Walking on Thin Ice: Exploring Demands and Means of Coping During an Extreme Expedition." *Journal of Human Performance in Extreme Environments* 17, no. 1(7), January 2022. https://doi.org/DOI: 10.7771/2327-2937.1148.

82. United States Department of the Interior and National Park Service. "Helicopter Rescue Techniques: Civilian Public Safety and Military Helicopter Rescue Operations." *National SAR Academy Training Manual*. Mountain Rescue Association, October 23, 2013. https://mra.org/wp-content/uploads/2016/05/Helicopter_Rescue_Techniques-_NSARA_Manual-_10-23-2013.pdf.

83. Howe, Nicholas S. *Without Peril: 150 Years of Misadventure on the Presidential Range of New Hampshire*, Tenth Anniversary Edition. Appalachian Mountain Club, 2009.

84. Szumowska, Malgorzata, and Michal Englert. *Infinite Storm*. Bleeker Street, 2022. 1:32.

85. Whately, Francis, director. *The Last Five Years*. BBC Worldwide, 2017. 1:30.

86. Kennedy, John F. "We Choose to Go to the Moon." Rice University, Houston, September 12, 1962. https://www.rice.edu/jfk-speech.

87. Tremmel, Manuela, and Ingrid Wahl. "Gender Stereotypes in Leadership: Analyzing the Content and Evaluation of Stereotypes about Typical, Male, and Female Leaders." Frontiers in Psychology 14, no. 1, January 26, 2023. https://doi.org/ 10.3389/fpsyg.2023.

88. McLaglen, Andrew V. *Shenandoah*. Universal Pictures, 1965. 1:4'

89. "Civil War Batte, Cedar Creek." American Battlefield Trust, Updated September 2021. https://www.battlefields.org/sites/default/files/2022-01/Cedar%20Creek--Oct%2019%201864--530%20to%20630%20am%20%28September%202021%29.pdf

90. Silver, Ike, and Alex Shaw. "When Staying Neutral Backfires." *Harvard Business Review*, August 24, 2022. https://hbr.org/2022/08/when-staying-neutral-backfires.

91. Page, Rick. *Hope Is Not a Strategy: The 6 Keys to Winning the Complex Sale*. McGraw Hill Professional, 2001.

92. Frei, Frances. "How to Build (and Rebuild) Trust." TED, April 1, 2018. Video, https://www.ted.com/talks/frances_frei_how_to_build_and_rebuild_trust?subtitle=en.

93. Horsager, David. *Trusted Leader: 8 Pillars That Drive Results.* Berrett-Koehler Publishers, 2021.

94. Covey, Stephen M. R. *The Speed of Trust: The One Thing That Changes Everything*. Simon & Schuster, 2006.

95. ———*Trust and Inspire: How Truly Great Leaders Unleash Greatness in Others.* Simon & Schuster, 2022.

96. "Plant of the Week: Purple Pitcherplant, Saddle Flower (*Sarracenia purpurea* L.)." United States Department of Agriculture, U. S. Forest Service, https://www.fs.usda.gov/wildflowers/plant-of-the-week/sarracenia_purpurae.shtml.

97. "Stream Crossing Safety while Hiking and Backpacking." Pacific Crest Trail Association (PCTA). https://www.pcta.org/discover-the-trail/backcountry-basics/water/stream-crossing-safety/.

98. Sandberg, Sheryl, and Nell Scovell. 2012. *Lean In: Women, Work, and the Will to Lead*. Alfred A. Knopf, 2013.

99. "Path to a Cure: Many Routes, One Mission." Cystic Fibrosis Foundation. https://www.cff.org/research-clinical-trials/path-cure-many-routes-one-mission.

100. Roche, David, and Megan Roche, M.D. "Feels Vs. Facts: Why You Still Need a Rest Day, Even When You're Feeling Good." Whoop, April 14, 2022. www.whoop.com/us/en/thelocker/feels-vs-facts-why-you-need-rest-days-in-training.

101. Williams, Florence. "The Nature Fix: The Three-Day Effect." REI Co-op, May 29, 2017. https://www.rei.com/blog/camp/the-nature-fix-the-three-day-effect.

102. Sluss, David. "Becoming A More Patient Leader." *Harvard Business Review*, September 2, 2020. https://hbr.org/2020/09/becoming-a-more-patient-leader.

103. Anderson, Dave. "250th Anniversary of the Pine Tree Riot: The Spark that Led to the Revolutionary War." Society for the Protection of New Hampshire Forests, March 2, 2022. https://www.forestsociety.org/blog-post/forestry-friday-250th-anniversary-pine-tree-riot.

104. Wells, Jessica C. "Leading Organizational Learning." *HCA Healthcare Journal of Medicine* 2, no. 2(6). Feb 26, 2021: 29–33. https://scholarlycommons.hcahealthcare.com/hcahealthcarejournal/vol2/iss1/6.

Index

Index

C

H

I

O

P

W

X

Y

Z

Made in the USA
Columbia, SC
07 August 2025

964dc9dc-b08b-4560-9f2b-0a45df085ef5R01